The Supernatural Cinema of Guillermo del Toro

The Supernatural Cinema of Guillermo del Toro

Critical Essays

Edited by JOHN W. MOREHEAD

Foreword by Doug Jones

McFarland & Company, Inc., Publishers
Jefferson, North Carolina

LIBRARY OF CONGRESS CATALOGUING-IN-PUBLICATION DATA

The supernatural cinema of Guillermo del Toro : critical essays / edited by John W. Morehead ; foreword by Doug Jones.
     p.   cm.
Includes bibliographical references and index.

ISBN 978-0-7864-9595-5 (softcover : acid free paper) ∞
ISBN 978-1-4766-2075-6 (ebook)

1. Toro, Guillermo del, 1964– —Criticism and interpretation. I. Morehead, John W., 1964– editor.
PN1998.3.T583S87 2015
791.4302'33092—dc23   2015016496

BRITISH LIBRARY CATALOGUING DATA ARE AVAILABLE

© 2015 John W. Morehead. All rights reserved

No part of this book may be reproduced or transmitted in any form or by any means, electronic or mechanical, including photocopying or recording, or by any information storage and retrieval system, without permission in writing from the publisher.

On the cover: Director Guillermo del Toro and Doug Jones as the Faun in *Pan's Labyrinth*, 2006, Mexico (Photofest)

Printed in the United States of America

McFarland & Company, Inc., Publishers
  Box 611, Jefferson, North Carolina 28640
  www.mcfarlandpub.com

Table of Contents

Foreword DOUG JONES   1

Introduction JOHN W. MOREHEAD   7

The Magical Spirituality of a Lapsed Catholic
   Atheism and Anticlericalism
      S. T. JOSHI   11

At the Mountains of Mexico
   The Echoes and Intertexts of Lovecraft and Dunsany
      KEVIN J. WETMORE, JR.   22

Slime and Subtlety
   Monsters in del Toro's Spanish-Language Films
      ANN DAVIES   41

Time Out of Joint
   Traumatic Hauntings in the Spanish Civil War Films
      KARIN BROWN   58

The Child Transformed by Monsters
   The Monstrous Beauty of Childhood Trauma
      JESSICA BALANZATEGUI   76

The Ambivalence of Creative Desire
   Theogonic Myth and Monstrous Offspring
      SIDNEY L. SONDERGARD   93

Henry's Kids
   Othered Children and Karloff's Frankenstein Monster
      JOHN KENNETH MUIR   112

Table of Contents

Where the Wild Things Are
   Monsters and Children
      ALEXANDRA WEST   130

Bloodsucking Bugs
   Horacio Quiroga and the Latin American Transformation of Vampires
      GABRIEL ELJAIEK-RODRÍGUEZ   146

The Birth of Fantasy
   A Nietzschaen Reading of Pan's Labyrinth
      JACK COLLINS   163

Menstruation as Heroine's Journey in *Pan's Labyrinth*
      RICHARD LINDSAY   182

About the Contributors   201

Index   205

Foreword
Doug Jones

Guillermo del Toro. A name that makes film fans buckle at the knee in reverence. A name that has forever changed my life.

I will never forget the day I met Guillermo. It was on the set of *Mimic* in 1997. Long after principal photography was completed in Canada with another actor in the "Long John" bug costume, I had been called in just to do a few days of pick-up re-shoots in Los Angeles. I hadn't actually met the director the first night, as I was on the roof of a brick building being pelted by a rain machine and yelled at by a man with a megaphone on the ground below I couldn't see through my mask. But my second day, it happened. I was sitting at the lunch table, and directly across from me, a jolly, round, scruffy fellow sat down, put his chin in his hands and said, "So tell me everything you've been in before." This was our director, Guillermo del Toro, finishing up his first big budget American film, and still unknown to many Americans like me who hadn't seen his first Spanish-language masterpiece, *Cronos*.

I dutifully listed highlights from my resume that included *Batman Returns*, *Tank Girl*, and *Hocus Pocus* at the time. Then he wanted to test his memory for who did the make-ups on me in these films—Ve Neill, Stan Winston, and, "*Hocus Pocus* was Tony Gardner, right? Is he a nice guy?"

His love for monsters and make-ups was readily apparent, and his love for the artists who create them, even more so. I confirmed that Tony Gardner is a great guy, as the energy at that lunch table rose to a level that would make twelve-year-old boys proud. Guillermo told me how he started in Mexico, making monsters of his own and filming them for television and movies there, appeasing his longtime love for all things creepy

Foreword by Doug Jones

and crawly. We connected as two fan boys, giggling about our love of classic monster movies, and then remembered we had to go back to "director" and "actor" when lunch was over that day. Little did I know, that was my first encounter with the genius who would later create the defining moments of my career.

He found me again five years later when the creature shop Spectral Motion was creating the Abe Sapien character make-up for *Hellboy*. Shop owner Mike Elizalde, designer Steve Wang, and sculptor Jose Fernandez were presenting the finished maquette sculpture for director Guillermo del Toro's approval. Legend has it, he fell to his knees and quietly said, "Wow. I am so fat." We think this means "What a beautiful, thin, aquatic creature." It was at this moment when the Spectral Motion guys all chimed in that the perfect person to play this role was Doug Jones.

"Doug Jones? I know Doug Jones," he said, as he pulled out of his wallet the business card I had given him five years earlier at our lunch table on *Mimic*. This is the Guillermo people fall in love with—the Guillermo who keeps people in his stable with whom he remembers creating magic. I have never known anyone who is better at surrounding himself with people who inspire him, who motivate him, who can collaborate with him, who share his artistic vision, no matter which filmmaking department they are in.

He doesn't just meet people. He absorbs them. He studies them. He wants to know what fibers each of us possess and how they weave together to make us the people we are. He also absorbs this information from fine art sculptures, paintings, movies, music, dance, any form of artistic expression, and the people who create them. He doesn't just love the original *Frankenstein* movie like most fans. He loves actor Boris Karloff. He loves director James Whale. He loves the novel by Mary Shelley. And because of this love, he's had his own *Frankenstein* in development now for just long enough to imply that he doesn't want to do any of these people a disservice by making his own movie before it's ready to fulfill every childhood dream he carries to this day. I am attached to play Frankenstein's monster, and I have never been so happy to wait.

As an actor, I've observed his relationship with actors most keenly. Those personality-dissecting skills of his enable him to direct each of us very differently, based on what buttons we have. I noticed this most on *Hellboy II: The Golden Army*, watching his demeanor change between giving notes to Ron Perlman, Selma Blair, Jeffrey Tambor, and me. With me, he knows he doesn't have to say much. Like the scene in *Hellboy II* where I put contact lenses in my fishy eyes and sprayed my gills with a device that would allow me to not need my goggles and water-filled breathing apparatus. After the first take of all that business with those props, he simply said, "Cut! Cojones! You're boring me to tears." He knows that to make me laugh and give me a one-liner jab, I'll get the idea and fix it until it's more interesting. And yes, "Cojones" "with every vulgar double meaning intended, bless his heart," is just one of many nicknames he's called me over the years.

Hellboy II also gave birth to one of my favorite Guillermo quotes ever. We were a couple of months along in our six-month shoot ... 18 hours a day, six days a week. I have never felt so depleted by sleepless toil, yet so invigorated by the art we were making. A confusing mix. One day, between camera set-ups, I was dozing off in my set chair, and I heard his shuffling footsteps approaching. Like a loyal doggie, I perked up when I heard my master approaching. He put his hand on my shoulder and gently spoke. "I know we are killing you, my friend." I was about to agree when he continued, "But the good news is, there will be pilgrimages to your grave." And right there, he summed it all up. Making immortal art that will live long after we are gone from this Earth might just be worth the torment we were all putting our bodies through.

After he hand-picked me to play the Faun and the Pale Man in his masterpiece, *Pan's Labyrinth*, I argued that I couldn't be the best choice for the Faun, as I don't speak Spanish, and I'd ruin his film. But Guillermo insisted I was the only one who could play the Faun, adding, "You can count to ten, for all I care, and I'll dub it over later, but I need you in that role." He knows my strengths and weaknesses far better than I do, and he also knew that given this challenge, I'd never let him film me counting to ten. So I learned all that Spanish dialogue without a coach. Then in our second week of filming, he sat with me in a quiet moment between shot set-ups, put his hand on my arm and said, "I know you haven't heard much from me, my friend." And this was true. After I took in all his pre-production notes, he didn't offer much on-set direction. I knew this was his way, and he proved me correct when he continued with, "It's because you're simply getting it right." A dream director, who can see he's getting what he wants and doesn't spoil the soup by over-seasoning it.

This book is filled with very smart essays on del Toro's cultural, philosophical, and theological nods and hints throughout his films. Others here will be able to draw much better parallels and decipher deeper meaning behind his imagery. But what I can tell you is how much I have reveled in playing characters within his bigger schemes, themes, and production designs, which include a lot of old church iconography, sculptures, artifacts, and relics that respectfully bow to Guillermo's Catholic upbringing. He told me about his Catholic heritage during pre-production on *Pan's Labyrinth*, at the same time he was inquiring about my Christianity with fascinated attention. Now, when I watch *Pan's Labyrinth*, the Christ-like imagery of sacrifice, innocent blood, and taking one's rightful place at the right hand of the Father makes me tear up every time.

When Guillermo sent me home with the first *Hellboy* script and asked me to call him that night with my thoughts, all I could think was, "Oh dear, how am I going to word this when I have to decline this movie?" But then I read the script. Excited, I called him to say, "Guillermo! How is it that a story with a demon from hell as the centerpiece doesn't even come close to offending my Christian sensibilities?"

He replied, "It was never meant to offend you, my friend." Then he went on to explain how so many of us drag our pasts around with us, allowing our history and our faults to weigh us down like we're tied to a piano. This is a story about healthy rebellion that can make us stop and cut that past free from our present. And who better to exemplify having a past and inherent nature to overcome than a demon from hell? I was sold. My favorite scene from that first *Hellboy* film is one I'm not in. As Hellboy is about to make a bad decision to reclaim his evil roots in order to save his love, Liz Sherman, his sawed-down horns are growing back, indicating the dark change. But just then, young Agent Myers shouts from across the room, "Remember who you are!" as he tosses Hellboy the crucifix his earthly father figure, Professor Broom, taught him to honor. When Hellboy catches the crucifix, it burns a cross into the palm of his hand. Hellboy pauses to do just what Agent Myers implored, and he remembers what he stands for now, what he represents, and who he really is. He reaches up, and in a triumphant act of defiance of our film's villain, Hellboy breaks off his newly grown demon horns, thus breaking the evil spell that was being created to release chaos. A gorgeous, empowering moment we can all learn something from. We do have choices to make every day.

Foreword by Doug Jones

Enjoy all the essays to come in this collection from some very smart people who have researched and analyzed the work of Guillermo del Toro to peel back the many layers of a deep thinker, a deep feeler, and my favorite filmmaker with whom I have ever worked.

Guillermo del Toro. A friend and mentor. The man who breathed the life of old school Hollywood into my career. The director who just plain gets it. The man to whom I will forever be grateful for allowing my name to be associated with his in some of the most respected films in the history of cinema.

Doug Jones is a noted character actor with a strong connection to science fiction, fantasy, and horror film and television. His roles include Billy Butcherson the zombie in Hocus Pocus, *a Gentleman in* Buffy the Vampire Slayer, *Abe Sapien in the* Hellboy *films, and the Faun and Pale Man in* Pan's Labyrinth.

Introduction

Guillermo del Toro is one of the most prolific artists at present. At the time of this writing, his work as a film director includes *Cronos* (1993), *Mimic* (1997), *The Devil's Backbone* (2001), *Blade II* (2002), *Hellboy* (2004), *Pan's Labyrinth* (2006), *Hellboy II* (2008), and *Pacific Rim* (2013), with the film *Crimson Peak* scheduled to hit theaters in October 2015. Plans for him to direct *Pacific Rim II* have been announced, as has a del Toro version of *Pinocchio*. He has also worked extensively as a producer or executive producer, not only on his own films such as *The Devil's Backbone* and *Pan's Labyrinth*, but also on projects where he has identified talent in colleagues and their creative ideas and worked to see them become realized in films such as *The Orphanage* (2007), *Splice* (2009), and *Mama* (2013). Del Toro also has several writing credits to his name, including various screenplays for some of his own cinematic offerings, as well as efforts like *Don't Be Afraid of the Dark* (2010), as well as his work on the Strain series of novels, co-authored with Chuck Hogan and developed into a television series that aired in its first season in 2014. And if this wasn't enough, del Toro has also been involved in video game development with *Hellboy: Science of Evil* (2008).

I had heard of del Toro and his work previously, but I began to take serious interest in him with the release of *Pan's Labyrinth*. As a scholar of religion and popular culture also involved in religious studies and interreligious dialogue, I was intrigued by the pagan elements in the film, and the fact that the film came to be an item of interest and discussion in the pagan community online. I subsequently began my research on his work and discovered why this film incorporated these religious concerns.

Del Toro was born in Guadalajara, Jalisco, Mexico, where he grew up with a stern Catholic grandmother. In various interviews he has described

Introduction

the negative experiences he had with her and her religious faith which lead to his eventual rejection of Catholicism. Additional life experiences would further sour his confidence in organized religion altogether, including the trauma of the kidnapping of his father, and his work in a morgue where he came to question the existence of the human soul. Even so, he has not jettisoned spirituality completely. In a video for Big Think he has described himself as an agnostic, and has expressed a belief in the paranormal, and in an interview in *Time* magazine he referred to art as providing a "primal, spiritual function" in his life. Del Toro's life experiences, and his fantasy art as spirituality, are expressed in his body of work, particularly his films, and the way in which he incorporates them makes for a fascinating study.

Del Toro also embodies his artistic expression that comes as a result of creative passion coupled with deep reflection. An Internet search reveals a wealth of interviews that include del Toro's critical reflection on his art. This is extremely important in relation to the ways in which he brings his various expressions of genre to life. This includes his interests not only in filmmaking in general, but also various elements related to his approach to the art including monsters, metaphor, myth, archetype, and Jungian psychology.

The essays in this volume explore many of these elements through the key themes and facets of del Toro's work, and in so doing provide the reader with fresh insights into del Toro's art and the man behind it. As such it is a complement to other explorations of del Toro's work, including his own thoughts shared in *Cabinet of Curiosities: My Notebooks, Collections, and Other Obsessions* (Insight Editions, 2013) with contributions by Marc Scott Zicree, and the commentary of others, such as *Guillermo del Toro: Film as Alchemic Art* (Bloomsbury, 2014) by Keith McDonald and Roger Clark.

The book is organized by subject matter. The first two essays consider various elements that have shaped del Toro as a filmmaker, including his negative experience with religion, and literary influences. S.T. Joshi begins the volume with a consideration of the spirituality of del Toro as a "lapsed Catholic" and agnostic, and various (a)religious undercurrents in his films. In the second essay Kevin J. Wetmore, Jr., considers how del Toro personalizes H.P. Lovecraft and Lord Dunsany, filtering them through his own experiences, beliefs, and interests.

Introduction

The next two essays consider Spanish aspects of del Toro's work. Ann Davies discusses implications of del Toro's Spanish-language monsters for audiences both at home (Mexico and Spain) and abroad. Davies argues that it is possible to read Spanish and Mexican specificities, but the monsters lean to wider traditions of monstrosity that pick up on and emphasize the allegorical style of earlier Hispanic cinema while also drawing on production values reminiscent of Hollywood. Karin Brown then explores the figure of the traumatized child and the supernatural in connection with the setting of the Spanish civil war which provides del Toro with the perfect metaphorical space in which to exorcise ghosts from his personal past as well as explore those issues unresolved in Spanish culture.

Four essays follow that look at children in connection with the monstrous. Jessica Balanzategui analyzes two films, *The Devil's Backbone* (2001) and *Pan's Labyrinth,* and also the three child-centered horror films which del Toro has produced, *The Orphanage, Don't Be Afraid of the Dark,* and *Mama,* and considers these in light of del Toro's own childhood. Sidney L. Sondergard explores monstrous offspring by way of consideration of Hesiod's *Theogony* in contrast with del Toro's films to discover the strategic interactions between creator and created that are represented archetypally in theogonic myth. John Kenneth Muir identifies and enumerates the connections between del Toro's films and *Frankenstein* in literature and film, specifically Whale's adaptation starring Boris Karloff. Del Toro's works are viewed by Muir as deliberate contrasts to that mythic story of parenthood, ones which re-write "bad fathers" in more positive, humane terms. Alexandra West concludes this section by examining the films *Mimic, The Devil's Backbone,* and *Pan's Labyrinth.* Through these films she looks how del Toro cleverly uses his child characters to explore the themes and metaphors of the adult struggles, the child's experience of humanity through the monster, and how the monster is used as both friend and enemy.

The next essay explores one of the ways in which del Toro uses insects in his work, in this case the bloodsucker. Gabriel Eljaiek-Rodríguez discusses the ways in which the filmmaker transforms and adapts traditional European vampire narratives to a distinctly Latin American literary and sociopolitical context, following the path previously explored by Horacio Quiroga and other writers of the Latin American Gothic.

The final two essays consider alternative readings of one of del Toro's

Introduction

most significant films. Jack Collins argues that by manipulating both the conventions of traditional fantasy and classical drama, *Pan's Labyrinth* deconstructs the historically escapist social function of fantasy and reconstructs it as a postmodern analog to Nietzsche's "goat song," and in so doing, del Toro expands the symbolic vocabulary of tragedy and reappropriates fantasy to force the audience to confront what it once only allowed them to escape. Richard Lindsay's essay concludes the volume with a different perspective on this film. The author suggests a reading that takes into account the visual and mythological symbolism of the figure of Pan portrayed as the Faun, as well as the cultural context of menstruation in mythology and religion. It concludes that the strange and fertile symbolism of the film represents a coming-of-age struggle intimately familiar to women.

There are many people who work to make volumes like this possible. It is not possible to name them all, but I want to express a special note of thanks to Dave Canfield for making a connection for me to Doug Jones so that I could ask him to write the foreword. I offer my thanks to Doug as well for making time in a very busy acting schedule to write his contribution.

I hope the reader enjoys the essays that follow, and develops new insights about the work of Guillermo del Toro.

The Magical Spirituality of a Lapsed Catholic
Atheism and Anticlericalism
S. T. JOSHI

The emergence of atheism, agnosticism, and secularism in the West is by no means a recent phenomenon, even though the so-called New Atheists (Sam Harris, Richard Dawkins, and the late Christopher Hitchens) have raised the consciousness of both the religious and the irreligious by the incisiveness and at times polemical fire of their best-selling treatises, published in the early years of this century. But the history of atheism in the West can be traced back to the Greek philosophers of the seventh, sixth, and fifth centuries BCE: they were the first thinkers to our knowledge who abandoned the notion that a god or gods created the universe and that, instead, the world as we know it was created by natural forces.

The rediscovery of classical learning—especially the writings of the Greek Atomist Democritus and his disciples, Epicurus and Lucretius (the works of the first two exist only in extensive fragments)—in the Renaissance, and the simultaneous advance of scientific (especially astronomical and biological) discovery with the work of Copernicus, Kepler, Newton, and others, led to the ultimate dethronement of the Judeo-Christian worldview from intellectual supremacy. By the time Charles Darwin published *The Origin of Species* (1859), the intelligentsia—if not the general populace—was ready to embrace a worldview that entirely banished God or godlike forces from the universe. As Richard Dawkins has stated, "Darwin made it possible to be an intellectually fulfilled atheist."[1] This tendency continued in the later nineteenth and twentieth centuries with such thinkers as Friedrich Nietzsche, Bertrand Russell, Albert Einstein, Gore Vidal, Kai Neilsen, and many others.

Anticlericalism—a belief that a specific church, or perhaps all churches, are forces of evil rather than good, whether it be in the intellectual, cultural, political, or social sphere—is quite a different thing. Many strongly anticlerical thinkers would be horrified at the notion that they are atheists or agnostics. Voltaire, the most celebrated (but far from the most acute) thinker of eighteenth-century France, was strongly anticlerical, as his repeated utterance "Écrasez l'infâme!" ("Crush the infamy!"), applied to the Catholic Church, attests: while vigorously condemning the intolerance and corruption of the church, he just as vigorously scorned atheists as intellectually suspect libertines. Voltaire was a pronounced Deist (a believer that a god had created the universe and initiated its complex mechanism, but then sat back and admired his handiwork without any subsequent intervention in human or cosmic affairs), as were many of the America's Founding Fathers, notably Thomas Jefferson and James Madison. All would have rejected the imputation of atheism.

Del Toro and Religion

Guillermo del Toro has frequently referred to himself as a "lapsed Catholic." It is well known that he was raised in a strict Catholic household in Guadalajara, Mexico, chiefly under the influence of his grandmother. In his 2009 interview with Charlie Rose he stated: "I mercifully lapsed as a Catholic, I say. But as [Luis] Buñuel used to say, 'I'm an atheist, thank God.' You know, there is always, once a Catholic, always a Catholic in a way."[2]

The intersection of weird and fantastic fiction and atheism is a subject that still needs detailed exploration. Del Toro, thoroughly conversant with the long history of supernatural fiction—as most recently exemplified in his splendid introductory essay "Haunted Castles, Dark Mirrors" to the Penguin Horror series of 2013—is no doubt aware that there is no easy equation of weird fiction with atheism. While a few writers of the weird may have been atheists or agnostics (Poe, Lord Dunsany, and H. P. Lovecraft come to mind), others were emphatically otherwise: del Toro's longtime favorite Arthur Machen was a devout Anglo-Catholic; Algernon

Blackwood was a Buddhist mystic; and the contemporary British writer Ramsey Campbell is a lapsed Catholic like del Toro, but it is not clear he has gone all the way to atheism.

Del Toro's closest analogue may indeed be with Lovecraft, an author he has long held in high esteem. Lovecraft was, indeed, an outspoken atheist, once claiming to have shed the tenets of his Baptist upbringing so early as the age of twelve; but most of his discussions of atheism were included in private letters that only began publication in the 1960s. Del Toro is no doubt aware of this body of work, but he has probably been even more influenced by Lovecraft's fiction, which—when read with care—embody an uncompromising atheism that depicts a humanity "alone in the cosmos" and dwarfed by the immensity of space and time. Del Toro had long wished to adapt Lovecraft's great Antarctic novel *At the Mountains of Madness* (1931) as a film. It is precisely Lovecraft's creation of an invented mythology in many of his best tales that appealed to del Toro, whose rejection of orthodox religion in no way entailed a rejection of a sense of spirituality; indeed, rejection of religion may in fact have enhanced the spirituality that is at the core of his being.

Cronos (1993), the first feature film written and directed entirely by del Toro, employs a motif that is of very long standing in the history of weird fiction—the quest for eternal life. In its traditional literary modes—as, for example, in William Godwin's novel *Caleb Williams* (1794), Charles Robert Maturin's *Melmoth the Wanderer* (1820), and, imperishably, Goethe's *Faust* (1808–32)—the notion involves a sorcerer or alchemist who seeks the philosopher's stone, an object that at once grants eternal life and all-encompassing knowledge. *Cronos* is premised largely on this idea: an alchemist in 1557 created something called the "Cronos device" and lived until 1937, when he died in a building collapse in Mexico. The bulk of the film deals with the rediscovery of the device by an elderly antiques dealer, significantly named Jesús Gris (the gray Jesus), and the attempts by a dying man, de la Guardia, to secure it and rejuvenate himself.

The film treads lightly on a number of religious and metaphysical issues. Early in the film Gris, looking at the strange metallic device, which resembles a large mechanical insect, and asks, "What are you? A god?" The miraculous powers of the device would certainly lead most human beings—inclined, as del Toro is surely aware, to belief in gods and the supernatural whenever they encounter anything anomalous or incomprehensible—to attribute deific properties to the object. Gris is subsequently killed by de la Guardia's vicious nephew, but the device revives him; however, the result is that Gris becomes a kind of vampire, requiring human blood to continue his undead life. When he refuses to drink his granddaughter Aurora's blood, he dies a second time.

Cronos is, in its way, a perverted retelling of the death and resurrection of Jesus Christ—exactly the sort of thing that a lapsed Catholic like del Toro would have been led to fashion. In the end it becomes a touching love story between an old man and his granddaughter, who refuses to abandon him even after his death and grotesque revival. There are also a few Lovecraftian touches, notably in the notion that the "rules" for the use of the device are embodied in an ancient book—an adaptation of the "forbidden book" motif that Lovecraft utilized perhaps more extensively than any other author of weird fiction.

Religion and Fascism

The Devil's Backbone (2001) is one of the first of del Toro's films to fuse terror and political commentary, and religion inevitably enters the mix. Its setting during the earlier stages of the Spanish civil war is no accident: del Toro is keenly cognizant of the degree to which the outmanned Republicans were inclined toward atheism (as a facet of their communist or socialist politics), whereas the Loyalists under Franco had sought the assistance of the Catholic Church to aid their ruthless suppression of political freedom. The film only glancingly equates Catholicism with Fascism; more significant is the complex portrayal of Doctor Casares, a "man of science" who scorns superstition and denies the existence of ghosts, even though the ghost of a murdered boy, Santi, frequently appears in the orphanage that serves as the setting of the film.

In one of the most gripping scenes in the film, Casares shows the young boy Carlos, who has been abandoned at the orphanage by his parents, a series of bottles with mutant fetuses preserved in alcohol. One fetus in particular has a pronounced backbone—the "Devil's backbone" of the title. This image is derived from several episodes in del Toro's childhood. As Daniel Zalewski reports in his *New Yorker* article on the filmmaker, "As a young child, del Toro had read a book featuring laparoscopic photographs of babies in utero." Some years later, visiting a mental hospital, del Toro saw "a pile of fetuses, new arrivals [in the morgue].... Del Toro had been raised Catholic, but this sight, he said, upended his faith. Humans could not possibly have souls; even the most blameless lives ended as rotting garbage."[3]

In a sense, we are to admire Doctor Casares as a brave holdout against the brutal Franco regime; but in another sense, he is a contemptible figure, selling the fetus-laced alcohol to soldiers and (less culpably) seeming to use poetry and music as a replacement for the religion he has clearly abandoned. In a sense he embodies del Toro's view of humanity in general, a species that in his view is an inextricable mix of good and evil: "I believe in mankind ... as the worst and the best that has happened in this world."[4] Casares's denial of the very existence of the ghost of Santi is the immemorial response of the rationalist and materialist faced with the reality of the supernatural.

Pan's Labyrinth (2006) continues the fusion of politics and the supernatural. Here again the setting is the Spanish civil war, and both the political and the religious dichotomy of the two sides is etched more clearly than in *The Devil's Backbone*. A communist leaflet seen toward the opening of the film clearly states: "No God, no country, no Master." In contrast, a priest who has sided with the Loyalists states with unctuous viciousness of the rebels: "God has already saved their souls. What happens to their bodies hardly matters to Him." Meanwhile, the ruthless Captain Vidal, facing the severe illness of his pregnant wife, blandly instructs the doctor to save the baby's life (he assumes it will be a boy, and therefore his heir) over that of the mother. Sure enough, the mother delivers the baby early; it lives, but she dies.

The equation of Catholicism and Fascism was something that, as del Toro admitted later, emerged when he was working on *The Devil's Backbone*. It was then, he states, that "I found the absolutely horrifying—not only complicity—but *participation* of the Church in the entire Fascist movement of Spain." He goes on to say that the words of the priest quoted above are a verbatim transcript of what a priest actually told a group of Republican prisoners in a Fascist concentration camp.[5]

The film presents a kind of alternative religion or cosmology in the existence of fairy creatures who attempt to lure the young girl Ofelia, Captain Vidal's stepdaughter, into their clutches. Magic pervades the film—the form of the mandrake root that, soaked in milk, helps to cure Ofelia's mother when she suffers a serious illness; through the form of a huge grasshopper-like creature that leads Ofelia to an encounter with a Faun, who takes her to be the Princess Moanna, daughter of the king of the underworld; and especially in the form of the Faun's (Pan's) labyrinth itself, a structure not far from the Loyalist encampment where Vidal's forces are battling the rebels.

Del Toro is well aware of the symbolic import of these magical entities. Like Lovecraft, who certainly did not believe in the literal existence of Cthulhu, Yog-Sothoth, and other "gods" of his invented mythology, del Toro is proposing in *Pan's Labyrinth* a contrast to the Catholicism and perhaps even the broader Christendom that, to his mind, can only lead to intolerance and Fascism. And although he himself stated in an interview that, "for me, what she [Ofelia] sees is a fully blown reality, spiritual reality. I believe her tale not to be just a reflection from the world around her, but, to me, she actually turns into the princess,"[6] he does not necessarily intend us, as viewers, to interpret the magical elements of the story as literal reality. This seems to be confirmed at the very end of the film, when Captain Vidal, hunting down his own daughter (who has taken her baby brother and brought him to Pan's labyrinth as instructed by the Faun), fails to see the Faun when Ofelia sees him and talks with him. This can either mean that Vidal, as a man blinded by his own dogmatic faith and cruelty and without childlike imagination, cannot see the magic that really exists in the world, or that Ofelia herself is deluded as to the existence of the magical creatures she thinks she has encountered.

In the end, Vidal does indeed kill his own stepdaughter, after she refuses to sacrifice her brother to Pan; but, as the concluding voice-over narration informs us, she has indeed returned to her father's kingdom and lived there for many years. It is amusing that the concluding image of the king of the underworld is pointedly similar to standard (stereotypical?) conceptions of the Christian God as a long, bearded figure in a robe seated on a throne; but this god, del Toro is saying, is a very different entity altogether.

The Gods of Chaos

Our analysis of the religious elements in *Hellboy* (2004) must be tempered by awareness of what elements are found in the original graphic novels by Mike Mignola. The film is a reasonably faithful adaptation of the graphic novels, but with apparent touches—specifically some religious undercurrents—added by del Toro himself. (The screenplay was written by del Toro based on a story by del Toro and Peter Briggs.) The basic premise of the film follows that of the graphic novels: Hellboy, a demon summoned from another dimension by the Nazis in 1944, decides to follow a nobler path and battle occult forces of evil; but there is always a chance that he might let in the Ogdru Jahad (the gods of chaos) to overwhelm the earth.

At the very outset of the film, religious imagery enters in the form of a rosary held by Professor Trevor Bruttenholm (pronounced "Broom"). This rosary ultimately occupies a small but significant place in the overall narrative, for Hellboy—who has been raised by Bruttenholm and has come to regard him as his father—takes up the rosary when Brutteholm is killed. Still later, as Hellboy is indeed tempted to let in the Ogdru Jahad, FBI agent John Myers throws him the rosary and cries, "Remember who you are!" The tactic works, and Hellboy allows the inter-dimensional portal to close. The message we are to derive from this series of incidents is not that Hellboy himself is acknowledging faith in the Catholic Church; although Bruttenholm is himself a devout Catholic, Hellboy's attraction to the rosary is largely a matter of devotion to his "father," Bruttenholm. Myers's cry is meant to recall to Hellboy that he is half-human and therefore should show some sort of devotion to his species rather than to the extra-dimensional monster seeking to destroy the world and all its inhabitants.

There is a powerful influence of Lovecraft throughout the film, and it is a delicate question as to which of the Lovecraftian touches are derived from Mignola's graphic novels and which from del Toro's elaborations upon it. Some tips of the hat are amusing but frivolous, as in a passing radio broadcast from station HPLN, or the fact that Hellboy (like Lovecraft) is enamored of cats. One of Hellboy's monstrous assistants, Abe Sapien, has webbed hands, a nod from del Toro's with his love for *The Creature from the Black Lagoon*, but also exactly like the hybrid Deep Ones (described as an amalgam of human and fish) in Lovecraft's "The Shadow over Innsmouth" (1931).

But other elements are much more significant. The film opens with a passage from *De Vermis Mysteriis*, an imaginary book of occult lore similar to the celebrated *Necronomicon* of Abdul Alhazred, invented by Lovecraft so early as 1922. *De Vermis Mysteriis* was created by Lovecraft's young friend Robert Bloch, who cited it under its English title, *Mysteries of the Worm*, in the story "The Shambler from the Stars" (1935); Lovecraft supplied the Latin title. In the film, the passage states: "Seven Gods of Chaos ... slumber in their crystal prison, waiting to reclaim Earth ... and burn the Heavens." This notion—and, in general, the idea of letting in extra-dimensional creatures to overwhelm the earth—is taken directly from Lovecraft's novelette "The Dunwich Horror" (1928), where an elderly librarian, Dr. Armitage, realizes that there was "some plan for the extirpation of the entire human race and all animal and vegetable life from the earth by some terrible elder race of beings from another dimension."[7] Armitage's valiant efforts prevent Wilbur Whateley, a huge, goatlike figure from a backwoods Massachusetts town, from doing just that.

The creature that emerges toward the end of *Hellboy* bears striking resemblances to Cthulhu, the octopoid "god" who, in Lovecraft's "The Call of Cthulhu" (1926), came from the depths of space and became imprisoned in an underwater city called R'lyeh in the Pacific. Like Cthulhu, the entity in *Hellboy* is many-tentacled, and at one point it is itself referred to as a "god." Both creatures are, in fact, alien entities, but their immense power makes them seem like gods to the fragile and minuscule human beings who encounter them.

The ultimate "religious" significance of *Hellboy* is its bland acknowledgment of an alternate cosmology that has nothing to do with the Christian tradition. For all the fleeting Catholic references, the film is premised on the notion that the god of Christianity is simply an idle myth, and that the "real" gods are the "Seven Gods of Chaos" who, in their extra-dimensional realm, will pose a recurring threat to humanity.

The sequel to *Hellboy*, *Hellboy II: The Golden Army* (2008), is an interesting fusion of the original film with some elements seemingly derived from *Pan's Labyrinth* (and with some parallels from *Blade II* directed by del Toro). Here Hellboy battles a variety of entities led by Balor, the king of Elfland. While an entertaining action film and special effects extravaganza, the film does not raise any profound religious or philosophical issues beyond that contained in the original film.

A Film Not Made

Del Toro's most salient—and radical—religious or anti-religious vision might have been embodied in a film that he has (so far) not yet made—

his long-planned adaptation of Lovecraft's *At the Mountains of Madness*. This novel is indeed Lovecraft's most pungent exposition of his own atheism, providing a kind of humiliating "origin of species" that renders us the accidental by-products of an extraterrestrial race far greater in every regard than ourselves.

At the Mountains of Madness tells of the discovery by a small group of explorers of the existence of an immense city built in Antarctica millions of years ago by a race of alien entities whom the explorers deem the Old Ones. As the explorers continue to investigate the immense stone city, they are forced to the conclusion not only that it was not built by human hands but that

> the builders of the city were wise and old, and had left certain traces in rocks laid down before the true life of earth had advanced beyond plastic groups of cells ... rocks laid down before the true life of earth had existed at all. They were the makers and enslavers of that life.... They were the Great Old Ones that had filtered down from the stars when earth was young—the beings whose substance an alien evolution had shaped, and whose powers were such as this planet had never bred.[8]

Elsewhere it is stated that the creatures were "supposed to have created all earth-life as jest or mistake."[9]

It is this cosmic panorama that del Toro attempted for years—since at least the early 1990s—to adapt into a blockbuster film. He tells of his decades-long fascination with it:

> Reading this tale in my midteens was a revelation. I had never been exposed to any literature that so dwarfed our existence and hinted at the cold indifference of the cosmos. I became entirely enamored. Making a film of it became my quest.
>
> For the last fifteen years or so, I have attempted repeatedly to make a film based on this story. From 2009 to 2011 I dedicated my every waking hour to sketching, sculpting, and writing about every detail in the adaptation of Lovecraft's difficult prose. Difficult to adapt, that is, since it is a superb tonal work, peppered with brief but shocking episodes of devastating power. The adaptation took necessary liberties but remained faithful to every landmark of the novel.[10]

In his interview with Daniel Zalewski, del Toro underscores his understanding of the core atheistic message of Lovecraft's novel: "The book essentially says how scary it is to realize that we are a cosmic joke."[11]

Alas, the film has not been made, because Universal Studios denied del Toro the $150 million he wished to spend, as the studio felt that an R-rated film of this sort would not sufficiently make back its investment. In 2012 del Toro claimed that Ridley Scott's *Prometheus* "killed" his plan for *At the Mountains of Madness* because it seemed to duplicate the core element in the novel: the notion that an alien species created the human race.[12] In recent years, however, del Toro has backtracked somewhat, holding out faint hopes that an *At the Mountains of Madness* film may in fact one day be made.

Conclusion

Whether it does so or not, it has become clear that several central films in Guillermo del Toro's oeuvre address religious issues in a bold, dynamic, and at times anticlerical or actually atheistic manner. While fully recognizing the significance of religion as a critical component of many people's worldview (and, indeed, his own), del Toro challenges viewers of his films to consider alternate worldviews or cosmologies that dispense altogether with the metaphysical tenets of the Judeo-Christian religion or any other religions of the earth. We may or may not be alone in the universe, but in del Toro's vision it is unclear whether orthodox religion can provide even a modicum of comfort to assuage the awareness of our transience and fragility in the immensity of the cosmos.

Notes

1. Richard Dawkins, *The Blind Watchmaker* (New York: W. W. Norton, 1986), 6.
2. Charlie Rose, interview with Guillermo del Toro, 2 July 2009.
3. Daniel Zalewski, "Show the Monster," *New Yorker*, 7 February 2011, http://www.newyorker.com/reporting/2011/02/07/110207fa_fact_zalewski?currentPage=all.
4. Rose interview with del Toro.
5. Michael Guillen, "*Pan's Labyrinth*—Interview with Guillermo del Toro," twitchfilm.com, http://twitchfilm.com/2006/12/pans-labyrinthinterview-with-guillermo-del-toro.html.
6. Matthai Chakko Kuruvila, "Embraced by Many Religions, 'Labyrinth' Allows Broad Discussion of Faith Issues," sfgate.com, 2 March 2007, http://www.sfgate.com/entertainment/article/Embraced-by-many-religions-Labyrinth-allows-2612375.php.
7. H. P. Lovecraft, "The Dunwich Horror," in *The Dunwich Horror and Others*, S. T. Joshi, ed. (Sauk City, WI: Arkham House, 1984), 185.

8. H. P. Lovecraft, *At the Mountains of Madness,* in *At the Mountains of Madness and Other Novels,* S. T. Joshi, ed. (Sauk City, WI: Arkham House, 1985), 59–60.
9. Ibid., 22.
10. Guillermo del Toro, "Haunted Castles, Dark Mirrors," in *American Supernatural Tales,* S. T. Joshi, ed. (New York: Penguin, 2013), 25.
11. Zalewski, "Show the Monster."
12. Clark Collins, "'Prometheus' vs. 'At the Mountains of Madness': How Ridley Scott's 'Alien' Prequel Killed Guillermo del Toro's Dream Project," *Entertainment Weekly,* 10 June 2012, http://insidemovies.ew.com/2012/06/10/prometheus-ridley-scott-guillermo-del-toro-lovecraft/.

Bibliography

Collins, Clark. "'Prometheus' vs. 'At the Mountains of Madness': How Ridley Scott's 'Alien' Prequel Killed Guillermo del Toro's Dream Project." *Entertainment Weekly,* 10 June 2012. http://insidemovies.ew.com/2012/06/10/prometheus-ridley-scott-guillermo-del-toro-lovecraft/.
del Toro, Guillermo. "Haunted Castles, Dark Mirrors." *American Supernatural Tales,* S. T. Joshi, ed. New York: Penguin, 2013.
Guillen, Michael. "*Pan's Labyrinth*—Interview with Guillermo del Toro." Twitch-Film.com. http://twitchfilm.com/2006/12/pans-labyrinthinterview-with-guillermo-del-toro.html.
Kuruvila, Matthai Chakko. "Embraced by Many Religions, 'Labyrinth' Allows Broad Discussion of Faith Issues." SFGate.com. 2 March 2007. http://www.sfgate.com/entertainment/article/Embraced-by-many-religions-Labyrinth-allows-2612375.php.
Lovecraft, H. P. *At the Mountains of Madness.* In *At the Mountains of Madness and Other Novels.* S. T. Joshi, ed. Sauk City, WI: Arkham House, 1985.
———. "The Dunwich Horror." In *The Dunwich Horror and Others.* S. T. Joshi, ed. Sauk City, WI: Arkham House, 1984.
Rose, Charlie. Interview with Guillermo del Toro. PBS, 2 July 2009.
Zalewski, Daniel. "Show the Monster." *New Yorker,* 7 February 2011. http://www.newyorker.com/reporting/2011/02/07/110207fa_fact_zalewski?currentPage=all.

At the Mountains of Mexico
The Echoes and Intertexts of Lovecraft and Dunsany
KEVIN J. WETMORE, JR.

Well known to fans, del Toro's continual attempts to develop *At the Mountains of Madness* as a feature-length film mark both his dedication to Lovecraft and fandom's frustration at this imagined but still non-existent film. In his planned film, the narrative would be moved from Lovecraft's setting of twentieth century Antarctica to sixteenth century Mexico: "I wrote a version of it set during the time of the conquest of the New World with a bunch of conquistadors arriving at the Mayan ruins and finding another city beneath."[1] This statement is arguably the perfect summary of what del Toro does: takes his source material and filters it through his own experiences, sensibilities, and the culture of his youth. His "mountains of madness" are Mexican, even as they are Lovecraftian.

Del Toro has, however, mined Lovecraftian themes and imagery in previous films, but perhaps even more so the themes and images of Lord Dunsany, one of Lovecraft's greatest admitted influences. In *Supernatural Horror in Literature*, Lovecraft calls Dunsany "unexcelled in the sorcery of crystalline singing prose and supreme in the creation of a gorgeous and languorous world of iridescently exotic vision" and then continues for four more pages to sing his praises as one of the greatest fantasists, "a master of triumphant unreality."[2]

Others are there as well, to be sure, and del Toro is not lacking in his fantasy and horror genealogy, citing Algernon Blackwood (indeed, the auction house in *Hellboy II* is named Blackwood in tribute), Mary Shelley, Poe, Machen and others as shaping his vision of horror and fantasy.[3] But it is his blend of Lovecraft and Dunsany, I argue, that shapes his films of the first decade of the twenty-first century. In a letter Lovecraft bemoans the fact that he has "my 'Poe' pieces & my 'Dunsany' pieces," but no "Lovecraft" pieces, not realizing that his transformations of those two authors (and blending of them) were his Lovecraft pieces.[4] Similarly, del Toro has Lovecraft pieces and Dunsany pieces, but he mostly has del Toro pieces, filtering Lovecraft through Dunsany and his own sensibilities to develop an ethos of local (not cosmic) horror and fantasy.

The reader should note I am not positing an evolution or teleology to del Toro's films, but rather a sustained series of conscious echoes of Lovecraft and Dunsany that removes the cosmic aspect and focuses on fantasy and local horror. *Pan's Labyrinth* and *Hellboy II: The Golden Army* form intertexts with each other and with Dunsany's work, especially *The King of Elfland's Daughter*. In all of these texts, the cosmic horror of Lovecraft is filtered back through a Dunsanian sensibility to form a local horror. For del Toro, the horror being summoned is not a cosmic horror out there, but a horror summoned here that affects the people here.

As important to the Lovecraftian films of del Toro (if not more than the actual fiction of Lovecraft) are the Lovecraftian epiphenomena: other films based on Lovecraft, graphic novels, role-playing games, etc. Del Toro's Lovecraftian films are more "Lovecraftian" in this sense than Lovecraft's actual fiction. The similarity between del Toro's Lovecraftian films and his Dunsanian films is that both types rely upon the narrative and visual tropes of their sources, but the former tend to be the popular Lovecraftianism rather than actual Lovecraft and the latter tend to be much closer to the source, at least partly because "Lovecraft" is a brand name in a manner that "Dunsany" is not.

Del Toro blends elements of both in his films. Lovecraft is a "weird realist," rooting his stories of horror in everyday reality and then showing the cosmic horror lurking behind that reality.[5] Dunsany is an ironic fantasist, telling tales of elves, trolls and their interactions with men, but from an ironic distance. Del Toro is a blend of both, a weird, ironic, fantastic realist, so to speak. Lovecraft's gods are not actually gods: they are alien beings who came to this planet long ago or who live in the cold reaches of space. Dunsany makes the gods more human: fickle and shortsighted, petty and vengeful, or preferring to avoid contact with other races and beings entirely. Lovecraft took Dunsany's divinities and made them the gods of the Dreamlands (see, for example, *The Dreamquest of Unknown Kadath*, arguably Lovecraft's most Dunsanian work), detaching them somewhat from Dunsany's irony, although maintaining the distance. Lovecraft already took the gods and made them less "godish"; they are simply aliens or entities from another reality, not gods in the Dunsanian sense, in which they actually were divine beings. Del Toro takes this de-deification further and melded the dreamland gods with the ugly everyday reality of our world, domesticating both the fantastic and the cosmic horror, localizing them to specific places and areas while simultaneously embracing Dunsany's ironic treatment of fantasy. The mountains of madness become the mountains of Mexico, and specifically Guadalajara.

Although it is dangerous to conflate biography with artistic practice, one can see in del Toro's own philosophy a de-mystification of the religious elements of Lovecraft. Lovecraft himself was an atheist, but his stories concerned gods and ancient religions. Del Toro's rejection of his family's Catholicism, his experiences growing up in Guadalajara—a child's fantasy land intermingled with difficult reality, and his own cross-border work (moving between Mexico, the United States and Spain), all shape his unique vision as a filmmaker and one could argue predispose him to see gods as less than divine and instead part of a localized reality. In the DVD commentary for *Cronos*, del Toro compares his own grandmother to Piper Laurie's character in *Carrie*: "My grandmother sort of tortured me religiously for my own good quote unquote." He loved her, but her religion was seen as a negative aspect of her character and led him to reject Christianity altogether. He has also stated that "I am a skeptic. I love talking about supernatural stuff and fantastic themes but I am in real life very skeptical because I want to believe. This is out of my formation as a lapsed Catholic, if you would." His films are those of a skeptical believer who would love to learn these fantastic beings are real and the world posited by Lovecraft and Dunsany behind our own was true, but knows in his heart they are not.

All of del Toro's gods are local gods, faded divinities. The Faun at the beginning of *Pan's Labyrinth* is faded and mangy. It is only through the actions of Ofelia that he and the Elfland can be made whole looking again. The Pale Man is monstrous, but trapped in his small prison from which he seemingly cannot escape. Even a little girl is able to outrun him. The Angel of Death in *Hellboy II* has powers over life and death, but he is no sense a divinity. He even notes his own specificity, telling Liz Sherman, "At last, I have been waiting for you both, I am his death and I will meet him at every crossroad." The Angel of Death is revealed to be not *the* Angel of Death, but the Angel of Hellboy's death, a localized divinity at best. The tree elemental in that same film is described by Prince Nuada as a "Forest God.... The last of its kind. Like you and I. If you destroy it, the world will never see its kind again...." Yet it is dispatched with a shot to the head and affects nothing beyond its immediate environment. The death of the last Forest God changes nothing in the world. In short, in del Toro's films, to a greater extent than in Lovecraft and Dunsany, the godhead is removed from gods which are simply other, longer living beings with power in the local sphere.

I propose to consider del Toro's first film, *Cronos*, as his most Lovecraftian, with later films, especially *Pan's Labyrinth* and *Hellboy II: The Golden Army*, as Dunsanian blends, mixing in the fantasy of Dunsany but with both the removal of any real divinity and the localization of the cosmic horror in all three.

The *Cool Air* in *Cronos*

Del Toro's debut film, *Cronos* (1993), is often called a vampire film, but it is not. I argue it is perhaps the most Lovecraftian of del Toro's films. *Cronos* is not a story of cosmic horror, but rather one of local horror. For that matter, Lovecraft is not particularly "Lovecraftian" in *Cool Air*, the story that echoes through *Cronos*. Written in 1926 while Lovecraft was suffering his final days in Brooklyn before returning to Providence, and published in 1928, Lovecraft's story concerning a man whose neighbor is revealed to be a dead man kept alive through refrigeration reflects both the urban horror of apartment living as well as the horror of the discovery means by which the personality might survive bodily death. While both narratives encompass mythic imagery, tied to history, there is no cosmic horror present in either. In both narratives, the protagonist discovers a technology to change and preserve life (alien alchemy?), resulting in a reluctant zombie and his neighbor in Lovecraft and a reluctant vampire and his granddaughter in del Toro.

"It is a mistake to fancy that horror is associated inextricably with darkness, silence and solitude. I found it in the glare of mid-afternoon, in the clangour of a metropolis, and in the teeming midst of a shabby and commonplace rooming-house with a prosaic landlady and two stalwart men by my side," begins *Cool Air*, removing horror from its traditional darkness in Lovecraft.[6] *Cronos*, after its precredit prologue of a Spanish alchemist's death, begins in the glare of a Mexican morning, as Jesus Gris and his granddaughter Aurora open his antique store, finding horror in the shabby and commonplace houses and industrial factories of urban Mexico.

In the slum apartments of New York City, the narrator lives among "Spaniards," Herrero, the landlady, is from Barcelona. Dr. Muñoz, also Spanish, "a man of birth, cultivation, and discrimination" and trained by "Dr. Torres of Valencia" and who has been dead for eighteen years, moves into the building.[7] The narrator only sees him in passing. Muñoz uses chemicals and an engine to cool his room. When the pump in the engine breaks and Muñoz and the narrator are unable to repair it, his body disintegrates when to air grows too warm to continue his preservation.

Like Joseph Curwen or Ephraim/Asenath Waite, Dr. Muñoz had been interested in preserving himself after death and discovered a means to do so, a blend of science, alchemy and technology: Muñoz "did not scorn the incantations of the mediaevalists, since he believed these cryptic formulae to contain rare psychological stimuli which might conceivably have singular effects on the substance of the nervous system from which organic pulsations had fled."[8] He uses an engine to cool the air of his apartment until the rooms are cold enough to halt the decay of his flesh after the incantations and chemicals preserve his personality (soul? self?) after death. In short, technology plus alchemy equals a living dead man.

Similarly, Lovecraft's early tale *The Alchemist* offers a narrative of an ancient French family cursed by an alchemist so that the men of the family will all die shortly after their thirty-second birthday. Antoine, the last of the line after six hundred years of the curse, reaches his thirty-second birthday in fear of the curse and learns that the curse is not real. The explanation for the deaths of his forebears is both more prosaic and fantastic. Instead of a curse, the eponymous alchemist, gifted with immortality, has hidden in the family castle, emerging to secretly kill the men after their thirty-second birthdays. Antoine, alerted to the killer, sets him on fire, ending the "curse."[9]

Similarly, in *Cronos*, Jesus Gris uses a Spanish device from the Renaissance to preserve his life, which is also sought by De la Guardia, a wealthy industrialist who, like Dr. Muñoz, seeks to preserve himself after death by living in a hermetically sealed space, controlling his environment and using a combination of technology and alchemy. The film (in its English language version) begins with narration explaining the backstory of the Cronos device:

> In 1536, fleeing from the Inquisition, the alchemist Uberto Fulcanelli disembarked in Veracruz, Mexico. Appointed official watchmaker to the Viceroy, Fulcanelli was determined to perfect an invention which would provide him with the key to eternal life. He was to name it the Cronos device. Four hundred years later, one night in 1937, part of the vault in a building collapsed. Among the victims was a man of strange skin, the color of marble in moonlight. His chest mortally pierced, his last words, "Suo tempore." This was the alchemist.

Thus Fulcanelli lived four centuries and died from his wounds in the collapse of the vault in which he was presumably living. Is there something about achieving a kind of immortality that results in one's self-imprisonment to continue preserving life? Dr. Muñoz mostly keeps to his apartment, Fulcanelli left Spain at some point and dies in a collapsed vault in which he was presumably living in Mexico, saying, "At one's own time," again presumably speaking of his own death. De la Guardia hides all day in his own chambers, dying by his own admission. He shows Gris a glass casket containing organs, telling him, "Half my body is here in this case." Like Muñoz, De La Guardia hides away in a chamber where he is protected from the world and death, causing Angel to spurn when he hears his uncle wants the Cronos device in order to live longer: "That fucker does nothing but shit and piss all day, and he wants to live longer?" It would seem the price of immortality is seclusion and only occasional emergence into the world, like Lovecraft's alchemist.

As the film unfolds, Gris finds the device in the base of a statue. He tricks De la Guardia to reveal information about the device, as it has begun piercing his flesh, drawing out blood and in exchange he has grown younger, more vigorous, as the film makes clear. The device itself is revealed by del Toro to be a combination of watchmaking technology and an alien insect, which drinks the blood and revitalizes its host. "The matter of the resurrection is related to ants," the viewer is told, "to spiders. They can remain inside a rock for hundreds of years until someone comes along and frees them." Thus, the film itself ties immortality to imprisonment. Ants and spiders may live "hundreds of years" if enclosed in rock, but live a normal short life when released. The alien insect that grants immortality is truly Lovecraftian, an example of "weird realism."

Gris is beaten by Angel, and his body placed in a car and pushed off a cliff. His body is prepared for cremation and he awakens in his casket to escape the crematorium. He finds himself decaying, until instructed by De la Guardia to "peel it off" and it is revealed that like Fulcanelli his skin is "marble in the moonlight" as he is "being reborn" as a living dead man who needs blood to survive with the aid of the Cronos device. Like the other dead men who continue to live, however, Gris finds resurrection requires imprisonment. After fleeing the crematorium he finds his way back to his house where Aurora places him inside a toy chest in a storage room to sleep until sunset. He has gained eternal life but at the cost of self-imprisonment to preserve it.

The imagery of the film is in keeping with del Toro's approach to Lovecraftian themes. The device is found in the base of a statue of an angel. De la Guardia has been purchasing and opening such angels for years, apparently, as the décor of his chambers consists largely of the angel statues hung from ropes, their bases broken and shattered, the angels half encased in plastic. Like the rest of the room, they are paradoxically decaying and sterile, a metaphor for a corrupt and rotting and ultimately meaningless belief system. It is a visualization of a metaphor for the Catholic Church del Toro had already left behind, promising an eternal life it cannot deliver.

The Cronos device itself is a clockwork vampire. Gears and switches (an engine, if you will) drive a needle that draws blood for the insect inside the device and delivers a fluid that preserves the donor, fills him with vitality and gives an appetite for blood. The alien insect inside forms a symbiotic relationship with the user of the device. The supernatural (vampirism) is revealed to be the combination of technology and alien life, just as in Lovecraft. The horror is all local, and rooted in fantasy, not an idea that behind this reality lurks a cosmos at best indifferent to us and at worst malevolently out to purge humanity from existence. Both *Cronos* and *Cool Air* are the horror-next-door. While others find Lovecraftian elements throughout del Toro's work, for me, *Cronos* remains his most Lovecraftian.

Del Toro and Dunsany

Del Toro refers to Lovecraft as his "spiritual godfather" and observes, "I have devoted more time to Lovecraft than virtually any other author in the genre."[10] And yet, his work is as much, if not more so, reflective of the work of Edward John Moreton Drax Plunkett, known colloquially as "Lord Dunsany." If del Toro devotes time to Lovecraft, then he devotes time indirectly to Dunsany. Lovecraft singles out Dunsany's work for "humour and irony," and notes, "beauty rather than terror is the keynote of Dunsany's work."[11] It could easily be argued that del Toro shares Dunsany's use of humor, irony, and beauty above Lovecraft's vision of terror.

Dunsany, initially known for plays and short stories, produced a series of early novels that echo through del Toro's work: *Don Rodriguez: Chronicles of Shadow Valley* (1922), set in Spain during the "Golden Age" and concerning the eponymous knight who sets off to find fame, fortune and a bride, *The King of Elfland's Daughter* (1924), which is the most influential work on del Toro, as discussed below, *The Charwoman's Shadow* (1926), again set in Spain's Golden age, in which a king sends his son to a magician to gain a fortune and meets a cleaning woman without a shadow, and *The Blessing of Pan* (1927), the first novel set entirely in the real world (in rural England), in which a vicar hears a haunting song from the hills outside the village and discovers the worship of Pan has continued. The last novel obviously holds echoes for del Toro, considering that *Pan's Labyrinth* concerns a captain in Fascist Spain who is concerned with the rebels in the hills outside the village. Del Toro links the rebels with the natural world, with the labyrinth and with the magical world Ofelia discovers. Like Dunsany's vicar, the captain fears and hates both what is happening in the hills and the magic that is unfolding within his own home. Witness his reaction to discovering Ofelia's mandrake under the bed and one realizes Captain Vidal is a destructive force opposed to freedom, life and magic. Ofelia, who represents all three, is eventually stabbed and killed by him. And yet, the story ends with a blessing from the Faun—Ofelia is reunited with her Elfin parents and the Captain is killed by the rebels, his son to be raised without knowing his true nature, just as Ofelia did not know hers.

In an interview about *Pan's Labyrinth* for a Spanish website, del Toro revealed that Tolkien and Robert E. Howard's fantasy work "never called out to me," but, "aunque hay dos escritores de fantasia que me parecen sublimes: Clark Ashton Smith y Lord Dunsany" ("although there are two writers of fantasy that I think are sublime: Clark Ashton Smith and Lord Dunsany").[12] In another interview, del Toro claims to have influenced for that same film by "[Jose Luis] Borges, [Algernon] Blackwood, [Arthur] Machen, Dunsany," noting the last's *The Blessing of Pan* as a "compelling" influence.[13] As noted above, there are strong echoes of that novel in the structure and themes of *Pan's Labyrinth* that go far beyond the sharing of the pagan deity.

In his 1995 study of Dunsany, S.T. Joshi identifies the major themes of Dunsany's work, all stemming from a desire to return to nature: "the diminution of the human (because it is so clearly tied to the rise of cities and industrialism), the glorification of the past, the preference for dreams (and art, the distillation of dreams) over mundane reality, and a sympathy for the animal world, frequently at the expense of the human."[14] Del Toro's work also features many of these themes. The mythic past is certainly glorified in the animated history of Elfland at the beginning of *Hellboy II*, as well as in Ofelia's personal and mythic past in *Pan's Labyrinth*. Dreams and art rise to the level of the transformative in del Toro's work, where even a simple piece of chalk can create a gateway to another reality. Likewise, the human world in del Toro is small and the humans petty. Every encounter with mundane humans (as opposed to those who know the true nature of reality) results in misunderstanding and fear in *Hellboy II*. After Hellboy slays the forest god, the police draw their guns and threaten to arrest him and Liz. The soldiers of *Pan's Labyrinth* are small-minded petty individuals, incapable of seeing the beauty around them and torturing those whom they oppose.

A major theme in Dunsany's work and in del Toro's is the idea of the fallen prince. Alveric in *The King of Elfland's Daughter* abandons his throne, his son and his responsibilities to the kingdom in order to search for his missing wife for years. His son, Orion, abandons any duty to the kingdom and spends most of his time hunting, killing a unicorn over the course of the novel. In del Toro's canon, Jacinto from *The Devil's Backbone*, Nomak from *Blade II*, Nuada from *Hellboy II* (and Hellboy, as well, who as a prince of hell may challenge Nuada for the right to control the Golden Army), and Captain Vidal from *Pan's Labyrinth* are all "fallen princes," literally in some cases.[15] While the fallen princes tend to be villains, the same films have exiled princesses serving as heroines.[16] *The King of Elfland's Daughter*, with elfin princess Lirazel in exile from Elfland for the first third of the novel and then in exile from her family for almost the last two thirds is matched by Ofelia, a fallen princess in *Pan's Labyrinth*, both in this world, in which she destroys her best dress to fight a toad and cannot function in the society of her mother and the Captain, as well as an elfin princess who has fallen into this world. Princess Nuala is a fallen princess whose sacrifice ends her brother's assaults on humans and Hellboy.

While del Toro is famous for his child characters—Ofelia in *Pan's Labyrinth*, the orphans of *The Devil's Backbone*, Aurora in *Cronos*—it is important to remember that many of his protagonists are adults as well: *Hellboy*, *Mimic*, *Pacific Rim* and *Cronos* are all fairy tales about adults with grown-up protagonists. Perhaps that is why Hellboy is the ideal del Toro character: a child-like man with super powers. Hellboy (even the name suggests his eternal child state) has impulse control issues, no sense of patience, and no respect for authority. In *Hellboy II: The Golden Army*, the adult Hellboy behaves very much the same way as the child Hellboy at the beginning of the movie: demanding rewards, resisting orders, and refusing to take responsibility. It is only the realization that he is about to become a parent that transforms Hellboy into a responsible being.

In the majority of del Toro's films, it is actually the combination of adult and child that saves the world: Hellboy and his more mature companions Abe, Liz, and eventually Johann Krauss, must cooperate to stop Nuada, a man-child out to destroy the world. In *Pacific Rim* the adult Stacker Pentecost rescues the child Mako Mori, but it is the adult Mako whom he must allow to drift with the adult Raleigh Beckett (himself a man child, lost when his older brother dies) so the Kaiju might be stopped. Ofelia works with the Faun to restore the universe and her place in the Elven kingdom. Aurora protects her grandfather when he returns from the dead and in return he protects her and their family from Angel. A theme in Dunsany (although not in Lovecraft) that echoes through del Toro's work, is the maturation of the young hero who is then able to enter and defeat the threat to and from the fantasy world.

The King of Elfland's Labyrinth

Pan's Labyrinth forms an intertext with Dunsany's *The King of Elfland's Daughter*, a pioneering fantasy novel from 1924 about the quest of a lovesick husband for his bride, the titular king's daughter, whose father uses his power to transform part of the real world into an eternal, enchanted world in which they both may live happily forever. Obviously similar to del Toro's penchants for the link between the real world and an enchanted one, for unhappy young children escaping this world into a fantasy one, and for powerful magical beings serving to reshape reality as a means to deal with evil, Dunsany's novel both influenced and forms a powerful intertext with *Pan's Labyrinth*.

Neil Gaiman notes in his introduction to *The King of Elfland's Daughter* that it is "a book about magic; about the perils of inviting magic into your life; about the magic that can be found in the mundane world, and the distant, fanciful, changeless magic of Elfland."[17] He could, for all intents and purposes, also be describing *Pan's Labyrinth*. Ofelia invites magic into her life, and finds it in the mundane world and eventually ends up as a princess in Elfland, although her mortal body seemingly passes away, killed by her stepfather in a fairy tale in which the wicked stepparent wins before losing. Like Dunsany's novel, "it is not a comforting [story], neither is it a comfortable one."[18]

Dunsany writes about the borderland between the fantasy world and our own. In *The King of Elfland's Daughter*, the border is a porous one in which trolls and elves may wander into the lands of men, and men, through determination, may end up in the Elflands. However, the border is also controlled by the King of Elfland, who can cause it to not merely close but recede altogether so the border itself cannot even be found. Likewise, in *Pan's Labyrinth*, Captain Vidal has brought his wife and stepdaughter to the borderlands in more sense than one. He is responsible for the border between Fascist Spain and the wilderness controlled by the rebels. The film's beginning, however, with Ofelia's encounter with the fairy, demonstrates that the border is also between the real world of Fascist Spain and the lands of fairy and elves, to which Ofelia properly belongs. The rebels, like the elves in Dunsany, can recede back into the forests and not be found when they do not want to be.

In *The King of Elfland's Daughter* the inciting incident is the request of the Parliament of Erl, twelve old men who advise the king, that the men of Erl "would be ruled by a magic lord," and encourage him to send his son to Elfland, despite seven hundred years of excellent rule by the chiefs of men.[19] Later on, they believe that there is too much magic when

Orion summons the trolls of Elfland to Erl. In a chapter entitled "The Coming of Too Much Magic," the Parliament of Erl suffers buyer's remorse, voting to outlaw magic due to the presence of too many trolls.[20] When Orion slays a unicorn, the Parliament discusses the issue and eventually votes that the creature was, in fact, not a unicorn. They deny reality by vote.

Captain Vidal, likewise, ignores the magic occurring around him. He is unaware that the doctor caring for his wife and Mercedes, the head of the household servants, are both in league with the rebels, giving them aid and access. He fails to recognize the power of the mandrake root under his wife's bed. He fears the power of the rebels and the mysterious knowledge which makes no sense to him. He is unaware of the dangers that surround him, from the monstrous toad under the tree to Mercedes, who will eventually stab and mutilate him, finally overseeing his execution by the rebels, telling him his son will "never know your name." Like the Parliament of Erl, he believes the force of his will can overcome magical reality.

Even Ofelia, who believes, must adjust to the magical reality. She cannot understand the fairies from the moment they appear to the quest to the Pale Man's lair. Conversely, in Dunsany, when the troll Lurulu first arrives in the human realms he wants to tell the pigeons he meets the legends of Elfland, "but found that he could not make them understand troll talk."[21] A major theme in both Dunsany and del Toro is the cultural differences between the human and magical worlds. Just as Dunsany, an Irishman in England, and del Toro, a Mexican in the United States, are border-crossing artists, their characters understand the challenges of transitioning from culture to culture. Alveric must adjust to Elfland, Lurulu must adjust to the human realms, Lirazel as well must come to understand the ways of men, just as Ofelia must learn how to behave appropriately in the magical world. In both narratives, when taboo or cultural rule is broken, the consequences are serious.

At heart, both *Pan's Labyrinth* and *The King of Elfland's Daughter* are actually tales of magical beings living in the human world where they must transcend the mundane reality and gain their way back to the magical kingdom as well as children being reunited with their real parents. Dunsany's tale begins with Lirazel, the eponymous daughter of the king of Elfland, meeting and marrying Alveric, who has come to Elfland in search of a magical bride. She returns with him to the human realm, much to her father's displeasure. Lirazel misses Elfland, but is happy with her husband and child. Her father sends a troll to her bringing a rune which, when she reads it, transports her back to Elfland, and she seemingly forgets her time among men, remembering her family through a haze. Orion, her son by Alveric, is raised by the witch Ziroonderel. Alveric searches for his wife, and eventually all three are reunited in Elfland.

Del Toro's tale also begins with the Faun narrating a fairy story similar to this:

> A long time ago, in the underground realm, where there are no lies or pain, there lived a Princess who dreamed of the human world. She dreamed of blue skies, soft breeze, and sunshine. One day, eluding her keepers, the Princess escaped. Once outside, the brightness blinded her and erased every trace of the past from her memory. She forgot who she was and where she came from. Her body suffered cold, sickness, and pain. Eventually, she died. However, her father, the King, always knew that the Princess' soul would return, perhaps in another body, in another place, at another time. And he would wait for her, until he drew his last breath, until the world stopped turning...

Del Toro's story also concerns a princess who escapes to the human realm. With the entry to the human land and the loss of the magical realms, pain and mortality become a reality. In Dunsany, the Elf King was once married to a mortal woman who died, "for she would often stray to the hills of Earth to see the may again, or to see the beechwoods in Autumn; and though she stayed but a day when she came to the fields we know, and was back in the palace beyond the twilight before our sun had set, yet Time found her whenever she came; and so she wore away, and soon died in Elfland."[22] Ofelia is a daughter of the magical realms who abides, like the Elf King's queen, among the humans and then returns. The Faun warns her that since she has failed to complete the task, "the moon will be full in three days. Your spirit shall forever remain among the humans. You shall age like them, you shall die like them, and all memory of you shall fade in time. And we'll vanish along with it. You will never see us again." Both narratives link the daughter of the magical king to the possibility of dying and forgetting.

While some hints of Lovecraft lurk in the corners of *Pan's Labyrinth*, it is a Dunsanian tale: "For Lovecraft, however, the horror of the stories comes when the characters are alerted to a reality far more terrifying than anything they had previously known."²³ Not so in del Toro. The new reality can be terrifying, as when Ofelia encounters the Pale Man or the monstrous toad, but it can be just as satisfying, as when she discovers she is, in fact, a lost princess. And while the toad and the Pale Man are dangerous, they are easily defeated. Not so Captain Vidal, who is actually far more dangerous than either of the magical threats. He is, in fact, the only one to actually hurt Ofelia, possibly killing her. But in dying, she returns to the magical kingdom, where she is welcomed by the King, her true father, and her mother, resurrected in the magical lands as well.

"Elfboy"? *Hellboy II* and Dunsany

In his director's commentary on the DVD of *Pan's Labyrinth*, del Toro states that that film forms an intertext with *The Devil's Backbone*. Subsequently, in the director's commentary on the DVD for *Hellboy II*, del Toro states that that film forms an intertext with *Pan's Labyrinth*. All three are texts about lost children seeking to make the world right again and share many common factors. *Hellboy II*, like *Pan's Labyrinth*, contains multiple echoes of Dunsany and especially *The King of Elfland's Daughter*, to the point of showing the story of King Balor of Elfland via animation while Professor Broom narrates the background of the Golden Army to a young Hellboy. As much as his previous film, *Hellboy II* employs the elements and tropes of Dunsany's novel to tell a fairy tale for adults about the relationship between the magical world and our own.

While they see *Hellboy* as an "apocalyptic, Lovecraftian, cosmic horror" (indeed, del Toro himself sees Sammael from the original as "from the nightmarish Old Ones of *At the Mountains of Madness*"),²⁴ Keith McDonald and Roger Clark find Dunsany in *Hellboy II: The Golden Army* "far more influence by another, less well-known fantasy writer, Lord Dunsany, whose classic *The King of Elfland's Daughter* (1924) involves a questing prince, son of the King of Elfland, and which juxtaposes human and magical worlds."²⁵ *Hellboy II* features scenes set in Elfland, and feature the King of Elfland and his daughter, while also introducing a psychotic son, Prince Nuada.

Tony Vinci argues that "del Toro's treatment of Dunsany is somewhat of a reversal. While in Dunsany's *The King of Elfland's Daughter,* part of the human world is transformed into a parcel of Elfland, and Lirazel and Alveric live eternally in an earthly paradise, in del Toro's world the opposite happens: families and lovers are separated and the Elven qualities of the world disappear."[26] This statement, however, is simply not true. Alveric and Lirazel are separated from each other for most of the novel, and he spends decades searching for a new way into Elfland while their son, Orion, is separated from both parents and raised by a witch. The borderlands in Dunsany, as noted above, are fluid and can recede, flow and ebb, being described as being at "high tide," and being described as "Elfland came racing back as the tide over flat sands."[27] Del Toro's Elfland is also always present, but has receded somewhat.

The audience is shown that the Troll Market (and again, note that Dunsany places Trolls and Elves together in Elfland, working together—Tolkien, on the other hand makes Trolls and Elves enemies) is actually under the Brooklyn Bridge, and Prince Nuala lives directly underneath it. King Baylor, Princess Nuala and the rest of the Elf court exist nearby. Darrell Schweitzer, examining Lovecraft's debt to Dunsany, observes that "there is a clear implication ... that if one goes down into the ghoul tunnels under Boston one arrives, not at the earth's molten core, but in dreamland, as if our mundane world were just the top layer covering another reality."[28] This could also be a description of the world of *Hellboy II,* in which the Troll Market is found directly under the Brooklyn Bridge.

As with *Cronos* and the erasure of cosmic horror in favor of a local, Mexican one, *Hellboy II* desacralizes, if not desecrates the magical reality and divinity of its magical world. The film depicts an auction of supernatural and religious items at Blackwood Auction House. Among the items for sale is a fifteen-thousand-year-old statue of a fertility goddess. It sells for $375,000. Hellboy subsequently uses it to kill a number of tooth fairies. The figure was once worshipped as a god, and now it is décor for some wealthy individual. In the end, it is only as valuable as its use, which is to kill little monsters attacking the Bureau of Paranormal Research and Defense team, and Hellboy joyfully pushes it over. Idols literally fall and magical things die. The deity the statue represents is shown to be a myth, just as all other gods in the Hellboy milieu. Hell is real, demons are real, but God or the gods are not.

While Nuala has much in common with Ofelia, both daughters dedicated to fathers (Ofelia's real father, not Vidal, in her case) who sacrifice themselves to repair the rift between magical and mundane worlds, and both are princesses, like Lirazel, who find themselves trapped between the two worlds, it is the princes that are the center of *Hellboy II*. Orion has much in common with Hellboy himself: a child from between worlds who grows to be a warrior, barely tamed, with supernatural abilities, raised by a stepparent. Nuada also points out the similarities between himself and Hellboy: "You have more in common with us than with them. You could be a king." Nuada seeks not to mend the rift between magic and mundane worlds, but to conquer the human one in order to reassert Elfland's dominance.

Nuada's war is, from his perspective, a religious one: "The humans … the humans have forgotten the gods, destroyed the earth, and for what? Parking lots? Shopping malls? Greed had burned a hole in their hearts that will never be filled! They will never have enough!" The humans have forgotten the gods and Nuada plans to remind them that the gods are real. Except no gods are ever seen or shown. Tooth fairies, the Angel of Death (or, as discussed above, the Angel of Hellboy's death), trolls and goblins might be real, but the gods are not. The magical creatures are just as petty and lost as the humans they surround and occasionally fight. Prince Nuada Silverlance does not remind anyone of the gods they have forgotten. He finds the Golden Army, is challenged by Hellboy for control of them and is first defeated by Hellboy and then killed when his sister, with whom he is linked psychically as well as physically, kills herself so that he will die too. The elven realms are not lands of forgotten gods and magical divinities. Instead, del Toro depicts a world in which the Golden Army is located somewhere in a magical borderland in Scotland, the market is under the Brooklyn Bridge and the only divine presence is an ancient statue, destined to be decoration or a giant flyswatter.

Hellboy II contains echoes of Dunsany, making direct references to *The King of Elfland's Daughter* and other themes found in Dunsany's writing. What del Toro adds is actually a subtraction: the removal of any religious elements and the domestication of the magical and mysterious. In short, del Toro demystifies the magical world, transforming it into just another border region of our own. Whereas Dunsany presents a mythical Elfland from prehistory, del Toro's Elfland is subsumed into the recognizable contemporary world.

Conclusion

It is no great revelation that Lovecraft and Dunsany echo through del Toro's films. He admits his influences freely and frequently. Instead, I posit that what the audience sees in del Toro's work are a series of echoes and intertexts with the narratives of those two authors, particularly *Cool Air* in the case of *Cronos* and *The King of Elfland's Daughter* in *Pan's Labyrinth* and *Hellboy II*. In all three cases, del Toro does what Lovecraft and Dunsany already began in their narratives: removing the supernatural, un-deifying the gods, and reducing the border between magic and mundane, domesticating the horror. Whereas Lovecraft remained firmly ensconced in the realm of cosmic horror, del Toro localizes that horror. On the other hand, del Toro embraces Dunsany's ironic vision of a magical world that ebbs and flows next to our more mundane world. In Lovecraft, narrators discover the horrific reality underlying ours. In Dunsany, the characters are already aware of the other world and can move between them. In del Toro, the characters often discover the magical world, realize it is a part of our own, and move freely between them.

Notes

1. Guillermo del Toro and Marc Scott Zicree, *Guillermo del Toro Cabinet of Curiosities* (San Rafael, CA: Insight Editions, 2013), 260.
2. H.P. Lovecraft, *Supernatural Horror in Literature* [1927] (New York: Dover, 1973), 98, 99.
3. del Toro and Zicree, *Cabinet of Curiosities*, 66–67. Del Toro, in the director's commentary track on the DVDs for *Pan's Labyrinth*, *Hellboy II: The Golden Army*, and *Cronos*, the films considered here, is quick to cite and site his influences and frequently draws attention to where he has paid visual tribute to his literary heroes.
4. H.P. Lovecraft, *Selected Letters, Volume I* (Sauk City, WI: Arkham House, 1965), 315.
5. The term is Steven Mariconda's, after Graham Harmon. Lovecraft is a "weird realist" ("Easy as Falling Off Logic: A Consideration of Lovecraft and Ligotti as 'Weird Realists,'" *Lovecraft and Influence: His Predecessors and Successors*, edited by Robert Waugh [Lanham, MD: Scarecrow Press, 2013], 168). For that matter, so is del Toro.
6. H.P. Lovecraft, *The Dunwich Horror and Others* [1963] (Sauk City, WI: Arkham House, 1982), 199.
7. Ibid., 201, 203.
8. Ibid., 203.

9. H.P. Lovecraft, "The Alchemist," in *Dagon and Other Macabre Tales* (Sauk City, WI: Arkham House, 1965).
10. del Toro and Zicree, *Cabinet of Curiosities*, 25, 67.
11. H.P. Lovecraft, *Supernatural Horror in Literature*, 99.
12. "Guillermo del Toro." *Elmundo.es*, October 9, 2006, http://www.elmundo.es/encuentros/ invitados/2006/10/2192/.
13. Laura Garrido Eslava, "Spanish Language Movie: El labertino del Fauno" *The Spanish Blog*, February 16, 2012, http://www.thespanishblog.com/2012/02/spanish-language-movie- el-labertino-del-Fauno-pans-labyrinth.
14. S.T. Joshi, *Lord Dunsany: Master of the Anglo-Irish Imagination* (Westport, CT: Greenwood, 1995), 3.
15. del Toro and Zicree, *Cabinet of Curiosities*, 100.
16. Ibid.
17. Neil Gaiman, "Introduction," *The King of Elfland's Daughter* by Lord Dunsany (New York: Del Rey, 1999), xii.
18. Ibid.
19. John Edward Dunsany, *The King of Elfland's Daughter* (New York: Del Rey, 1999), 1.
20. Ibid., 209.
21. Ibid., 157.
22. Ibid., 173.
23. Alex Houstoun, "'Harken ... I can tell you the whole story': Monologues and Confession in the Early Works of H.P. Lovecraft and Edgar Allen Poe," in *Lovecraft and Influences: His Predecessors and Successors*, edited by Robert H. Waugh (Lanham, MD: Scarecrow Press, 2013), 52.
24. del Toro and Zicree, *Cabinet of Curiosities*, 134.
25. Keith McDonald and Roger Clark, *Guillermo del Toro: Film as Alchemical Art* (London: Bloomsbury, 2014), 181–2.
26. Tony M. Vinci, "Remembering Why We Once Feared the Dark: Reclaiming Humanity through Fantasy in Guillermo del Toro's *Hellboy II*," *Journal of Popular Culture* 45, no. 5 (2012): 1046.
27. Ibid., 124, 120.
28. Darrell Schweitzer, "Lovecraft's Debt to Dunsany," in *Lovecraft and Influence: His Predecessors and Successors*, edited by Robert H. Waugh (Lanham, MD: Scarecrow Press, 2013), 63.

Bibliography

del Toro, Guillermo, and Marc Scott Zicree. *Guillermo del Toro Cabinet of Curiosities*. San Rafael, CA: Insight Editions, 2013.
Dunsany, Edward John Moreton Drax Plunkett, Baron. *The Blessing of Pan*. New York: G.P. Putnam's Sons, 1927.
_____. *The Charwoman's Shadow*. New York: Del Rey, 1999.
_____. *Don Rodriguez: Chronicles of Shadow Valley*. New York: G.P. Putnam's Sons, 1922.
_____. *The King of Elfland's Daughter*. New York: Del Rey, 1999.

Eslava, Laura Garrido. "Spanish Language Movie: El labertino del Fauno." *The Spanish Blog*. February 16, 2012. http://www.thespanishblog.com/2012/02/spanish-language-movie- el-labertino-del-Fauno-pans-labyrinth.

Gaiman, Neil. "Introduction." *The King of Elfland's Daughter* by Lord Dunsany. New York: Del Rey, 1999. xi-xiii.

"Guillermo del Toro." *Elmundo.es*. October 9, 2006. http://www.elmundo.es/encuentros/ invitados/2006/10/2192/.

Houstoun, Alex. "'Harken ... I can tell you the whole story': Monologues and Confession in the Early Works of H.P. Lovecraft and Edgar Allen Poe." In *Lovecraft and Influences: His Predecessors and Successors*, edited by Robert H. Waugh. Lanham, MD: Scarecrow Press, 2013, 45–53.

Joshi, S.T. *Lord Dunsany: Master of the Anglo-Irish Imagination*. Westport, CT: Greenwood, 1995.

Lovecraft, H.P. "The Alchemist." In *Dagon and Other Macabre Tales*. Sauk City, WI: Arkham House, 1965,308–316.

_____. *The Dunwich Horror and Others*. [1963] Sauk City, WI: Arkham House, 1982.

_____. *Selected Letters, Volume I*. Sauk City, WI: Arkham House, 1965.

_____. *Supernatural Horror in Literature*. [1927] New York: Dover, 1973.

Mariconda, Steven J. "Easy as Falling Off Logic: A Consideration of Lovecraft and Ligotti as 'Weird Realists.'" In *Lovecraft and Influence: His Predecessors and Successors*, edited by Robert H. Waugh. Lanham, MD: Scarecrow Press, 2013, 165–179.

McDonald, Keith, and Roger Clark: *Guillermo del Toro: Film as Alchemical Art*. London: Bloomsbury, 2014.

Schweitzer, Darrell. "Lovecraft's Debt to Dunsany." In *Lovecraft and Influence: His Predecessors and Successors*, edited by Robert H. Waugh. Lanham, MD: Scarecrow Press, 2013, 55–67.

Vinci, Tony M. "Remembering Why We Once Feared the Dark: Reclaiming Humanity through Fantasy in Guillermo del Toro's *Hellboy II*." *Journal of Popular Culture* 45, no. 5 (2012): 1041–1059.

Slime and Subtlety
Monsters in del Toro's Spanish-Language Films

ANN DAVIES

This essay focuses on the Spanish-language films of Guillermo del Toro with the aim of arguing that the director combines the tenets of the fantasy and horror genres with a more muted approach to his material that is regularly associated with foreign language film. It does this by looking specifically at the different permutations that del Toro offers to the figure of the monster. The latter days of del Toro's career to date have been dedicated to big-budget blockbusters in English, and although *Pan's Labyrinth* (*El laberinto del Fauno* in the original Spanish) has received widespread critical acclaim, his directorial work in film and now TV continues to draw on an apocalyptic-style of monster familiar from the *Hellboy* films and *Pacific Rim*. In this chapter I propose that the Spanish-language approach to monstrosity merits celebration because of its subtler and often more surprising approach to the horrors of monsters.

There are good reasons for the subtlety. According to the Internet Movie Database, all del Toro's English-language films apart from *Mimic* have had budgets of over $50 million, and *Pacific Rim*, the most recent film at the time of writing, had a budget of approximately $190 million. Compare this to the budget of *Pan's Labyrinth*, which had a budget of $13,500,000, the biggest budget of del Toro's three Spanish-language films but barely comparable to the budgets of the *Hellboy* films made either side of it ($66 million and $85 million dollars, respectively).[1] *Pan's Labyrinth* shares in the high production values of the English-language action adventure films, drawing on prosthetics, CGI, and special effects. The differences between this film and one like *Pacific Rim*, that would account for a lower budget, are also, however, fairly obvious: an inability of characters to escape their environments that arises from fewer sets; an avoidance of action-adventure style that leads to smaller casts; and a greater emphasis on child actors at the expense of big-name stars. The Spanish-language films—*Cronos* and *The Devil's Backbone* (*El espinazo del diablo*) as well as *Pan's Labyrinth*—have a more claustrophobic feel about them due to the limited range of action for the plot and characters: only *Mimic* out of the English-language films comes close in comparison. *The Devil's Backbone* and *Pan's Labyrinth* in particular have isolated settings that reinforce the sense of entrapment, a strong contrast to the wide-ranging *Hellboy* and *Pacific Rim*: the children's home and the old mill become places of suffocating tension. The small scale of the Spanish films enhances the tensions and subsequent violence, which occur precisely because there is no room for co-existence.

These films owe their artistic success in part precisely because they are small-scale. The claustrophobia and isolation match the circumscribed remit of the Spanish-language films compared to the English-language ones, where the action ranges over many countries. It also matches the idea that foreign-language cinema and Hollywood blockbusters don't mix. With the blockbusters, the world is their stage; the limited settings of *Cronos*, *The Devil's Backbone* and *Pan's Labyrinth* are in strong contrast. Critique of del Toro's films in the early days tended to make a neat division between them according to language, with the Spanish side seen as less obviously commercial. Although initial grosses for films are a fairly rough and ready point of comparison (they take no account, for example, of DVD sales), they are indicative. *Pan's Labyrinth* made a gross of over $37 million in the U.S., but *Hellboy II*, the film that followed, took over $75 million.[2]

These differences are pronounced enough for some del Toro experts to argue for the Spanish-language films as a sort of trilogy.[3] My own feeling is that we could argue for a diptych of *Devil's Backbone* and *Pan's Labyrinth* based on their historical settings, the mirror images of before and after the end of the Spanish civil war and the arrival of General Franco's dictatorship; the contrasting settings of barren plain and dense forest; and male and female child protagonists. But it is hard to see how *Cronos* meshes with these two films beyond the shared language. The three films do share themes, style and personnel, but this sharing is not confined to the Spanish-language films: it includes for instance, themes such as a resistance against corrupt power or malignant bureaucracy, and the heroic defiance of the individual, all of which can be found in del Toro's films regardless of language. What also links the films, more obviously, is the fact that they all draw on variants of fantasy, even if the elderly vampire of *Cronos* seems very far removed from the Kaiju and Jaegers of *Pacific Rim*. Del Toro also scatters references to other writings and films almost indiscriminately throughout his work, to the extent that he becomes self-referential in later films (such as the jars of deformed fetuses, the motif from *The Devil's Backbone*, which reappear in the Bureau for Paranormal Research in *Hellboy*).

Del Toro's Monsters

More specifically, del Toro makes copious use of monstrous figures in all his films. CGI and prosthetics allow crossover here too, from the hellhounds and troll markets of the Hellboy films to the Faun and the Pale Man of *Pan's Labyrinth*. For those who like their monsters slimy and repulsive there is much to fascinate. The permanent cloud of blood and scum that surrounds Santi of *Devil's Backbone*, the revolting goo spewed out by the toad of *Pan's Labyrinth* or the gaping jaws of the Reapers in *Blade II* go a long way to satisfy such fascinations. Death, or the prospect of it, at the hands (or other trappings) of the monsters, is often horrific: gnawed to death in a matter of seconds by a tooth fairy, drowned in a tank of dirty water by a ghost, the potential to be eaten by a monster with eyes in his hands. Many of del Toro's monsters are also heroes, such as Jesús Gris in *Cronos* or Hellboy, but even these sympathetic characters have monstrous traits. The image of Gris licking blood from a washroom floor is one of the most arresting and horrible of the film, literally showing the depths to which he has sunk. The shaved horns of Hellboy fit with the quirky humor with which the character is presented, along with a love of kittens and Baby Ruth bars, but the moment when Hellboy allows his horns to grow back in response to Rasputin's threats is more disturbing, suggesting that a more threatening monster has always lurked behind Hellboy's wisecracking façade. There are also parallel motifs across the language divide, such as the Angel of Death in *Hellboy II* with eyes in the wings that recall the eyes in the Pale Man's hands in *Pan's Labyrinth*.

Mechanical monsters, however, suggest a point at which the films might divide along blockbuster/arthouse lines and thus to some extent along language lines as well. The mechanical device in *Cronos* that turns Gris into a vampire is itself a monster just like its user, a hybrid of machinery and insect life that probes delicately but sharply under Gris's skin. The Cronos device itself is an intriguing cyborg, spider-like with its claws and probe yet with a carapace of golden beauty. Although it does not have a humanoid shape it bears comparison with the other cyborgs of del Toro's work such as the Golden Army or Rasputin's helper Kroenen, all mechanical yet animated. The device is small—thus easily transportable to the New World, unlike the Golden Army trapped under the Giant's Causeway in Northern Ireland. It is easily hidden inside Aurora's teddy bear, indicating how the sinister lurks even within the everyday world of a child, a motif that del Toro would repeat in *Devil's Backbone* (such as Jaime's sketchbook) and *Pan's Labyrinth* (Ofelia's storybook). As Gris uses the device, del Toro cuts to a close-up shot inside it in which the insect lurks amongst whirling cogs. Those cogs reappear a decade and a half later in the climatic fight with Prince Nuada and the Golden Army in *Hellboy II*. The cogs are now, however, on a much larger scale, while the cyborgs that form the Golden Army are brash weapons of mass destruction as opposed to the small-scale but deadly Cronos device. This comparison hints at an aspect that continues to differentiation the English- and Spanish-language films to date: the simple matter of scale.

Another clear difference between the two sets of films is that the Spanish-language films are less apocalyptic. While the heroes of *Pacific Rim* fight a worldwide scourge of Kaiju, and Hellboy saves the human race from extinction—twice—the monsters of the Spanish-language films do not threaten the end of the world in the manner of Hollywood monsters. The monsters of *Cronos*, *Devil's Backbone* and *Pan's Labyrinth* lean to wider traditions of monstrosity that draw on production values reminiscent of Hollywood (vampires, ghosts, and fairy tale creatures), while emphasizing an allegorical style often to be found in earlier Hispanic cinema. The result is that the Spanish-language films offer monsters that inspire fear and repulsion through misshapen decaying or slimy bodies, but the threats they embody or respond to are small-scale or local, in which the human race by and large are never in danger. Nevertheless, in order to resonate with audiences beyond the immediate context they refer to, these monsters must respond to or embody threats that are readily transferable. Their battles to the death are inherently local affairs, often inextricably joined to local conflicts. The local conflicts themselves are indicative of wider sociopolitical concerns—the fear of neocolonialism in *Cronos*, the fight against Fascism in *Pan's Labyrinth* and *The Devil's Backbone*—but the monstrous threat is up close and personal.

The Devil's Backbone: Ghosts as History and Horror

Take Santi in *The Devil's Backbone*, for example: the action of the film takes place against the background of the Spanish civil war in its final days, and Franco's conquering troops are an ever-present but never seen menace lurking off screen. Yet the dead boy Santi has no concern with this, and his whispered promise that many of the living boys in the children's home will die is a forecast as much of the violence among the home's occupants as of the Francoist doom just beyond the horizon. Santi is not out to save any of his friends but to avenge his own death at the hands of Jacinto. Unlike the world of *Pacific Rim*, 1930s Spain does not experience the relief of a threat averted. Instead, at the end of the film the surviving boys leave the home for an uncertain future, walking towards that very horizon where Franco's troops are likely to appear. Since their father fought on the losing Republican side, against Franco, the boys' futures do not promise much.

The Spanish civil war is an example of a local conflict that nonetheless had, and still has, wider echoes in world history and politics. In some measure a de facto rehearsal of the dividing lines of World War II, the Spanish civil war was seen by many on both sides, in Spain and abroad, as not simply a fight about political control of Spain but a conflict of good and evil. Where the two sides were split was over what that evil generally was. The eventually victorious forces of General Franco believed the greatest dangers to Spain to be inherent in Marxism or socialism, in a loss of power of the Catholic Church, in a secular state that permitted divorce, and in a government that allowed regional areas, such as Catalonia and the Basque Country, a greater say in their own affairs, which hinted at the possible break-up of the Spanish nation. Those who fought on the side of the elected Republican government fought against the rise of Fascism, for freedom of beliefs and self-determination at the regional and local level, for secular education and better rights for women, and for an end to the grinding poverty in which many Spaniards lived. These ideas speak to more universal values in which many people share beyond Spain. In this way, del Toro's films set in Spain can be perceived at both a local and a universal level: a knowledge of Spanish history is not essential to view the films, although if you do know the history there are resonances to each film that are not apparent at the generic level. The idea of fighting against Fascism is still a powerful one today for many people in many countries, even though Fascism was only one element of a coalition of right-wing forces under Franco. The death of children and the corruption of their innocence also speaks to a wider audience beyond—but encompassing—the Spanish one. (It is worth bearing in mind that many Spaniards fled to Mexico, del Toro's country of birth, during and after the war, while Mexico was a rare example of a country openly supporting the Republican government.)

Santi of *The Devil's Backbone* is one of a number of ghostly children in Spanish cinema who could be thought to stand for the lost Republican victims of the Spanish civil war. He is in good company alongside the ghosts from *The Orphanage* (*El orfanato*, 2007), *The Haunting* (*NO-DO*, 2009), *Darkness* (2002), *The Nameless* (1999), and *The Others* (2001). Not all these ghosts have a direct connection with the Civil War: the ghosts of *The Others*, for instance, derive from World War II Jersey and those of *The Orphanage* derive from the childhood of the central character Laura, now grown up. Nonetheless many commentators have made the connection between the ghosts and the Civil War—these children are lost victims in search of justice. During the war and the early Franco era many people died, were executed without trial, were imprisoned, went into hiding or simply disappeared. While there were atrocities on both sides—Franco's forces and those of the Republican government—there is still bitter dispute in Spain as to whether one side was more culpable than the other. A law passed in 2007, to allow families access to historical records in order to track down missing relatives, and to prohibit the glorification of the Franco era, has proved highly controversial. What is beyond doubt, however, is that once in power Franco showed no tolerance at all for those who had fought against him; and throughout his regime the defeated had no voice. They were censored, or indeed censored themselves, for fear of reprisals by the regime. It is not hard to imagine, then, that the equation between the fictional and the real ghosts of the Spanish past is easily made. Del Toro's Santi is an easier fit than most given that *The Devil's Backbone* is clearly set in the Civil War period, and while his murderer avows no political allegiance he shares many characteristics of the Francoist Right, dismissing the rest of the members of the home as "reds" (rojos).

Yet to insist on a straightforward political or historical reading of Santi neglects the pleasures of the ghost. Many of the films listed above as examples of Spanish ghost films do not necessarily set out deliberately to invoke Spanish national history, and indeed audiences outside Spain can and do get by without any knowledge of the historical background. Alongside the efforts to recover the memories and the stories of those who were denied a voice, is a surge in Spanish horror and Gothic. Spain's contribution to horror film has been of long-standing if largely unrecognized until recently (as Antonio Lázaro Reboll has detailed in his recent book *Spanish Horror Film*),[4] but it is better known now and del Toro is one of the filmmakers who have brought it to international attention, not only through films such as *The Devil's Backbone* but also through his work as producer, lending his talents and his name to films such as *The Orphanage*. Many Spanish directors are now doing as del Toro has done, switching between language and industries. Jaume Balagueró made English his default screenplay language until the *[REC]* films, Alejandro Amenábar's *The Others* was also made in English, with star Nicole Kidman heading an Anglophone cast, and J. A. Bayona of *The Orphanage* has become involved in the TV series *Penny Dreadful* by way of disaster movie *The Impossible*, again with Anglophone actors.

Santi as ghost readily invokes the horror genre, and makes a satisfyingly slimy monster (an extension, perhaps, of his original pursuit of slugs in the underground cellar that led to him being caught by Jacinto and murdered). His final resting place in the underground water reservoir is fittingly nasty, filled with a murky ochre water that dyes him a similar color. His most notable trademark is the stream of blood that flows from the wound in his head, his eternal mark as a murder victim. Although we are very likely to feel sympathy for Santi as an innocent, he functions nonetheless as the focus of horror. He was the boys' friend, but now they whisper fearfully about "the one who sighs," and notice that when Carlos arrives, he is given Santi's bed in the orphanage. Carlos in fact replaces Santi, the new friend of many of the boys and ultimately Jaime, who was with Santi as he died and who knows what happened. Their fear of and implicit rejection of their former friend is hardly surprising: Santi is the one who intones that many of the members of the home will die, a prophecy all too accurate. In addition, Santi's pursuit of Carlos through the corridors of the home is as unnerving for Carlos as for us. The chilling pause of suspension as Carlos cowers in the linen cupboard is reinforced by the sudden shock of Santi's monstrous eye peering through the keyhole. (There seems to be no danger, however, of Santi passing through the cupboard door, which logically poses questions as to how he got out of the cellar and into the home in the first place.)

In many ways these marks of horror are hard to square with the concept of Santi as representative of victims of the Spanish civil war. This is perhaps one of the most intriguing elements of *Devil's Backbone*: the child as monster inspires both pity and fear. This is not the case for all child monsters—we feel no pity for Damian in *The Omen* (1976), or the mysterious children of *Village of the Damned* (1960). But it is the case for many such children. Examples that come readily to mind include Joseph of *The Changeling* (1980), Tomás in *The Orphanage*, even Sadako in *Ringu* (1998). They become monsters because of the wrongs done to them by adults. The child remains nonetheless the monster to be feared. The horror vehicle that contains the child monster may not necessarily aspire to the arthouse values of *Devil's Backbone*, but child monsters from such as Santi to those such as the vomiting Regan of *The Exorcist* (1973) share in both gross-out value or frissons of horror (or both) and also their sheer domesticity. Child monsters do not threaten the world, but the home, and as such are all the more menacing. Santi may symbolize forgotten Civil War victims, but his monstrosity also derives from del Toro's effective use of horror style.

Pan's Labyrinth: The Most Frightening Monsters Are Human

The double storyline of *Pan's Labyrinth* offers a different approach to history and monstrosity. Ofelia is engaged on her own personal quest for salvation and a fairy tale happy ending, yet she follows her mission amidst the violent events of the Civil War's aftermath. Although the war ended in 1939, guerrilla resistance to Franco continued in the hope that the victorious Allies would oust Franco just as they had helped to oust Mussolini and would go on to vanquish Hitler. What actually happened was that the Allies left Franco in power, although ostracized for a few years; then, with the threat of the Soviet Union, there was increasing rapprochement between the West and the virulently anti–Communist Franco. As these events occurred, guerrilla warfare from the Resistance petered out and it would be a while before concerted and active opposition to Franco's regime would reappear. Since *Pan's Labyrinth* is set in 1944, all these events are in the future, and the Resistance fights on in the belief that the Allies will eventually come to their aid. The victory of the Resistance over Captain Vidal at the end of the film gives no hint of the wider defeat that is to come. Although the ending of *Pan's Labyrinth* is hardly upbeat, we do have a sense that the "right" side won the battle even as Ofelia's sacrifice is redeemed through her entry into her magic kingdom as Princess Moanna. This idea that things have been set right is also enhanced by the parallels between Vidal and the Nazi villains that stride across many a World War II film only to be defeated in the final reel. The ending is of a piece with fairy tales and fantasies that often wrap things up with a settling of accounts and a restoration of order, particularly when it comes to fantasy royal dynasties. *Pan's Labyrinth* suggests that even historical facts can be susceptible to a fantasy rejigging, softening the sharp distinction between fact and fiction. Yet there has been some concern that del Toro is rewriting Spanish history and neglecting the historical outcome of the Spanish resistance.[5] The defeat of Vidal gives the impression that right-wing oppression was ended in Spain. This was far from the case: the ending runs the risk of skating over the long years of a dictatorship that already had a strong grip in 1944.

Ofelia's resistance to Vidal is easily read as both a resistance to the Franco regime he represents and more widely a resistance to Fascism and dictatorship: in this sense we could argue that like the heroes of del Toro's English-language films she works to make the world a better place. Many critics have commented on the parallels between the historical level of the film and the fantasy one[6]; but this neglects the very personal nature of Ofelia's quest. She seeks redemption for herself above all: this is not to make her out to be a selfish character, but it is to say that her desire to escape a highly unpleasant reality takes on a very specific form in terms of an improvement of her own status. It is also to say that one of the pleasures we take in this film is the quest narrative itself, the chance of transforming one's life through a well-known fairy tale formula of three tasks. Where del Toro most successfully blurs the boundaries of the divide between fantasy and reality is in his ability to combine both levels of the storyline through the outcome of Ofelia's quest. Her refusal to surrender her baby brother to be killed turns out to be both a triumph and a defeat. The refusal to sacrifice her brother means that Vidal catches up with her and shoots her dead, by far the most shocking moment in a film that nonetheless has plenty such. Yet this sacrifice of herself in place of her brother is the final test of Ofelia's worthiness, and she is welcomed back to her magic realm by her father. She is reunited with her mother and brother (intriguing that he should be there given that he is still presumably Vidal's child), and applauded by the Faun and the assembled multitude.

In terms of fantasy, then, this is an appropriate end to a quest narrative: the quest is successful, yet success depends on a twist and apparent failure (the refusal to carry out the Faun's final instruction to kill the baby). Ofelia's refusal shows that she has the true instinct of a heroine, to do what is right rather than to do what she is told. Such an instinct is well established by the time we get to this point, since in following her quest at earlier points in the film Ofelia goes directly against her mother's instructions, to abandon the idea of fairy tales and to be sure to look nice for Vidal's dinner party. The contrast with Ofelia's failure in the second quest, where she refused to obey the Faun's command to eat nothing from the banquet table, further underscores the fact that Ofelia relies on what her heart tells her: despite the apparent lesson from the second quest (her failure to obey awakens the Pale Man), she still will not do what the Faun tells her.

Yet on the "historical" level of the narrative the ending is a tragedy: a child dies. I can still remember my shock at that moment when I first saw the film, not knowing what was going to happen. Surely the young girl protagonist couldn't *die* at the end of the film? It is a surprising outcome given the traditions of quest narratives, in which the self-sacrifice is somehow rejigged so that the quester survives in some manner. Their own survival may not always be so triumphant as Ofelia's return to the magic kingdom: Frodo's end in *The Lord of the Rings* (both novel and final film of the trilogy), for instance, is a bittersweet one. Rarely does the quester simply die, however. We can also see Ofelia's death in terms of the antagonist relationship between herself and Vidal, in which for once the wicked stepparent wins the contest, albeit briefly. This line of narrative has much to do with fairy tales, while the antagonism between the two has little to do with the historical setting. Nonetheless the historical reading (or perhaps misreading) in terms of Spanish history is still available to us, even if you do not have to know the history in order to see the tragedy. Ofelia's death can be seen as the victimization of those who dared to resist the forces of Franco, and it is fitting in that sense that Vidal himself is shot dead soon afterwards by the *maquis*, and that Mercedes informs him that his son will never even know his father's name. Children certainly suffered during the Civil War and under Franco, and many films recognize this, though the death of a child protagonist is still very unusual. We can see this latter point clearly by comparing *Pan's Labyrinth* with *Devil's Backbone*, where, as Santi rightly prophesizes, many of the boys die, but the protagonist survives. There is an intriguing sequel to this in that Carlos and Jaime from *Devil's Backbone* (or at least the actors playing them) turn up in *Pan's Labyrinth* as part of the dead and dying *maquis* forces defeated in a skirmish with Vidal's troops. This continuity across the films suggests childhood resistance during the war as part of a continuum in which people resist and die as commonplaces of war. Ofelia's death against this backdrop stands out for the tragic emphasis that del Toro awards it.

This emphasis on the ending is not to deny the success of other parallels in the film, including those of monstrosity, which here is handled differently than *Devil's Backbone*. Many commentators have noticed, for instance, the parallel between the Pale Man and Vidal seated at banquet tables, equally willing to victimize the helpless children under their control. Indeed, both turn out to be child killers, while at the same time both place a very high and exploitative value on children, though in different ways (the Pale Man prizes them as food, while Vidal is obsessed with his son who will, he hopes, carry on the Vidal family name). *Pan's Labyrinth* pushes this comparison further by setting up Vidal as monster even to the extent that he becomes misshapen after Mercedes slices his mouth open with her knife. The Pale Man and the toad are truly horrible, while even the Faun, Ofelia's guide, is no cuddly Mr. Tumnus from *The Lion,*

The Witch and the Wardrobe; yet Vidal is the one that will do Ofelia most harm. This sense of monstrosity on the human level carries difficulties in definition in that the term 'monster' is applied to anything shocking rather than to possibly threatening creatures from the fantasy realm. Nevertheless danger comes above all from the violence of other humans, something we also see in *Devil's Backbone*. The boys may be scared of the vague threat of Santi's whispers, but they are far more nervous of the bully Jacinto, who murders Santi, and whose actions bring about both death and resolution at both the human and fantasy level. Jacinto's dislike of the people who surround him, as well as his brutal methods, suggests he shares much common ground with the overtly Francoist Vidal. The ever-present human menace is both more subtle and more frightening than the apocalyptic dangers of the English-language films, and on one level precisely because the terror is so local, so close to home. While humans in the English-language films might ally themselves with evil (Rasputin in *Hellboy*, for example), they have no power without the support of magic or of non-human monsters. Vidal and Jacinto need no such help to be malevolent and for that reason are all the more terrifying, appearing to loom larger than any actual monster. (The use of child protagonists reinforces this point.) The ooze and deformities of the fantasy monsters such as the Pale Man satisfy the requirements of the mix of horror and fantasy genres in *Pan's Labyrinth*, but none of these monsters have Vidal's quiet menace. It is slime *or* subtlety, and the latter is by far the more frightening.

Cronos: Elderly Monsters, Worn-Out Economics

The nuances of slime and subtlety play themselves out in slightly different ways in *Cronos*, ironically the only film set in Mexico despite del Toro's Mexican nationality. This apparent scarcity of Mexican scenes in del Toro's work has arisen for a variety of reasons, not least the troubled relationship of del Toro with the Mexican film industry. The government film body IMCINE (the Mexican Film Institute) showed a distaste for del Toro's early style of filmmaking: they contributed little funding to *Cronos*, were unwilling to distribute a horror film to international festivals, offered a minuscule budget for a Cannes screening, and restricted distribution of the film within Mexico.[7] (*The Devil's Backbone* was originally envisaged with a Mexican setting, but del Toro then decided to merge his script with the Spanish-set plot envisaged by eventual co-writers David Muñoz and Antonio Trashorras[8]; and Spanish film funding proved more forthcoming.) Despite this uneasy relationship between del Toro and his 'home' industry, there have been strong efforts on the director's part to support Mexican film, through production, collaboration, and lobbying for greater support from the Mexican government. Yet *Cronos* at times appears to be the child left behind, slightly detached from the rest of del Toro's work. The motif of vampires reappears, of course, in later work such as *Blade II* and The Strain novels and TV series; while some of del Toro's team of collaborators were in at the very beginning with this film, such as actors Perlman and Luppi, and crew members such as cinematographer Guillermo Navarro.

There is nonetheless a wider conflictual background to *Cronos* as to the other two films, but this time it is the difficult relationship between Mexico and the United States. Part of the southern States (notably Texas, New Mexico, and parts of California) was originally Mexican territory until a war between the two countries which led to defeat in 1848. The United States has also involved itself in Mexican politics, notably supporting the president Porfirio Díaz who was ousted at the start of the Mexican Revolution, as well as specific political figures of the revolutionary era such as Victoriano Huerta. More recently the potential flashpoints of Mexican-American relations are the border, the frontline of tensions related to immigration and drug trafficking, but also the North American Free Trade Agreement (NAFTA) that opened up trade between the two countries. In the relationship between Jesús Gris and the de la Guardias this history is invoked, and in particular we are reminded that the traffic between the two countries has not been one way. The de la Guardias with their decrepit factory have been read by some academics as symbolic of American neo-colonialism and the encroachment of U.S.–style capitalism.[9] The ruined state of the factory suggests that this is an economic and political model that is now worn out, but neo-colonialism, like the de la Guardias themselves, remains a threat. Gris's resistance to them can be—and has been—read in terms of a Latin American resistance to the encroachment of U.S. influence, a Mexican gatekeeper aiming to protect a future generation of Mexicans represented by his granddaughter Aurora.

However, the wider context grabs our attention less than the up-close and personal conflict between Gris, Dieter de la Guardia and Angel that incorporates the monstrous motif of slime. Dolores Tierney has argued cogently that Dieter de la Guardia is the true vampire of the film: "Cinematically, with his combed-back hair, pale countenance, and nocturnal habits (he's around 'all night'), de la Guardia evokes the sinister, gentlemanly appearance of various film Count Draculas (Bela Lugosi in Browning's *Dracula* or Christopher Lee in various Hammer Films productions)."[10] Kept artificially alive beyond his natural lifespan through medical intervention, de la Guardia wants to prolong his life nonetheless, to his nephew's bemusement. Why live so long, when the old man "does nothing but shit and piss all day?" Angel's reference to such noxious bodily fluids hints at the regular association of the monster with ooze: they are part of the monster's everyday existence and thus no bar to the monster wishing to prolong his life. Our attention is also drawn more to the personal battle Gris undergoes with the Cronos device and his metamorphosis into a vampire. Through use of the device he transforms himself from a doddery old man into a suave, dapper gentleman of mature years. The new sophistication comes at a price: the debasement of craving for blood and the addiction to the device. The moment where Gris attempts to lick blood from the washbasin and then the floor of a lavatory offers an arresting image of abjection. Once he is dead, Gris's appearance reverts to the monstrosity that lay underneath the earlier smooth veneer, his pale, lumpy skin peeling away to reveal new layers underneath. Gris's final destruction of the Cronos device in a suicidal gesture ensures protection for Aurora, the only source of blood left to him at the end of the film's climactic fight scene—but it also arrests the total disintegration of corporeal identity into an abject mess.

Vampires are, of course, long associated with the abject nature of blood: their desire for it is why they are monstrous. Many vampire films and novels make a point of contrasting the vampire's sophistication, goodness or beauty with their abject craving, a trend that has become particularly pronounced in vampire vehicles aimed at teens and young adults (though the audiences are actually more varied than that). The contrast between the gentle Gris and his monstrous habits reflects this. Gris also offers a contrast with vampires elsewhere in del Toro's work, where vampires are on the whole unsympathetic. The Reapers of *Blade II* are repulsive beings who threaten other vampires who are for the most part arrogant and hard: on the whole we root for the latter only because Blade—the only one touched with humanity—is working with them. The vampires of *The Strain* trilogy (the novels del Toro has co-written with Chuck Hogan) are voracious killers who threaten New York, in the other vampire tradition of unredeemable and shameless monsters, as in Murnau's *Nosferatu* or more recently the film adaptation of Matheson's *I Am Legend*. The battles with, by and for vampires are, however, those of a younger generation. Gris is of an older generation. (It is striking how the generation of young adults and people in their prime, who would normally supply the heroic fighting figures, are missing from this film.) Just like de la Guardia, Gris too is living beyond his natural lifespan.

Far from the international face-off suggested by NAFTA, we could also perceive the film as the competition of two equally abject monsters to continue to be slimy in perpetuity. The battle of elderly monsters renders it quieter—none of the flourishes of Hellboy or even a veteran such as Pentecost in *Pacific Rim*—but desperate and to the death for all that. Del Toro's battle of slimy senior citizens is an odd, low-key beginning in feature filmmaking for a director who would go on to command the larger budgets of action-adventure blockbusters. Yet it paves the way for the continued development of restrained horror throughout del Toro's career. The ironic, wisecracking nature of the English-language heroes are perhaps simply the flipside of the concentrated horror of the Spanish-language monsters. There is ooze aplenty to be found in all del Toro's films, and in that regard we can argue against an analysis of the Spanish films as a separate set. I think, however, that the Spanish films show the monster at its most truly frightening: not simply part of real human history with specific dates and places, but also inescapable and at times even banal. We may (or may not) prefer the Spanish films because of their supposed art house quality, which is perhaps simply another way of saying they have a subtlety the English-language blockbusters do not possess: I would argue it is undeniable that the monstrosity of the Spanish-language films hits harder precisely because of their quiet restraint.

Notes

1. All budget figures are taken from Internet Movie Database, www.imdb.com. The budgets for *Cronos* and *The Devil's Backbone* were $2 million and $ 4.5 million, respectively.

2. These figures again are from the Internet Movie Database. UK figures also suggest that *Hellboy II*'s gross was greater than that of *Pan's Labyrinth* (£7,379,488 and £1,887,542, respectively). However, the IMDb gives a gross of €7,172,602 for *Pan's Labyrinth* in Spain, while the Spanish government's Ministerio de Cultura suggests a gross of €4, 542, 344 for *Hellboy II*. (They also put the gross for *Pan's Labyrinth* at over €8 million). The latter's audience figures give over a million and a half spectators in Spain for the Spanish film, but under 800,000 for *Hellboy II* (http://www.mecd.gob.es/cultura-mecd/areas-cultura/cine/datos-de-peliculas-calificadas.html). This is suggestive of how *Pan's Labyrinth* functioned as an '"event" film in Spain.

3. See, for example, the chapters by Dolores Tierney and Juan Carlos Vargas in *The Transnational Fantasies of Guillermo del Toro*, Ann Davies, Deborah Shaw and Dolores Tierney, eds. (New York: Palgrave Macmillan, 2014). Peter Hutchings, in the same volume, argues for a stronger continuity across the language divide.

4. Antonio Lázaro Reboll, *Spanish Horror Film* (Edinburgh: Edinburgh University Press, 2012).

5. See, for instance, Deborah Shaw, *The Three Amigos: The Transnational Filmmaking of Guillermo del Toro, Alejandro González Iñárritu and Alfonso Cuarón* (Manchester: Manchester University Press, 2013), 80–81.

6. A good discussion of these parallels can be found in Mercedes Maroto Camino, *Film, Memory and the Legacy of the Spanish Civil War: Resistance and* Guerrilla *1936–2010* (Basingstoke: Palgrave Macmillan 2011), 120–126.

7. Shaw, 21.

8. Miriam Haddu, "Reflected Horrors: Violence, War and the Image in Guillermo del Toro's *El espinazo del Diablo*," in Davies, Shaw and Tierney, 145.

9. See, for instance, John Kraniauskas, "*Cronos* and the Political Economy of Vampirism: Notes on a Historic Constellation," in *Cannibalism and the Colonial World*, eds. Francis Barker, Peter Hulme and Margaret Iverson (Cambridge: Cambridge University Press, 1998), 142–157; Shaw, 19–26.

10. Dolores Tierney, "Transnational Political Horror in *Cronos* (1993), *El espinazo del diablo* (2001) and *El laberinto del Fauno* (2006)," in Davies, Shaw and Tierney, 164–5.

Bibliography

Camino, Mercedes Maroto. *Film, Memory and the Legacy of the Spanish Civil War: Resistance and* Guerrilla *1936–2010*. Basingstoke: Palgrave Macmillan, 2011.

Haddu, Miriam. "Reflected Horrors: Violence, War and the Image in Guillermo del Toro's *El espinazo del diablo*." In *The Transnational Fantasies of Guillermo del Toro*, Ann Davies, Deborah Shaw and Dolores Tierney, eds. New York: Palgrave Macmillan, 2014, 143–59.

Kraniauskas, John. "*Cronos* and the Political Economy of Vampirism: Notes on a Historic Constellation." In *Cannibalism and the Colonial World*, Francis Barker, Peter Hulme and Margaret Iverson, eds. Cambridge: Cambridge University Press, 1998, 142–157.

Lázaro Reboll, Antonio. *Spanish Horror Film*. Edinburgh: Edinburgh University Press, 2012.

Shaw, Deborah Shaw. *The Three Amigos: The Transnational Filmmaking of Guillermo del Toro, Alejandro González Iñárritu and Alfonso Cuarón.* Manchester: Manchester University Press, 2013.

Tierney, Dolores. "Transnational Political Horror in *Cronos* (1993), *El espinazo del diablo* (2001) and *El laberinto del Fauno* (2006)." In *The Transnational Fantasies of Guillermo del Toro,* Ann Davies, Deborah Shaw and Dolores Tierney, eds. New York: Palgrave Macmillan, 2014, 161–82.

Time Out of Joint
Traumatic Hauntings in the Spanish Civil War Films

Karin Brown

> *The time is out of joint. O cursèd spite,*
> *That ever I was born to set it right!*
> —*Hamlet*, 1.5.211–212

Why quote *Hamlet* in an essay about the films of Guillermo del Toro? What play better provides a blueprint for the ghost story and the theme of traumatic haunting: a country at war, a murdered father, a tyrannical substitute, the supernatural erupting through the real but turbulent and violent world, a child set with the task to redress wrongs. For those familiar with del Toro's work these are recognizable recurring tropes. In *Pan's Labyrinth* he directly references Shakespeare's most ghostly play by naming his central character Ofelia. Like the Ophelia in *Hamlet* her future is cut short by the devastating effect on her mind by an oppressive tyrannical regime. The ghost story genre itself can be crystalized by two quotes from the play: "Remember me!"—so powerfully enforced by the Ghost's demand for revenge—and "Time is out of joint…"—the despairing cry of the protagonist whose personal safety and sanity is put at risk by their encounter with another dimension, a revenant from another time. These quotes encapsulate major issues facing Spain as they officially deal with their violent past, and point to two central truisms in del Toro's handling of this traumatic episode in history and its repercussions. This essay will explore how through his exhumation of the past del Toro provides a conduit for the very primal need of the Spanish people to release and deal with its ghosts.

Remember Me

From Shakespeare to Christina Rossetti, the word "remember" is a ghostly verb.[1] The act of remembrance resurrects people, places and events that have long passed. Borges refers to it as a "sacred verb" in the opening lines of *Funes the Memorious*—to remember someone being an act of devotion to them. In the normal healing process after the trauma caused by war there is an intense period of remembrance which takes place after the acute pain of that trauma has diminished enough for comprehension and understanding to develop. However, in the case of civil war where family member fights against family member, allegiances are tested, communities broken down, cities destroyed by the people who once inhabited them, remembrance and healing are hard tasks to establish, especially when the winning side is a Fascistic violent and controlling one. By its very nature a Fascist country must be one that lives in stasis as it has to suppress freedoms and alternative ideologies. Until the death of Franco, Republican sympathizers were forbidden to mourn their dead. The inability of individuals and families to come to terms with the war, to find a sense of resolution, has only recently come to the fore as the country deals with its release and new found freedoms to explore its political past. Labanyi refers to the sentiment expressed as "'recuperación de la memoria histórica' (recovery of historical memory) that has, since the creation of the ARMH (Association for the Recovery of Historical Memory) in 2000, become obligatory when referring to the need for present-day Spaniards to engage with the unresolved legacy of the civil war and ensuing repression."[2] In 2007 the Ley de Memória Historica (Historical Memory Law) was passed by the Congress of Deputies. The provisions of the law include: the recognition of political, religious and ideological violence on both sides of the Spanish civil war; condemnation of the Francoist regime; state help in tracing, identification and eventual exhumation of victims of Francoist repression whose corpses are still missing, often buried in mass graves; temporary change to Spanish nationality law granting the right of return and *de origen citizenship* to those who left Spain under Franco.

In his Spanish civil war films del Toro shows how the ghosts of the past come back to be heard, to have their history revealed, their makeshift graves opened, to claim the future from the past. Initially del Toro set the script for *The Devil's Backbone* in the Mexican revolution but transferred the plot to Spain due to the fact that

> I realized that the Mexican Revolution has never ended, and secondly it was a very complicated mess with factions being subdivided into other factions. There were a series of intestinal wars in Mexico that didn't stop until the 1930s or later. It was very dirty metaphorically, and I wanted the war to be a war that happened within a family, an intimate war where brothers killed brothers—and that was the Spanish civil war.[3]

In order for del Toro's microcosm of the orphanage to work he needed a conflict in which the family functioned as a central metaphor. Civil wars throughout history have divided and changed familial relationships, opposing values and beliefs often leading to allegiance to opposing sides within one family. The Spanish civil war was ideal for del Toro, not only because of the Spanish language but because an international sense of idealism captured the imagination of ordinary people, artists, and intellectuals rather than politicians. Politically there was very little intervention in the rise of Fascism in Spain by other European governments, but people who believed in the idea of freedom and justice joined the fight. That sense of idealism and belief against all the odds is essential to del Toro's handling of that violent historical period.[4]

Franco's regime inflicted a severe State control over national identity and the Republican "story" was effectively ideologically cleansed from the country's history. Michael Shapiro refers to a "nation-state's attempt to colonize time as part of its more general attempt to mythologize a national culture."[5] What better way to colonize time than to try and obliterate the memory of Republicanism from the national consciousness. However, as is usual, the very act of repression puts the repressed to the forefront of the mind. Spain has found that the ghosts of those unacknowledged for more than 70 years have come back to claim their presence in history. The exhumation of Republican mass graves has brought the past hard up against the present. One of the hopes of the ARMH is surely for the creation of a new more complete national identity for the future through the unification of the temporal zones in which Republicanism, Fascism and Democracy existed.

In her affecting work *Exhuming Loss* Layla Renshaw writes extensively about the various sites where exhumations have taken place and peoples' reactions to the work. In it she describes how acts of exhumation and human identification lie at the intersection of different moral, metaphysical, and psychological preoccupations and anxieties concerning mortality, individuality, the fallibility of memory and historical narrative, the infallibility of physical proof, and the possibility of redemption and closure in the wake of trauma.[6]

It is no coincidence that these themes around exhumation are central to del Toro's films on the Spanish civil war—only through a confrontation with the dead can wrongs be uncovered and redressed. Del Toro's films deal with the problems of coming to terms with death, and life lived under traumatic, often violent circumstances. As Shapiro states:

Storytelling allows death a presence. It is the genre of imagination that recognizes the pervasive presence of death in life. Its ultimate presence is inevitable, but the when of its appearance is a matter of uncontrollable contingencies.[7]

In *The Devil's Backbone* the cinematography acts as the storyteller and embeds a deathly presence in the fabric of the film. The camera glides and floats through the action in a voyeuristic way, almost as if it were another character; the unseen ghostly presence, or ourselves—the viewer integrated into the story as another ghost. Thus del Toro opens up the story to the present and we, the audience, are included in Carmen's statement in her first dialogue with Casares, "Sometimes I think that we are all ghosts."

For del Toro the orphanage in *The Devil's Backbone* was a metaphor for Spain. As he explained in an interview for *Cineaste*,

The civil war could be broken into elements easier inside the orphanage: the older professor being the republic and the young, class-conflicted Fascist being the Fascists, and the young children being Spain, essentially. So I started working within the confines of this metaphor and found this freedom.[8]

Jacinto, as the embodiment of Fascism in the film, is the creator of ghosts—both Santi and Casares are killed by his actions. He returns to the orphanage to find gold but also to tear it down. Like the Fascists, Jacinto perversely attempts to destroy his past in order to create a new future but at the same time creates a trap for himself. Like Vidal in *Pan's Labyrinth* he is a conflicted character haunted by his past: Vidal, by the overwhelming influence of his father; Jacinto by the fact that he is "nobody's child," a prince without a kingdom. Jacinto wishes to eradicate his past in order to obliterate his origins and his deep self-hatred. Jacinto's photograph floats to the surface as he is dragged by the ghost of Santi to his death—the past cannot be destroyed or forgotten. In the nineteenth century photographs were thought to record the ghostly remains or spirit of their subjects and del Toro's use of the photographic image here too contains that belief. Jacinto will always remain the prince without a kingdom, trapped in a blurred image of a man who cannot establish his own identity through the violent path he has chosen.

The narration and the composition of shots used by del Toro at the start and end of *The Devil's Backbone* mirror each other. In the first shot of Casares he is tightly framed within a window looking out at the antics of the boys in the courtyard, his face partly eclipsed in dark shadow. At the end of the film he is framed in the open doorway of the orphanage, completely silhouetted against the stark sun-drenched landscape outside. The camera's point of view is behind him. Del Toro called *The Devil's Backbone* a Gothic Western and in the final shot the allusion to the Western genre is at its most potent and poignant, the shot directly referencing the final image of John Wayne in John Ford's *The Searchers*. At the end of *The Searchers*, the character Ethan makes his way out into the western landscape unable to settle down or exist within the confines and comforts of home life. Near the start of the film as Ethan and a posse pursue the Comanches who have murdered his sister's family he shoots out the eyes of a dead Indian they find on their trail. His curse on the murdered Comanche, "he can't enter the Spirit Land. Has to wander forever between the winds," is his own curse at the end of the film. His words come back to us as he turns his back on the family home and wonders out into an uncertain future. Dr. Casares likewise cannot enter the "spirit land" but as an antithesis to Ethan is trapped forever within the confines of the orphanage, one of its many shadows. Before he dies he states he will never leave the boys. It is his fate to continue his static existence in death as in life—like a fly trapped in amber.

The archway into the cellar of the orphanage is pictured during the opening narration on the nature of ghosts. It is a doorway to the discovery of a supernatural world; through doorways other worlds wait and can be glimpsed. Doors, gateways, and boundaries have, for centuries, been connected to supernatural activity, offering a link between this world and another—they are heavily utilized in this way by del Toro in this and his other films involving the supernatural. Every horror film needs its major scare. What del Toro considered his "Hitchcock moment" comes when Carlos, forced into a pantry by the approaching specter of Santi, peaks through the lock on the door only to witness the yellow eye of the ghost suddenly appear. The doorway functions as a physical and metaphysical boundary where the spirits of the dead are most active; as Aristotle stated, "Death is most frightening of all, since it is a boundary."[9] When the boys seem to be trapped in the storeroom and faced with certain death at the hands of Jacinto the door is unlocked. We hear the faint buzzing of flies on the soundtrack and see them outside the door on the ground; the injured boy then tells us that Casares unlocked the door, despite the fact that we have already witnessed his death.

At the end of the film Santi's ghost is not liberated by the destruction of his murderer. In a chilling shot we see him framed in the arch of the basement—he stares directly at the camera hovering above the pool of water in which his body lies. *Remember me*. The orphanage, like Spain itself is still haunted by the death of innocents. Santi's body, like those in the war's mass graves has not been given proper burial; it has not been laid to rest.[10] As the boys leave the site of Santi's death at the end of the film, del Toro fades them from the image as if they too have become spirits. In *Pan's Labyrinth* the appearance of the Republican rebels from the woods is signaled by the same magical pollen that precedes the appearance of the supernatural, indicating that they will soon be entering a supernatural realm. Del Toro used the actors who played Carlos and Jaime in *The Devil's Backbone* as Republican fighters in *Pan's Labyrinth*. After Vidal's attack on the rebel encampment we see the dead bodies of those characters. Carlos and Jaime defeat and escape one Fascist only to be killed by another. In her review of *The Orphanage* Delgado points out that

> as in *The Devil's Backbone* and *Pan's Labyrinth*, the focus is on children damaged by the ravages of dictatorship in both its domestic and institutional forms ... the horrors unleashed deliver a pertinent lesson for a country where the consequences of fratricidal conflict remain all too visible.[11]

Ghosts are a symbol of a breach in time, a presence that according to nature shouldn't be there—the past impinging on the present and the future. When death occurs at the start of life or in the young there is a paradox that cannot be resolved and in these films enables the life force to break through the dimensions of time. In *The Devil's Backbone* the opening credits are played out over the image of an aborted fetus in a jar; later we hear that the fluid in which the fetus is kept is believed to have rejuvenating powers, the power to hold back time and physical decay, to promote fertility and new life. The flower that blooms on the branch of a barren fig tree at the end of *Pan's Labyrinth* takes the shape of the female reproductive organs, and is a sign that new life and growth can take place, it points to the hope of a more matriarchal, strong and caring future, which liberates the imagination and the ethos of choice as epitomized by Ofelia herself. The children, representing Spain, triumph in *The Devil's Backbone*. However, in *Pan's Labyrinth* del Toro's vision darkened. In the audio commentary to the film he recalls how after the terrorist attacks of 9/11 the optimism of *The Devil's Backbone* seemed at odds with the times. The international trauma caused by that event called for a new and darker treatment of the subject.

Time Is Out of Joint

Del Toro filmed his initial entry into the world of *Pan's Labyrinth* in the ruined town of Belchite, a village in the Zaragoza province of Spain. Between August 24 and September 7, 1937, Republican and Nationalist forces in the Spanish civil war fought the Battle of Belchite and reduced the town to a series of ruins. Franco ordered that the remains of the town be left untouched, a monument to all of the prevailing success of Nationalist forces and the superiority of their ideology. It remains today as it was at its surrender on September 7, 1937. The new village of Belchite was built adjacent to the ruins of the old one—a reminder of the devastation of the civil war, a memorial, a double, a ghost town and yet a "live" monument to war.

The ruin of Belchite at the end of the civil war was like an open wound in the psyche of a divided nation. Over time it has become a memorial to the dead of that war. Belchite, like the character of Ofelia, is the past that returns. It is a ghost, a physical presence from the past travelling through time in the state in which its existence ended. Having the car which carries Ofelia and her mother journey through Belchite not only forcibly reminds the viewer of the destructive force of Fascist tyranny and the endurance of war; it is a signal that our protagonists are entering a gateway to an environment which already lies beyond time. Through the ghost town they enter the forest, a primeval and wild space untamed by modern civilization with relics of ancient worlds by the rough roadside. The old mill which has been turned into a Fascist encampment and the labyrinth itself are reminders of times past, recent and distant. Del Toro's use of setting to evoke different time periods is reminiscent of Hitchcock's most ghostly film, *Vertigo*; the use of San Francisco's city ruin, the Palace of Fine Arts with its mock Roman and Greek architecture, the old Spanish mission, the forest of giant redwoods, the sea—all pointing to a sense of timelessness, of the past infringing and existing in the present and into the future. Against this background the mortal world seems at odds with the natural and past or ancient world. They exist together but are conflicted. Individual trauma in Hitchcock's *Vertigo* becomes national trauma in *Pan's Labyrinth*. Del Toro indicates that the disturbance caused by the Spanish civil war is the direct catalyst for the displacement of time; the rupture of a society, a nation's identity and continuity with itself and its past. Within the context of the film it also creates a schism that allows for the possibility of travel between two different temporal spaces, present time and an immortal world.

Del Toro's treatment of traumatic space echoes Freud's theories on the effect of traumatic experiences on the perception-consciousness layer of the mind. Freud argued that trauma penetrated the perception-consciousness and that those experiences were stored in the unconscious which exists outside of time.[12] As Lisa Starks points out in her essay on *Hamlet*, "Thus, in Freud's view, the subject is split into conflicting but interconnected layers—one caught up in the transient present, the other bound to a timeless past."[13] Spain is made flesh, a character that exists in two time zones that need to be reconciled before it can heal, recover and move forward. Of course, this is also true of the central protagonists in *Pan's Labyrinth*, Ofelia and Captain Vidal, who have a tenuous and fragile hold on the present and are drawn to the eternal.

As Paul Julian Smith noted in his review of *Pan's Labyrinth* for *Film Quarterly*, "Francoist Spain is a world of suspended time, symbolized by the Captain's stopped watch."[14] The unexploded bomb in *The Devil's Backbone*, the orphanage from the film of that title also stand as symbols of a world suspended and focus on characters that cannot move forward.

In *The Devil's Backbone* the characters, both living and dead exist in stasis. In the opening sequence to the film we witness the death of a child, Santi, and his immersion into amber colored water. This image melds with the image of fetuses of babies born with spina bifida preserved in rum, "the devil's backbone" of the title. Dr. Casares tells Carlos that the Spanish people are superstitious and ready to believe in the rejuvenating power of the rum from the jars. Del Toro colors the palette of the film in amber hues to indicate that all of those who reside within the orphanage are going to be faced with the supernatural in some way but also to show that they too are suspended, trapped like flies in amber, whether by cowardice, impotence, self-hatred, or patterns of violence. The central metaphor for this temporal schism in the film, the lack of ability to deal with the past and the anticipated future, is an unexploded bomb that sits in the middle of the orphanage complex. The bomb at times appears as a living, sentient being, uttering noises when tapped; the ribbons attached to it moving like the tentacles of some strange creature. When the ghost of Santi appears he is suspended in water; the air around him flows and small air bubbles surround him. From the gash in his head the blood flows freshly, floating from a wound which will never heal. The spirit of Santi and the bomb are intrinsically linked; it drops the night Santi dies, both his ghost and the bomb are the repressed; the ticking presence, the reminder of the ever presence of Fascistic violence and oppression waiting to erupt, but also of the past waiting to find its own resolution in the present and future.

Cyclical narrative patterns are obviously very attractive to del Toro as is the playing with time, as we have discovered with *The Devil's Backbone*. *Pan's Labyrinth* begins and starts with the same image. As Ofelia lies dying at the start of the film it appears that time is being reversed. The shot shows the blood going back into her body rather than leaving it. The narrative is replayed in what appears to be her dying moments. *The Devil's Backbone* begins and ends with an almost identical narration relaying a supposition on the nature of ghosts. By the time we reach the end of both films it becomes clear that we have witnessed events that have resulted in the death of a central protagonist, hinted at in the opening moments. The opening narration in *The Devil's Backbone* asks the audience, "What is a ghost?" The answer given is "An emotion, a terrible moment condemned to repeat itself over and over again." As Tabea Linhard points out, "the connections between the spectral and the structure of trauma have never been more clearly stated."[15] It leaves the viewer with the sense of the narrative being endlessly repeated, the film itself becoming like a ghost, reliving the same traumatic events, moving forward in time but condemned to endlessly repeat its story. Ghost stories which begin and end with the same wording or pattern of images have a special potency. This narrative technique is used at the beginning and ending of one of the most powerful ghost films, *The Haunting*, directed by Robert Wise (1963). Eleanor Lance, a character who has not had a chance to live her own life due to caring for her sick mother, is seduced by a false sense of belonging by the haunting at Hill House and ends up one of its many ghosts, trapped and alone. Her words at the end of the film directly mirror the opening narration with one minor alteration:

> **Dr. Markway at the start of the film:** "Hill House had stood for ninety years and might stand for ninety more. Silence lay steadily against the wood and stone of Hill House, and whatever walked there ... walked alone."
> **Eleanor in the final words of the film:** "Hill House had stood for ninety years.... And we who walk here ... walk alone."

Likewise in del Toro's film the narrator, Dr. Casares, at the end of the film, answers his question at the beginning: "What is a ghost? ... A ghost is what I am." This cyclical pattern of story gives the film a poetic framing, a chilling and melancholy reminder of the start of the story and the journey travelled to that point.[16] It marks the shift of a central character from one world to another, from a state of imperiled reality to a fantastic unwelcomed (or welcomed) form of existence; the transition or elevation to another world only dreamed about—an alternative immortal dimension.

Ruptures and channels between this world and other fantasy spaces created by the violence of war are not new to cinematic history[17]—one need only look at Michael Powell and Emeric Pressburger's *A Matter of Life and Death* (1946) made about and directly after the Second World War or Adrian Lyne's *Jacob's Ladder* (1990) about a traumatized Vietnam War veteran as precursors to this theme. *Jacob's Ladder* follows a narrative convention which del Toro is heavily drawn to—the fantasy action of the film in which Jacob Singer battles with demons and angels takes place within the dying hours of his life as surgeons battle to save him. In *A Matter of Life and Death*, Squadron leader Peter Carter argues his case for life in a heavenly court as his head wound brings him closer to death or possible madness. Physical and mental trauma bend and shape time psychologically and metaphysically in both *A Matter of Life and Death* and *Jacob's Ladder*. In both films the central protagonists have fantasy characters who lead and protect them into and through the realm of the eternal. However, at times it is unclear whether Peter Carter's Conductor, Jacob's friendly chiropractor, Louis or Ofelia's Faun are there to save them or damn them.

> Be thou a spirit of health or goblin damned,
> Bring with thee airs from heaven or blasts from hell,
> Be thy intents wicked or charitable,
> Thou comest in such a questionable shape
> That I will speak to thee [*Hamlet* 1.4.43–46].

The perplexities of time, memory, dreams and the afterlife—states of being and conception that are beyond time play throughout del Toro's work. In *Pan's Labyrinth*, the mechanics of measuring time feature strongly within the narrative and mise-en-scène. Past, present and future constantly play in and out of the narrative and the character's consciousness. Where Ofelia is introduced to us via a shot of her book of fairy tales, Captain Vidal is introduced by a close-up shot of his watch; he impatiently looks at it as he waits for Carmen and Ofelia to arrive. This fusion of time brings with it ghostly presences. In the scene where Vidal and Ofelia initially meet, the ghosts of their respective fathers also meet, embodied in her fairy tale book and his watch. Ofelia's book of fairy tales contains the spirit of Ofelia's father. It is the one item that she holds on to tightly as she travels into the new world of the Fascist encampment. Del Toro himself makes a direct link between the father and fairy tale in his commentary to the film, mentioning that the father's profession is a tailor—the families depicted in fairy tales often being working class tradesmen. Ofelia assimilates her father into the world of her imagination and her eventual entry through the labyrinth is her journey back to him. Fairy tales have a timeless quality by the fact that they are passed on by word of mouth from generation to generation. They are ever present in Ofelia's imagination and her way of coping with her traumatic situation, uniting the ghost of her father with her traumatic present. In his Introduction to *The Uses of Enchantment*, Bruno Bettelheim states: "If we hope to live not just from moment to moment, but in true consciousness of our existence, then our greatest need and most difficult achievement is to find meaning in our lives."[18] To Bettelheim fairy tales were a way of achieving this, enriching a child's life by stimulating imagination, developing intellect and clarifying emotions; being attuned to anxieties and aspirations, giving full recognition to difficulties and suggesting solutions.[19]

Ofelia's mother makes the mistake of denying the importance of imagination and fantasy in coping with their dangerous situation. As she travels into the woods she is sick when she tells Ofelia that fairy tales are nonsense, from then on her deterioration is steady as she tries to assimilate the world that Vidal lives in, to play the kind of wife he would want. As Ofelia's journey takes her into a fantasy world and eternal life, Carmen's journey into Vidal's world seals her fate. From the love of a humble tailor to military Fascist—her choice of husband could not be more different. Has the union been one of necessity? Ofelia asks her, "Why did you marry?" echoing the sentiments of Hamlet when his mother marries his uncle. Her dreams of security in violent times cannot be met by living under the wing of a man who perpetrates violence—Carmen turns out to be more of a fantasist than her daughter in that regard. Vidal criticizes her for letting her read fantasy stories, his Fascistic and war-like ego's need to crush imagination and all that the spirit of Ofelia and her father stands for. When they meet Ofelia would rather hold on to her book than shake hands with her Fascistic stepfather. It's when Carmen denies the world of imagination that she dies, turning against her own nature, the possibility of hope and acts of faith as embodied in Ofelia.

The part of the mill in which Vidal lives is dominated by giant cogs. We see him tinkering with his watch against this background and it appears as if he is trapped within the workings of a great timepiece. The watch and his strict adherence to time become symbols of Vidal's controlling Fascistic nature. Vinci, in his article on *Hellboy II*, quotes del Toro when describing the significance of the Golden Army, stating that

> a "clockwork army" is the perfect image to "embody a lack of choice." In this way, the relationship between the crown and the army—images of power and those it influences—becomes an allegory for the effects of capitalist [Fascist] ideology on humanity.[20]

In many ways Vidal is a character fated by his adherence to a code of combat espoused by his father, a tyrannical mode of behavior which, like Fascism itself, is restrictive and inflexible. Captain Vidal's broken watch is directly related to lineage through the male line. His father deliberately broke it, literally stopped time, just before he was killed in order that his son may know the exact moment of his death. As a result the ghost of Vidal's father is physically embodied in the watch, a constant reminder of his past. Vidal's unwillingness to acknowledge this story of his father at the dinner table is an exercise in control, not just, as Jennifer Orme suggests, as a way of setting himself apart from the female world of the storytellers, but in allowing people access to his personal history. The watch is so much part of him that it has become an essential element of his character; for others to know this would be to allow others to know him and it is clear that in his world the acknowledgement or revelation of personal feelings is a weakness. As Vidal waits for Ofelia and her mother to arrive his attention to his watch indicates he is thinking of his father and the prospect of being a father. As the film progresses it's clear that Vidal wishes to mythologize himself, for the masculine war-like ego of Fascism to be a legend passed to his son, for the same mode of behavior to be heralded and inbred into his next generation. He wishes to extend his life beyond his own in the same way that his father sought to haunt him.

> If, like Vidal, your desires lead you to try to master story—to create and control monologic master narratives to support patriarchal militaristic oppression, you'll not only end up dead—your stories will die with you.[21]

His request that his son know his name is not met by the Republican forces because the watch, like the town of Belchite, is a broken and timeless reminder of a Fascistic ideology. It represents a lack of choice for the next generation. Politically it also points to a move away from a patriarchal society—the masculine war-like ego and the emergence of the repressed feminine peaceful ego. It is also a means of breaking the cyclical pattern of haunting—Vidal's son will not be haunted by the moment of his father's death in the way that Vidal has been haunted. By denying Vidal the Republicans stop his story and close the labyrinth. In doing so del Toro provides a cinematic and metaphoric revenge for all the Republicans who were never given a chance to mourn their fathers.

> *Remember Me*
> But in the black corners
> in the blackest ones, they lie down
> to weep for the fallen,

mothers who gave them milk,
sisters who bathed them,
brides once of snow
but now in the black of mourning,
and now with fever;
dazed windows,
shattered women,
letters and photographs
which portray them as they were,
there, eyes bursting
from seeing them so much and so little,
from so many silent tears,
from so much absent beauty [Miguel Hernandez,
   Llamo a la Juventud, 1937].[22]

In the V&A's Memory Maps project, which focuses on people and their relationship with place, Marina Warner pointed out that "mapping memories involves listening in to other people's ghosts as well as your own."[23] *Pan's Labyrinth* and *The Devil's Backbone* may be set in the Spanish civil war but they are about stopping repeated cycles of violence through time, from generation to generation. Children die in these films, a fact which demonstrates the remorselessness of history. The death of a child is the death of the future. As countries battle with the consequence of the crimes of their past, the crimes that erupt into the lives of present generations, and will grieve future generations, these films remind us how much "the history of the world is the revenge of the old."[24] Haunted or cursed families, phantoms and psychological ghosts recur repeatedly—a sense of the unresolved, unabsolved or unredeemed haunt del Toro's films. In his imaginative engagement with the Spanish civil war "the whole of modern Spanish culture ... can be read as one big ghost story."[25] Nevertheless, Warner believes in a positive outcome from death's presence in storytelling and the power of remembrance:

> In his fine study, "Postwar: Europe since 1945," the historian Tony Judt discusses the uses of memory, and argues passionately for finding new ways of telling the past, not to shrug off guilt and overlook horror, but also not to let them fill the horizon end to end. As Seamus Heaney wrote, in a different context, "it is not, the grudge but the grief, that matters." There is no reason to repeat the past, in more ways than one.[26]

In *The Orphanage*, the medium Aurora tells the character Laura about the nature of ghosts: "When something terrible happens in a certain place, it sometimes leaves a mark, a wound. It's like ... like an echo repeating time and again waiting to be heard, like a mark from a pinch asking for a soothing caress." For a country that has experienced so much internal tragedy and especially tragedy within the family itself this is a clear statement about the impossibility of burying the past; that the pain of something untreated will continue to hurt and damage the people of Spain. Jan Kott stated in *Shakespeare our Contemporary*, "the sequence of time is an illusion.... We fear most the past that returns."[27] The present generation of Spain is cursed with the task of setting things right, ensuring that acts of remembrance can unite the ghosts of past with the present. As Andrzej Wajda stated on his film *Katyn*,[28] "We are shaped by our history.... Some wounds heal only when we become aware of them, and that is the role and duty of art."[29]

Del Toro's Spanish civil war films *Pan's Labyrinth* and *The Devil's Backbone* deal with unresolved grief and the importance of remembrance. In *Exhuming Loss*, Layla Renshaw examines how "the exposure of graves has opened up a discursive space in Spanish society for multiple representations to be made of the war dead and of Spain's traumatic past."[30] Del Toro's films are part of that discussion and part of that story. Grief and remembrance are at the heart of those multiple representations and at the heart of every ghost story. The mass murder of Republicans is an important story to remember, but each individual in that "mass" has their own story that till now has been denied.

The Republicans at the end of *Pan's Labyrinth* triumph over the Fascists, but it is momentary. Vidal's history, his story, will not be passed on but neither will theirs; from history we know that the lives, deaths and activities of the murdered republicans were denied, their voices and the grief of their families silenced.[31] The flower of Ofelia's spirit blossoms on a barren tree. Del Toro offers us the possibility of hope, of transformation. The most delicate things in life are can also be the most powerful. In these films innocence and goodness do not triumph; they resist and provide hope for humanity, in the possibility of a better world, in reconciliation, in peace. They are ever present despite the forces of darkness which are often more powerful and that is their strength, their importance, their essential part in the survival of the human soul in adversity. For a country that has come out of the other end of years of Fascism that is a very important message; and for a world dominated by the politics of fear it is, like faith, an important thing for us all to hold on to.

Notes

1. Linhard uses this phrase in the title to her chapter on fictional representations of women's stories from the Spanish and Mexican Civil War.
2. Jo Labanyi, "Memory and Modernity in Democratic Spain: The Difficulty of Coming to Terms with the Spanish Civil War," *Poetics Today* 28, no. 1 (2007): 106.
3. Jason Wood, *The Faber Book of Mexican Cinema* (London: Faber, 2006) 110.
4. Ken Loach's *Land and Freedom* demonstrated how this sense of belief and idealism survived in the stories of others, passed on from generation to generation. Where a flower blooms with Ofelia's spirit, David Carr's granddaughter, through uncovering and empathizing with his story, raises her hand in a communist salute as her grandfather is buried.
5. Michael J. Shapiro, *For Moral Ambiguity: National Culture and the Politics of the Family* (Minneapolis: University of Minnesota Press, 2001), 121.
6. Layla Renshaw, *Exhuming Loss: Memory, Materiality, and Mass Graves of the Spanish Civil War* (Walnut Creek, CA: Left Coast Press, 2011), 11.
7. Michael J. Shapiro, *For Moral Ambiguity: National Culture and the Politics of the Family* (Minneapolis: University of Minnesota Press, 2001), 87.
8. Kimberly Chun and Guillermo del Toro, "What Is a Ghost? An Interview with Guillermo del Toro," *Cinéaste* 27, no. 2 (2002): 29.
9. Aristotle, *Nicomachean Ethics*, translated by Terence Irwin (Indianapolis: Hackett, 1985), 40.
10. The legacy of a buried past is adeptly explored and revisited in Bayona's film *The Orphanage*, produced by del Toro. As one reviewer pointed out, "The coal shed in which the murdered children's ashes rest is a reminder that the tentacles of the Civil War found their way into every corner of the country."
11. Maria M. Delgado, "The Young and the Damned" (review of *El Orfanato*), *Sight and Sound* 4 (2008): 44.
12. "Mourning and Melancholia" in *The Standard Edition of the Complete Psychological Works of Sigmund Freud*, edited and translated by James Strachey, 24 vols. (London: Hogarth Press, 1953–74), 14:239–58.
13. Lisa S. Starks, "'Remember Me': Psychoanalysis, Cinema, and the Crisis of Modernity," *Shakespeare Quarterly* 53, no. 2 (Summer 2002): 183.
14. Smith, Paul Julian, "Pan's Labyrinth (El laberinto del Fauno)," *Film Quarterly* 60, no. 4 (Summer 2007): 9.
15. Tabea Alexa Linhard, *Fearless Women in the Mexican Revolution and the Spanish Civil War* (Columbia: University of Missouri Press, 2005), 229.
16. The poetic structure of the filming of both *The Devil's Backbone* and *Pan's Labyrinth* are crucial not only within the films themselves but between the films as companion pieces.
17. What could possibly be new is the removal of the Christian ideal of heaven and hell and the replacement of a fantasy world of immortality based on predominantly pagan symbols.
18. Bruno Bettelheim, *The Uses of Enchantment: The Meaning and Importance of Fairy Tales* (London: Penguin, 1991), 3.
19. Ibid.
20. T. M. Vinci, "Remembering Why We Once Feared the Dark: Reclaiming Hu-

manity through Fantasy in Guillermo del Toro's *Hellboy II,*" *Journal of Popular Culture* 45, no. 5: 1258.

21. Jennifer Orme, "Narrative Desire and Disobedience in *Pan's Labyrinth*," *Marvels & Tales* 24, no. 2 (2010): 232.

22. Quoted by Paloma Aguilar in "Agents of Memory: Spanish Civil War Veterans and Disabled Soldiers," *War and Remembrance in the Twentieth Century*, edited by Jay Winter and Emmanuel Sivan. (Cambridge: Cambridge University Press, 1999: 84). Hernández was incarcerated for 30 years after the end of the Spanish civil war but died in 1942 from tuberculosis. In 2010 his family received a posthumous "declaration of reparation" from the Spanish government.

23. Marina Warner, "Memory Maps: About the project," V&A website, http://www.vam.ac.uk/content/articles/m/memory-maps-about-the-project/.

24. David Hare, "A Map of the World," *David Hare: Plays 2* (London: Faber and Faber, 1997), 191.

25. Jo Labanyi, ed., *Constructing Identity in Contemporary Spain: Theoretical Debates and Cultural Practice* (Oxford: Oxford University Press, 2002), 1.

26. Marina Warner, "Memory Maps: About the project." V&A website, http://www.vam.ac.uk/content/articles/m/memory-maps-about-the-project/

27. Jan Kott, *Shakespeare Our Contemporary*, 2d rev. ed., translated by Boleslaw Taborski; Preface by Peter Brook (London: Methuen, 1967), 76.

28. Wadja's Katyn is a film about the massacre of over 4000 Polish officers and civilians by the Russian army in 1940. The director's father was killed in this massacre.

29. Wajda quoted by Brigid Grauman, "Face to Face with a Terrible Truth," *The Times*, 17 April 2008, 17.

30. Layla Renshaw, *Exhuming Loss: Memory, Materiality, and Mass Graves of the Spanish Civil War* (Walnut Creek, CA: Left Coast Press, 2011), 11.

31. According to a report by Danny Wood for the BBC one survey showed that 50 percent of Spaniards had not talked about the Spanish civil war at home and 35 percent said they were never taught what happened in 1936, in school.

Bibliography

Aristotle. *Nicomachean Ethics*. Trans. Terence Irwin. Indianapolis: Hackett, 1985.
Bettelheim, Bruno. *The Uses of Enchantment: The Meaning and Importance of Fairy Tales*. London: Penguin, 1991.
Chun, Kimberly, and Guillermo del Toro. "What Is a Ghost? An Interview with Guillermo del Toro." *Cinéaste* 27, no. 2 (2002): 28–31.
Delgado, Maria M. "The Young and the Damned" (review of *El Orfanato*). *Sight and Sound* 4 (2008): 44–45.
Grauman, Brigid. "Face to Face with a Terrible Truth." *The Times*, 17 April 2008.
Hare, David. *A Map of the World*, 2d rev. ed. London: Faber, 1983.
Kott, Jan. *Shakespeare Our Contemporary*, 2d rev. ed. Translated by Boleslaw Taborski; Preface by Peter Brook. London: Methuen, 1967.
Labanyi, Jo. "Memory and Modernity in Democratic Spain: The Difficulty of Coming to Terms with the Spanish Civil War." *Poetics Today* 28, no. 1 (2007): 89–116.

Labanyi, Jo, ed. *Constructing Identity in Contemporary Spain: Theoretical Debates and Cultural Practice*. Oxford: Oxford University Press, 2002.

Linhard, Tabea Alexa. *Fearless Women in the Mexican Revolution and the Spanish Civil War*. Columbia: University of Missouri Press, 2005.

Orme, Jennifer. "Narrative Desire and Disobedience in *Pan's Labyrinth*." *Marvels & Tales* 24.2 (2010): 219–34.

Renshaw, Layla. *Exhuming Loss: Memory, Materiality, and Mass Graves of the Spanish Civil War*. Walnut Creek, CA: Left Coast Press, 2011.

Shakespeare, William. *Hamlet*. Edited by Neil Taylor and Ann Thompson. London: Thomson Learning, 2006.

Shapiro, Michael J. *For Moral Ambiguity: National Culture and the Politics of the Family*. Minneapolis: University of Minnesota Press, 2001.

Smith, Paul Julian. "Pan's Labyrinth (El laberinto del Fauno)." *Film Quarterly* 60, no. 4 (Summer 2007): 4–9

Starks, Lisa S. "'Remember Me': Psychoanalysis, Cinema, and the Crisis of Modernity." *Shakespeare Quarterly* 53, no. 2 (Summer 2002): 181–200.

Vinci, T. M. "Remembering Why We Once Feared the Dark: Reclaiming Humanity through Fantasy in Guillermo del Toro's *Hellboy II*." *Journal of Popular Culture* 45, no. 5: 1041–59.

Warner, Marina. "Memory Maps: About the project." V&A website. http://www.vam.ac.uk/content/articles/m/memory-maps-about-the-project/.

Winter, Jay, and Emmanuel Sivan, eds. *War and Remembrance in the Twentieth Century*. Cambridge: Cambridge University Press, 1999.

Wood, Danny. "Civil War legacy divides Spain." *BBC News, Madrid,* July 18, 2006. http://news.bbc.co.uk/2/hi/europe/5192228.stm.

Wood, Jason. *The Faber Book of Mexican Cinema*. London: Faber, 2006.

The Child Transformed by Monsters
The Monstrous Beauty of Childhood Trauma

JESSICA BALANZATEGUI

Guillermo del Toro has said, "I have spent 32 years recuperating from my first 10 years,"[1] yet he consistently positions his traumatic childhood as a fertile source of inspiration and creative vitality for his films—as is implied even by this brief statement, which positions his film career as his process of working through his childhood traumas. Del Toro's supernatural horror films are deeply underwritten with the lingering effects of childhood trauma: a vision of trauma that exists at the interface between personal and cultural identities, expressed via a vacillation between supernatural and material horrors. These films circulate around embattled, traumatized child figures, whose fractured perspectives re-inscribe the disturbing events which constitute the narrative. This creative response to trauma is expressed in the films through the eruption of fantasy and the supernatural into the realist framing narratives, a technique which serves to powerfully register the trauma the child encounters not only as painful and harrowing, but as an opportunity to access a rich deeper layer of meaning. Thus the combined interlacing of the personal/cultural and supernatural/material which constitutes del Toro's filmic expression of childhood trauma enacts disturbances to ontological and temporal coherence, but these very disruptions are figured as opportunities for regeneration that employ the power of traumatic pasts to stimulate creative re-interpretations of rigid linear narratives. Thus, in his films, as well as in his interviews, sketches and writings, del Toro casts the traumatic event as a powerful transformative experience, which shifts and enriches understandings of reality. In its exploration of del Toro's approach to childhood trauma, this essay discusses two films del Toro has termed his "brother" and "sister" pieces, *The Devil's Backbone* (2001) and *Pan's Labyrinth* (2006), and ends with a brief consideration of the three child-centered horror films which he has produced—*The Orphanage* (2007), *Don't Be Afraid of the Dark* (2010) (for which del Toro also wrote the screenplay), and *Mama* (2013).

The Aesthetic Power of Traumatic Experience

The child's symbolic temporal function as the passed state of adulthood which yet lingers within the depths of the adult's present psyche is often equated in del Toro's works with the simmering of traumatic historical pasts within the socio-cultural present. Del Toro extends this tendency beyond the diegetic universe of his films not only through intermeshing supernatural occurrences with real historical events, namely the Spanish civil war, but also through the way in which he associates his own childhood with the events experienced by his child characters. For instance, he has stated that both *Pan's Labyrinth* and *The Devil's Backbone* are based "on things that happened to me,"[2] and surprisingly in both cases it is the film's supernatural elements that he claims are based on his own childhood, not, as one might expect, the instances of childhood abuse and neglect present within these films. Thus, the supernatural and the fantastic, so often positioned as an "escape" from childhood trauma, become a powerful way to face trauma's affront to normality and coherent meaning. As del Toro states, "I really think that the most creative, most fragile part of the child that lives within me is a child that was literally transformed by monsters. Be they on the screen or in myth or in my own imagination."[3]

In tandem with this personal privileging of the value of traumatic experience, del Toro often expresses his belief that it is only through art that the creative mode of perception sparked by trauma can be fully realized and appreciated: "it's only through art that we are able to glimpse otherness."[4] Extending del Toro's justification of the function of his work,

Zicree, editor and interviewer for *Cabinet of Curiosities*—del Toro's compendium of his notebook sketches, writings and storyboards—points out that del Toro's works encourage consideration of "the repulsive and the rejected with compassion and empathy—to expand our definitions of ourselves by encompassing the range of human (and even inhuman) experience."[5] The child is an apt vessel through which to access this alternative mode of perception in del Toro's films because she is forced onto the fringes of the situations of social or personal turmoil presented, and is disallowed or not offered a clear understanding of the events of the narrative. But the child's enforced status as a helpless observer ensures that he experiences trauma in a different way to the adult characters, who desperately attempt to cling to rigid structures of meaning in the face of turmoil and trauma. As del Toro explains, "the best witness you can have for anything is a child, because it's a non-judgemental, fully emotional character."[6] The child character's fractured yet creative perception of trauma thus functions in parallel to the ways in which del Toro himself develops and employs his art: both as a personal method of harnessing the subversive nature of traumatic experience, and as a way for society to approach and contemplate the darkest, most traumatic recesses of history and cultural consciousness normally submerged beneath accepted discourses of socio-cultural progress.

The Power of the Fantastic Childhood Imaginary

A common element that structures all of del Toro's child-centered horror films is the tension established between the child's physically oppressed and disempowered position in the realist framing narrative, and the overwhelming audio-visual power of the world conjured by his or her imagination. The child characters' imaginative realm comes to shape their (and the viewers') interpretation of the events of the film's diegetic real and disturbs the rigid framing narrative. Thus, the films dramatize the eruption of the previously subjugated realm of the child's imaginary (and, by extension, children's culture wholesale) into the adult's reality—an escalating engagement with the fantastic which mirrors the adult audience's engagement with the film's narrative.[7] This is realized in the structural fabric of the films as the imaginative and cultural material associated with childhood—fairy tales, lullabies and bogeymen—seeps into and eventually overwhelms or displaces the realist framework which makes up the adult characters' narratives. Thus, del Toro's construction of the child's imaginative perspective of traumatic events simultaneously incarnates the empowerment of the child and the empowerment of the inscrutable "otherness" of traumatic experience. Seminal trauma theorist Cathy Caruth describes trauma as a "breach in the mind's experience of time, self and the world.... [Trauma] is always the story of the wound that cries out that addresses us in the attempt to tell us of a reality or truth that is not otherwise available."[8] In harnessing this fissure in coherent discourse and linear time and rendering it a productive means of self-expression, the child characters in del Toro's films are empowered to shape a *new* discourse, which stands in contrast to the staid, inflexible grasping of logic and reason which characterizes the adult character's response to traumatic experience.

In all of del Toro's child-centered horror films, this harnessing of a traumatic breach in coherent meaning is expressed through the richly realized fantastic or supernatural realms that the child perceives—a world of ancient Fauns and fairies in *Pan's Labyrinth* and of emotionally-charged specters in *The Devil's Backbone*, *The Orphanage*, and *Mama*, and of ghoulish "tooth fairies" in *Don't Be Afraid of the Dark*. Thus rather than attempting to suture the gap in rationality raised by trauma, del Toro's child characters relish the opportunity for an alternative mode of perception to emerge into the traumatic breach, one that is not bound by reason, linearity, and ontological binaries. McDonald and Clark suggest that del Toro's use of fantasy provides a means of self-actualization via escape: speaking of the child figure in *Pan's Labyrinth*, they assert that "Ofelia 'writes' herself into existence as an autonomous being, employing the realm of the imagination as a retreat from trauma as well as a space for self-actualization and resistance."[9] While I concur that this "re-writing" of traumatic experience represents a powerful mode of self-actualization and resistance, I do not see this to be a function of a fantastic "retreat" or "escape." Instead, del Toro's association of the fantastic with the child's perspective represents the child's creative way of interpreting traumas gaps and fractures—a mode of perception freed of rational grounding which is not readily available to the adult characters—in an enriching way that establishes an alternative discourse and historical narrative. Fantasy is thus employed in a manner that resonates with Rosemary Jackson's characterization of the fantastic: "By attempting to make visible that which is culturally invisible ... the fantastic introduces absences. Hence the tendency of fantasy towards non-signification.... The cultural, or counter-cultural, implications of this assertion of non-signification are far-reaching, for it represents a dissolution of a culture's signifying practice, the very means by which it establishes meaning. Undoing those unifying structures and significations upon which social order depends, fantasy functions to subvert and undermine cultural stability."[10] As del Toro himself argues, "When people say, 'Oh, fantasy's a great escape,' I reply, 'I don't think so.' Fantasy is a great way of deciphering reality."[11]

Interweaving Personal and Socio-Cultural Traumas: *The Devil's Backbone*

Del Toro has described *The Devil's Backbone* as his most personal and favorite of his films: following his first two films, the low-budget *Cronos* (1993) and studio-manipulated *Mimic* (1997), he sees *The Devil's Backbone* as the first work in which his vision could be fully and freely realized.[12] The film is set in Spain in 1939, the final year of the Spanish civil war (1936–1939), a liminal period in which the advancement of Spain's national narrative is disturbingly uncertain. The film takes place in an orphanage for young boys from Republican families whose parents have been killed or captured in the Civil War. Del Toro explains that the orphanage setting was inspired by his own experiences of growing up in an all-male Jesuit boarding school—a "brutal" experience he sees as "the equivalent of prison life in Mexico."[13] In the middle of the orphanage's courtyard stands an unexploded bomb, an ominous and volatile reminder of the war occurring outside the orphanage's walls—as del Toro points out on the Criterion DVD commentary, "all the stories, occurrences are tied around the bomb, this constant looming reminder of a terrible past."[14] As well as being haunted by this unexploded bomb, the orphanage is also haunted by a child ghost, Santi (meaning "the one who sighs"), a former inhabitant of the orphanage who disappeared on the same night that the bomb landed in the orphanage's grounds.

Santi, too, is derived from a traumatic childhood experience which has stayed with del Toro: at the age of eight, he believed he heard the ghost of his beloved uncle—whose bedroom young del Toro inherited after the man's death—sighing in his ear, a deeply melancholic sound which seemed to follow del Toro until he ran screaming from the room.[15] Thus the film is a complex interweaving of del Toro's own experiences of childhood traumas and the socio-historical traumas of a reality del Toro himself did not experience. Yet del Toro's personal trauma provides a creative point of access to this historical past which occurred outside the purview of his own experience, in a manner which retrospectively disrupts linear historical continuity and suggests that the past is by no means dead and gone. Santi, the child ghost, is the embodiment of this traumatic undermining of the solidity of the present.

Trauma and the Aesthetics of Haunting

We learn mid-way through the film that Santi in fact drowned in the orphanage's cavernous cistern. After finding the child playing near the cistern late at night, the angry caretaker, Jacinto, struck Santi on the head. Fearful of being apprehended for his violent outburst, Jacinto then tossed the child's unconscious body into the cistern. Left unable to swim, Santi is shown sinking helplessly into the water's murky depths. This traumatic experience punctuates the entire film. The shot of Santi drowning is part of the film's opening sequence, presented before the audience is offered any context through which to understand the shot, aesthetically rendering the incoherence of a trauma that occurs "too soon, too unexpectedly, to be fully known, and is therefore not available to consciousness until it imposes itself again, repeatedly, in the nightmares and repetitive actions"[16] of those who've experienced it. This function is reinforced by the fact that the shot reoccurs at multiple points throughout the film, and is characterized by a murky, sepia filter—representative of the cloudy amber water in which Santi drowned—which obscures the audience's clear view of the image. Both the ghostly Santi and the unexploded bomb in the courtyard exude an eerie power despite—or perhaps because of—their apparent physical incapacity. While neither directly acts upon the events in the film's realist present, they unsettle the present's primacy by insistently raising the specter of traumatic pasts and disallowing the unchallenged progression of present into future.

The young protagonist, Carlos, is the vessel through which the traumatic past represented by the ghostly Santi and the unexploded bomb gain power in the narrative. Carlos' father has recently been killed in the war, and subsequently the child is dropped off at the orphanage without a clear understanding of why or for how long. Thus Carlos is a disempowered, helpless figure within the film's realist narrative—even amongst the other boys, who have resided at the orphanage for some time and have at least some degree of understanding about the Civil War and the hopelessness of their situations. In fact, Carlos is completely unaware of some of the finer details of the film's narrative, which centers on the adult characters and is concerned with Jacinto's plot to overthrow the orphanage's administrator, Carmen, and physician, Casares, in a quest to steal the gold he knows is hidden somewhere on the orphanage's grounds. However, when Carlos starts to perceive the ghost, this narrative is overwhelmed by the spectral power of Santi's traumatic past—the affective turning point of the film occurs when Carlos first sees Santi, a frightening scene in which the ghost slowly pursues Carlos from the external kitchen and through the orphanage's hallway.[17] This scene occurs approximately half-way through the film, and from this moment the supernatural realm perceived by Carlos and incarnated by the ghost of the dead child collides with and finally overwhelms the adult-centric narrative. Initially Carlos is terrified of Santi, however eventually he comes to terms with his existence and fulfills the ghost's request to "bring me Jacinto." Towards the end of the film when Jacinto has launched an attack on the orphanage in a desperate attempt to locate the gold—using gasoline to blow up the kitchen, killing many of the inhabitants—the children band together and stage an attack on Jacinto in the cistern that echoes Jacinto's own murder of Santi: an intentional replaying of this previously displaced traumatic past. The boys wound Jacinto and push him into the same amber water in which Santi died, and the ghost emerges from the water's depths to drag down Jacinto's body, ensuring that he too drowns. Ultimately the child ghost embodies the power of traumatic pasts to re-emerge in and affect the present, as a past Jacinto has concealed from the other adult characters literally comes back to haunt him. It is only the child characters who are cognizant of the supernatural power of this past trauma.

Furthermore, this traumatic power is obviously *located* in the child ghost, who disrupts the coherent linear flow of the narrative. As a ghost,

Santi has escaped the bounds of linear time altogether, and is now forever fused to the moment of his drowning. His spectral presence warps the ether around him as if he is permanently underwater; similarly, the blood from his head wound floats upwards regardless of where he manifests in physical space. Santi appears like a broken porcelain doll, with cracks visible all over his body, emphasizing his fragility; however in his ghostly form it is this very fragility which becomes uncanny and powerful. Thus the ghost's visual construction echoes del Toro's equation of his creative vitality with his fragile inner child—a wounded creature "transformed by monsters" who inspires his work. Santi's cracked body also fetishizes his status as a subject who is not fully formed or complete. As del Toro explains on the DVD commentary, Santi represents his belief that "childhood is not a beautiful happy, benign time—but a mortal, fragile state of being."[18] The film thus presents the post–Civil War child as a being who has been shattered and broken while undergoing the delicate process of being formed: an eerie incarnation of a trauma that has occurred "too soon" and defies coherent integration. Santi's broken body visualizes the mechanisms whereby the violent conditions and mentalities of war permeate the child's being in irreversible ways. Because he is soldered to the space and time of his death, he is caught forever as an expression of trauma's challenge to coherent space-time. His haunting involves the intrusion of this liminal space onto the solid boundaries and binaries of the diegetic present; thus his abject presence disallows the displacing or papering over of the traumatic experience by rational narratives of progress, forcing other characters, and viewers, to experience the powerful frisson of this previously concealed traumatic encounter.

Due to the film's setting in the aftermath of the Civil War in an institution for war-orphaned children, Santi's embodiment of the lingering power of suppressed traumatic pasts also functions symbolically as an expression of socio-cultural trauma in a Spanish context. The film may be set in the final year of the Civil War, on the threshold of the new Franco dictatorship, however in blocking the narrative's linear progress Santi also prevents the straightforward temporal progression from the end of the war into the new era. The spectral child thus raises trauma's power to challenge the restrictive and oppressive construction of "national progress" typical of Franco's post-war victory propaganda and subsequent Fascist reign. The orphans, the deserted products of a political movement all but vanquished by Franco and his Civil War, are quite literally the rem(a)inders of this forcibly suppressed alternative to Franco's model of national progress. Thus, through their very existence, these children trouble Franco's postwar efforts to suppress all remnants of the Republicans' cause and set in place a triumphal national narrative. This subversive potential is aestheticized in the film's final scene: all the adult characters having killed themselves in a microcosm of the Civil War, the orphaned Republican children stand on the threshold of the orphanage's grounds, staring out into the vast expanse of desert before them.

The Forest and the Labyrinth: The Child's Creative Response to Trauma in *Pan's Labyrinth*

Pan's Labyrinth is often considered del Toro's masterwork, having acquired widespread critical acclaim culminating in an Academy Award nomination for Best Foreign Language Film and the awards for Best Art Direction, Best Cinematography, and Best Makeup. The film has many resonances with *The Devil's Backbone*, and del Toro characterizes it as a "spiritual successor" to the earlier film.[19] Like *The Devil's Backbone*, the film is set in the aftermath of the Spanish civil war, in 1944—five years after the war had officially ended, during which the remaining Republican rebels were being violently quelled by the Falangist forces of the new Francoist dictatorship. The film centers on young girl Ofelia, whose beloved father died during the war. The narrative commences in the liminal situation created by this wartime rupture, mid-way through the journey of Ofelia and her heavily pregnant mother, Carmen, to the home of Carmen's new husband, the Falangist Captain Vidal. Thus, as in *The Devil's Backbone*, the Civil War represents the past traumatic event that ripples throughout the film, and with which the child character's personal trauma interacts.

Notably both films are set in the direct aftermath of the traumatic rupture represented by the war, not during it, emphasizing the ways in which trauma's power resonates in a belated manner, undermining narratives of national progress and the concept of "moving on" from national or personal conflict. Of course, the Falangist quest to violently extinguish all remnants of the Republicans and their cause represents the most totalizing extreme of such discourse. In *Pan's Labyrinth*, however, the collision between the child's richly realized fantastic response to trauma and the adult character's attempt to contain it within a rigidly rectilinear set of binary oppositions is realized with more force and clarity than in *The Devil's Backbone*. This opposition in perceptual modes is expressed in the film through the conflict between Ofelia—an imaginative, bookish girl whose limited understanding of the turmoil surrounding her is enriched by her love of fairy tales, and her new stepfather, Captain Vidal—a violent Fascist despot whose life is strictly guided by clocks, order, and rules.

This opposition is enunciated throughout the film by the different locales to which these two figures gravitate, even though they have been forced to cohabitate in the same regional home. Vidal is most frequently seen planning military operations in his office—an Old Mill complete with huge grinding cogs which echo on a grand scale the clockwork with which he is often seen tinkering. In contrast, Ofelia is constantly drawn to the rich, green forest which surrounds the property, which also conceals the base of the Maquis who continue to rebel against Vidal and his Falangist forces. Thus, the forest in which Ofelia stages most of her fantastic imaginings is constructed as a site of both flourishing creativity and of resistance against Fascist oppression, underscoring the revolutionary potential of Ofelia's imaginary realm. Of course, the forest is also associated with the fairy tales that Ofelia ardently consumes and which frame her perceptions and response to her traumatic existence. The key image of the forest—and of the film itself—is the crumbling and overgrown stone labyrinth into which Ofelia repeatedly ventures throughout the film. She first notices the anfractuous, sprawling structure soon after she arrives at the house and meets Vidal; in fact, she sets foot inside the labyrinth before she goes inside Vidal's house. Thus the labyrinth is quickly established as the symbolic antithesis to the inflexible ideologies which characterize Vidal and his Falangist cronies.

It is within the labyrinth that Ofelia meets the ancient Faun, a figure who is simultaneously terrifying and beautiful and who functions as the agent of Ofelia's immersion in the fantastic. The Faun requests that the child fulfill three tasks in order to reclaim her long forgotten identity as "Princess Moanna" within the fantasy underworld from whence he came. Ofelia's conflicted relationship with the Faun is drawn from a haunting but memorable experience from del Toro's childhood. He claims that when he was a young boy residing at his grandmother's home—a large, eerie house at which del Toro never felt at ease, echoed in Ofelia's discomfort at Vidal's house—he would see a Faun emerging from the shadows in his bedroom. As he elucidates: "every night at midnight, punctually, I saw a Faun emerge from behind the armoire … a hand would come out from behind the armoire … and then the hairy leg, and face of a goat."[20] Del Toro casts this as a terrifying experience which crystallized his discomfort at his grandmother's home, an ominous vision which he became primed to dread each night as he fell asleep. Yet at the same time, his visions of the Faun led him to "[forge] an alliance with monsters"[21] which helped strengthen his resolve and sense of identity as he navigated his painful relationship with his overbearing grandmother—whose life was strictly guided by an oppressive expression of Catholic dogma[22]—and establish a strong identity of his own. In resonance with del Toro's own childhood trauma, the Faun at the heart of the labyrinth provides a way for Ofelia to harness the pervasive fear and sense of powerlessness she experiences in her new surroundings and employ it to strengthen her resolve and burgeoning sense of identity. Notably, Ofelia's relationship with the Faun is not one of guidance and warmth but of deep ambivalence, through which she learns the importance of developing and assertively expressing her own voice. At the close of the film she simultaneously disobeys the orders of both her stepfather and the Faun: Vidal demands that she hand over his newborn son—her half-brother—who she has carried out to the labyrinth amongst the turmoil of the latest Rebel attack, and the Faun demands that she sacrifice her baby brother in order to facilitate her transformation into Princess Moanna. Ofelia refuses to submit to either demand, which results in her death—Vidal shoots her—but in dying she finally transforms into Princess Moanna, and gains full access to the fantastical underground realm.

The Refusal to Grow Up: The Revolutionary Potential of the Child's Fantastic Imaginary

Ultimately, *Pan's Labyrinth*, like *The Devil's Backbone*, expresses the ways in which the child's harnessing of the traumatic breach in meaning poses a challenge to oppressive narratives of linear progress, a subversive effect which is directly associated in this film with the child's resistance to the process of growing up. Ofelia is a girl on the cusp of adolescence, and Ofelia's mother Carmen continually tells her daughter that she has become too old for fairy tales, attempting to spark the child's interest in the pretty clothing that interested Carmen when she was a similar age. However Ofelia's rejection of such adolescent and adult interests as clothing and dinner parties functions as a dismissal of adult culture in favor of her childish—but rich and creative—realm of fairy tales and mythical beasts. This rejection of the linear development from childhood into adulthood is embedded within the film's circular structure. The first shot is identical to one of the last shots of the film, depicting a close up of Ofelia's face with blood running from her nose, as she lies dying after being shot by Vidal. As per her desire, the child thus never grows up: a bitter-sweet ending which casts a dark pall over the climactic triumph of the Maquis over Vidal and his men, destabilizing the progressive development from disequilibrium to victory which constitutes the linear vector of the realist, "adult" narrative. In alignment with the disruption to narrative resolution produced by Ofelia's death, while the ending of the film depicts the heroic Rebels' victory as they overthrow the Falangists and finally kill Vidal, when embedded in the broader socio-historical context upon which the film meditates this fleeting suggestion of progress is exposed to be illusory. Franco and the Falangists were to reign over Spain for the next thirty-one years, and would violently suppress the Maquis and any other alternative voices to the Fascist regime. This diminishment of the ostensibly exultant conclusion to the realist framing narrative is further reinforced by the aforementioned circular structure, as the film swiftly shifts attention away from the triumphant Rebels and back to the image of the dying little girl. Thus, del Toro employs the figure of the child and her investment in the fantastic to resist relying on the kinds of linear narratives of progress which were a key component of Francoist propaganda post-war.

In honing in on the fantastically unconventional perceptions of an oppressed young girl who lived a fleeting life, *Pan's Labyrinth* belatedly celebrates the suppressed alternative responses to the traumas of the Civil War, aestheticizing the ways in which Ofelia's relishing of the traumatic breach in meaning subverts the rigid narratives of progress characteristic of Francoist propaganda post-war. The lasting, potent ripples of trauma empower the suppressed voices of those like Ofelia whose experience stands in stark contrast to the politically sanctioned narratives of triumph which became the established historical discourse following the war. In subverting accepted "truths," alternative experiences such as Ofelia's hold the potential to generate new meaning. This potential is expressed in the final scene of *Pan's Labyrinth* as the narrator suggests that although brief and seemingly insignificant, Princess Moanna's time on Earth has left traces for any who know where to look, before closing on a shot which depicts the blooming of a white flower upon a gnarled, previously dead tree.

Conclusion: Del Toro's Children and Their Monsters

While *The Devil's Backbone* and *Pan's Labyrinth* employ the setting of the Spanish civil war to express the potential and power of childhood trauma, del Toro continually returns to this theme in other works which do not circulate around the ruptures of Spanish history. The year after *Pan's Labyrinth* was released, del Toro produced *The Orphanage*, providing guidance and mentorship to the young J. A. Bayona on his first feature film. The film in many ways functions like a contemporary companion piece to *The Devil's Backbone*. The film is set in Spain in the present, taking place in a huge building that was once an orphanage. Protagonist Laura spent her childhood in the orphanage, and the film depicts her return in adulthood to the Gothic space to start a new life there with her husband and adopted son, Simón. As in *The Devil's Backbone*, unacknowledged and unassimilated childhood traumas take on a supernatural power in *The Orphanage*, derailing the adult characters' intentions. On moving to the orphanage, little Simón quickly befriends the child ghosts of the previous inhabitants—Laura's childhood friends—who were murdered in the walls of the orphanage, unbeknownst to Laura. Simón's relationship with the specters eventually leads to the child's own death and subsequent transformation into a ghost. Thus, especially when seen in relation to *The Devil's Backbone,* the film expresses the continuing reverberations and repetitious cycles of childhood trauma. As in del Toro's earlier films, the power of this supernaturally charged childhood trauma displaces the film's realist, "present" narrative centered on the adult characters: the film closes as a distraught Laura decides to take her own life, dropping out of the present to join the ghostly children in their spectral realm.

The escalating power of the child's fantastic response to trauma is also the subject of *Don't Be Afraid of the Dark* (2010), for which del Toro wrote the screenplay in addition to producing. In this film, only the child, Sally, is cognizant of the violent, tooth fairy-esque beasts which have long besieged the huge, Gothic mansion that her father and stepmother are painstakingly restoring. While the adult caregivers dismiss Sally's obsession with these monsters as "merely" a fantastic response to the traumatic experience of being ostensibly given away by her biological mother, Sally's previously subjugated perceptions of these monsters soon come to invade and overwhelm the adult characters' reality as well—culminating in her stepmother's capture by the beasts and subsequent transformation into one of the deformed tooth fairies.

The most recent child-centered horror film that del Toro produced is *Mama* (2012), a film he calls "autobiographical"[23] even though he did not write or direct it. The film depicts the story of two young girls who are left to fend for themselves in a derelict cabin in the woods after the breakdown of their family. As the prologue details, after a crushing professional failure, the girls' father killed his wife and drove the children to the secluded cabin with the intent of killing them before taking his own life. The children were saved by a female ghost who killed their father and became a ghostly surrogate mother to the children. Throughout the film, the girls refer to this monstrous creature as "Mama." The narrative of the film is largely constituted of the events that occur five years later, when the children's uncle finally discovers the girls in the cabin and adopts them with his girlfriend, commencing the difficult task of rehabilitating the children into "normal" social structures after they have grown up "wild." But the power of the supernatural realm within which the children have existed for the previous five years is not so easily cast aside. The monstrously possessive ghost follows the girls, and throughout the film this distorted creature terrorizes the audience and adult characters. While she is the source of the film's horrors, Mama remains a comforting but suffocating presence for the girls—both the sign of their trauma and of their salvation. Again del Toro connects this ambivalent relationship with his own childhood: "the girls survived five years because of that ghost. That ghost cared for them. The same thing that I say about my childhood ...

my grandmother, as suffocating as [her] influence was in certain ways, I survived my childhood because I had her love, in a way."[24]

Ultimately, del Toro's horror films refract both his own childhood traumas and the power of such trauma to spark new ways of perceiving reality which stand in contrast to rigid, accepted—adult—structures of meaning. Central to this expression of the potential power of trauma is an appreciation of the ways in which the horrific and the beautiful are not necessarily set in binary opposition, but can work in tandem to generate subversive insights in the face of oppressive dogma or suffocating social environments. As del Toro explains, "a horrific image can be as potent an image as what we normally qualify as art, because it depicts beauty. Some images of horror are very resonant, as fragile and as beautiful as things that don't deal with the ugly side of human nature."[25]

Notes

1. Cited in Mark Kermode, "*The Devil's Backbone*: The Past Is Never Dead," *The Criterion Collection*, 30 July 2013, http://www.criterion.com/current/posts/2850-the-devil-s-backbone-the-past-is-never-dead.
2. Cited in Mark Kermode, "Interview: Guillermo del Toro," *The Guardian*, 21 November 2006, http://www.theguardian.com/film/series/guardian-interviews-at-the-bfi+guillermodeltoro.
3. Cited in Kermode, "The Devil's Backbone," 2006.
4. Guillermo del Toro and Mark Scott Zicree, *Guillermo del Toro Cabinet of Curiosities: My Notebooks, Collections, and Other Obsessions* (New York: Harper's Design, 2013), 62.
5. Ibid., 162.
6. Cited in Mike Mendez and Dave Parker, "Guillermo del Toro Interview," *Masters of Horror*, Sci-Fi Channel, 2002.
7. While del Toro has suggested that he often creates his films with a child audience in mind (in particular, he expressed profound disappointment that *Pan's Labyrinth* received an R rating, and not PG-13), due to the frightening elements and gory imagery in his films they usually attract "adults only" ratings. Furthermore, the complex narrative structure and preoccupation with Spanish historical events characteristic of most of del Toro's work suggests that they speak primarily to adult audiences.
8. Cathy Caruth, *Unclaimed Experience: Trauma, Narrative and History* (Baltimore: John Hopkins University Press, 1996), 4.
9. Keith McDonald and Roger Clark, *Guillermo del Toro: Film as Alchemic Art* (London: Bloomsbury Academic, 2014), 157.
10. Rosemary Jackson, *Fantasy: The Literature of Subversion* (New York: Taylor and Francis, 1981), 40.

11. del Toro and Zicree, *Cabinet of Curiosities*, 16.
12. Ibid., 110. The film was produced by del Toro's mentor, influential Spanish auteur Pedro Almodovar, who allowed del Toro free rein over the project.
13. Cited in Mendez and Parker, "Guillermo del Toro Interview."
14. Guillermo del Toro, *The Devil's Backbone*, Criterion, 2004.
15. Cited in *Criterion Collection*, "Guillermo del Toro's Ghostly Encounter," Criterion.com, 2013.
16. Caruth, *Unclaimed Experience*, 4.
17. Notably, this scene is also drawn from del Toro's own childhood memories of being terrified when navigating the long, dark hallway at his grandmother's house (Kermode, "The Devil's Backbone," 2006).
18. del Toro, *The Devil's Backbone*, Criterion, 2004.
19. Guillermo del Toro, *Pan's Labyrinth*, Optimum Home Entertainment, 2010.
20. Kermode, "The Devil's Backbone," 2006.
21. Richard Crouse, "Guillermo del Toro Interview with Richard Crouse," *Richard Crouse*, 4 January 2013.
22. del Toro describes his relationship with his grandmother as suffused with "the horror of Catholic guilt and Catholic dogma. My grandma was like Piper Laurie in *Carrie* ... so I was like a chubby version of Carrie." Ibid.
23. Ibid.
24. Ibid.
25. Jason Bovberg, "DVDTalk Interview—Guillermo del Toro," *DVDTalk*, 2014, http://www.dvdtalk.com/guillermodeltoro.html.

Bibliography

Bayona, J. A. *The Orphanage*. Esta Vivo! Laboratorio de Nuevos Talentos, 2007.
Bovberg, Jason. "DVDTalk Interview—Guillermo del Toro." *DVDTalk*. 2014. http://www.dvdtalk.com/guillermodeltoro.html.
Caruth, Cathy. *Unclaimed Experience: Trauma, Narrative and History*. Baltimore: John Hopkins University Press, 1996.
The Criterion Collection. "Guillermo del Toro's Ghostly Encounter." Criterion.com, 2013. http://www.criterion.com/current/posts/2848-guillermo-del-toro-s-ghostly-encounter.
Crouse, Richard. "Guillermo del Toro Interview with Richard Crouse." Richard Crouse.com. 4 January 2013. http://www.richardcrouse.ca/richard-crouse-interviews-guillermo-del-toro-on-mama-frankenstein-and-much-more/.
del Toro, Guillermo. *Cronos*. CNCAIMC, 1993.
_____. *The Devil's Backbone*. Criterion, 2004 (cinematic release, 2001). Blu-Ray/DVD.
_____. *Mimic*. Dimension Films, 1997.
_____. *Pan's Labyrinth*. Optimum Home Entertainment, 2010 (cinematic release, 2006). Blu-Ray/DVD.
del Toro, Guillermo, and Marc Zicree. *Guillermo del Toro Cabinet of Curiosities: My Notebooks, Collections, and Other Obsessions*. New York: Harper's Design, 2013.
Jackson, Rosemary. *Fantasy: The Literature of Subversion*. New York: Taylor and Francis, 1981.

Kermode, Mark. "*The Devil's Backbone*: The Past Is Never Dead." *The Criterion Collection*. 30 July 2013. http://www.criterion.com/current/posts/2850-the-devil-s-backbone-the-past-is-never-dead.

Kermode, Mark. "Interview: Guillermo del Toro." *The Guardian*. 21 November 2006. http://www.theguardian.com/film/series/guardian-interviews-at-the-bfi+guillermodeltoro.

McDonald, Keith, and Roger Clark. *Guillermo del Toro: Film as Alchemic Art*. London: Bloomsbury Academic, 2014.

Mendez, Mike, and Dave Parker. "Guillermo del Toro Interview." *Masters of Horror*. Sci-Fi Channel, 2002.

Muschietti, Andres. *Mama*. Universal Pictures, 2013.

Nixey, Troy. *Don't Be Afraid of the Dark*. Miramax, 2010.

The Ambivalence of Creative Desire
Theogonic Myth and Monstrous Offspring

SIDNEY L. SONDERGARD

> *When you seek beauty only within a world of perfection,*
> *you end up with illustrations of fairies dressed in pink tutus,*
> *sprinkling dust, with cherubic babies and a flower garden.*
> —Guillermo del Toro

Apart from what they may signify as projections of the unconscious (either cultural, or personal to the author), of personal identity, of social semiotics (with cinematic sign systems ranging from film history to genre conventions to horror icons), of historical frissons (both political proclivities and specific events), and of popular culture vehicles (from trading cards to comic books), monsters are aesthetic personifications to Guillermo del Toro, and hence possessed of a terrible beauty. This oxymoron is equally central to Hesiod's *Theogony* (eighth century BCE), an intrinsically conflicted narrative, with its account of archetypal creativity: the birth of gods, both exquisite and grotesque. In particular, the interpersonal dynamics of progenitors and their offspring reflect an ambivalence of desire that includes the creator's love for the potential of what has been created, as well as fear of its agency in subsequent, autonomous creation.

When each of Hesiod's sky gods acts preemptively to suppress his progeny, the triggering motive is fear of usurpation, and ultimately of being replaced as the primary shaper of reality. This latter concern is implicit in the motives behind all artistic invention. As Abraham Maslow explains it, "creative people are people who don't want the world as it is today but want to make another world."[1] In the narratives of the three sky gods, the creation of monsters is synonymous with the genesis of gods: the misshapen and hideous is just as inevitably a product of the creator's imagination as the idealized and handsome. Del Toro want us to love the monsters in his films; not because they're good or moral—though they may well be—but simply because they're beautiful in their grotesquerie. But he also ensures that they retain the capacity to disturb or to frighten us, an extension of the creator's power over them. In working to "make another world," del Toro brings his cinematic children to life but then carefully controls them by giving them apparently impossible tasks to perform, and by placing them in seemingly insufferable circumstances. For the director, as for Hesiod's sky gods, the conflicted desire to create and to control results in conflict. In the *Theogony*, it evolves to produce a definitive strategy that ensures the final sky god's dominance in perpetuity; for Guillermo del Toro, it is the animating spirit of his film narratives.

Creative Restraint and Resistance vs. "everything they can think of that is scary"

In his proposal of archetypal theses associated with the presence of monsters in narrative, Jeffrey Jerome Cohen posits that monsters serve as the harbingers of category crisis, that they implicitly oppose "traditional methods of organizing knowledge and human experience" and hence occupy "a contested cultural space."[2] But he also hypothesizes that viewer/reader fear of monsters is also a form of desire, that the very creatures "who terrify and interdict can evoke potent escapist fantasies" of "aggression, domination, and inversion [that] are allowed safe expression in a clearly delimited and permanently liminal space."[3] This essay will suggest that the aesthetics of del Toro's art requires a synthesis of these positions: that the hybridity of del Toro's monsters represents not a deformation of some categorical norm but rather a personal aesthetic preference for such composite creatures; and that theogonic myth reveals three tactical interventions between creator and progeny that reflect the creator's ambivalence towards his creations while mapping a strategy of controlling them.

Del Toro's notebooks reveal the affection and care invested in the conception of each of his film monsters. This is exemplified in his illustrations, rendered in loving detail, that are surrounded by notes that frequently imagine reactions, emotions, and dialogue from the created figure's intended film milieu. The notebooks are his proofing/proving ground, a laboratory of the imagination where he experiments with possible looks and possible combinations (as he explains in *Cabinet of Curiosities*, "it's not a journal, really").[4] They allow him to observe his creatures as they evolve over time, making it possible to see what should not be included in their portraits: "the mistake most people make when designing a monster is they literally put in everything they can think of that is scary."[5] The logic that del Toro employs when constructing his own creatures is to exercise a kind of binary hybridity, a formula derived from his own experience as a filmgoer.

Hybridity, the quintessence of the grotesque in visual art (e.g., Bosch's bird-headed humans, or Arcimboldo's human-vegetables) and in mythology, appears frequently in Hesiod in the form of female monsters, half-human and half-creature, like the Sphinx, the Gorgons, the Echidna, or the Harpies. Richard Caldwell explains that, "these always have the face, and often the breast, of a woman, but their lower parts ... are a lion or serpent or bird of prey, all common animal symbols of powerful male sexuality."[6] The hybridity here is dual, then, consisting of both sexual difference and specie distinction. Del Toro's experimentation with visual depictions of monsters gravitates towards a more simple binary hybridity that resists incorporating "everything [one] can think of that is scary."[7] He explains in *Cabinet of Curiosities* that he began illustrating his own stories while still quite young, but "the three creatures I drew obsessively were the Gill-Man from *Creature from the Black Lagoon*, the Frankenstein monster, and Lon Chaney's Phantom of the Opera."[8] These three figures evoke terror because something non-human (or destructive of the human) has been grafted onto a recognizably human form. The result is unpredictable, and hence it provokes fear.

Del Toro's designs, then, are a synthesis of incongruity and otherness with the familiar and even cherished. The creatures evolve through his notebook depictions of them, as do his expectations for what can be done with cinematic verisimilitude. In discussing the "grimy" nature of his creatures in *Pan's Labyrinth*, he notes that the "fairies are these little imps that are dirty, naked, and kind of evil looking. The Faun is incredibly ambivalent, even menacing.... And having to feed the mandrake with blood, and the fetal implications of the mandrake? I mean, I tried to make the fantasy as gritty as reality because that's what it's supposed to be."[9] Yet for the unproduced *Mephisto's Bridge*, he proposes that the composite demon, Spanky, appear as a "slender, almost beautiful creature" with each of the demon's feathers representing "a soul he had taken. So he was a walking epic."[10] Piero Camporesi applies the description of one "who overturns physical laws, who reveals the unexpected, who prophesies a change of state, who inhabits another dimension full of remarkable, unheard-of and spectacular phenomena"[11] to what it means to be a saint. It's equally applicable to what it means to del Toro to be a creator. And a monster.

Ouranos' Solution: Exile and Adversity ([Under]ground Zero for Rebellion)

In all three facets of Hesiod's theogonic myths, the creator god fears being usurped by his creations, and consequently devises a central strategy for preventing this from happening. Within the three sign systems proposed here, the sky gods are read as archetypal artists/creators, manifesting their creative powers as the active agents in the propagation of gods and monsters. Also common to all three variants is the assumption that creative power can only be assured through dominance of the created. Thus the strategies employed by the three generations of Greek sky gods, Ouranos, Kronos, and Zeus, respectively, seek to ensure supremacy over their progeny—to exercise control of their creations.

Hesiod describes Gaia (Earth) bearing by Ouranos (Sky) the six male Titans and six female Titanides, the youngest being the Titan, Kronos,[12] followed by the Kyklopes "with over-proud heart, Brontes and Steropes and hard-hearted Arges."[13] Finally born to the couple were "three great and mighty sons, unspeakable Kottos and Briareos and Gyges, rash children. From their shoulders shot a hundred arms unimaginable, and fifty heads on the shoulders of each grew over their strong bodies; great and mighty strength was in their huge shape."[14] Without an explicit rationale to explain his response, the reader is told that Ouranos hates and dreads them all equally: "all who were born from Gaia and Ouranos were the most terrible of children, and their father hated them from the first."[15] The most immediate problem for the creator is the fact that as a "race of immortals who always are, who were born from Gaia and starry Ouranos,"[16] they cannot be destroyed.

Ouranos' solution is to remove these "most terrible" children from his sphere of influence: "when any of them first would be born, he would hide them all away, and not let them come up to the light, in a dark hole of Gaia; the evil deed pleased Ouranos."[17] This tactic of keeping his creations literally in the dark, preventing them from emerging from Gaia, is prompted by the two primary fears of having his dominance challenged, and of suffering some kind of harm at their hands. Thus when "first the father was angry at heart" with Briareos, Kottos and Gyges, "he bound them in strong bondage; when he noticed their great manhood, their looks and size, he put them under the wide-pathed earth. They lived there under the earth in pain."[18] As for the others, most particularly the Titans, Ouranos is described as "reproaching the sons whom he himself begot; he said they strained in wickedness to do a great wrong, but there would be revenge afterwards."[19] As if to imply the nature of such revenge without articulating it, Hesiod follows this assertion with a list of the children of Nyx (Night), most prominently including the death triumvirat: Moros (Doom), Ker (Destiny), and Thanatos (Death).

As an artist of visual narrative, del Toro creates characters that reflect a full spectrum of morality, philosophy, intelligence, power and potentiality, then controls his creations by placing them in circumstances that will catalyze the emergence of their true natures. Ouranos shuts away his progeny because he wants to create, but is unable to predict (and hence to control) what will result from that desire; fearing that this uncertainty might extend to his ability to maintain his authority over them, he forces them underground. When del Toro does this, he's also acknowledging the power of his characters, but he uses the enclosed setting as a more ambiguous staging ground for his creations, where they reveal whether they are truly god-like or monstrous.[20]

The self-imposed imprisonment of *Cronos*' Manuel de la Guardia in a sterile hermetic environment, for example, reveals the desperation of his resistance to the decay of his body. He chooses to exile himself but also makes his nephew, Angel, a prisoner to his will, forcing him to carry out the relentless search for the Cronos device in exchange for Angel's expectations of inheriting all of his wealth—thus creating a parody of Ouranos shutting away his heirs to preclude their usurping his authority, as de la Guardia's sending Angel out into the world is meant to be a sign of his control, but signifies instead his utter impotence. A different kind of inversion of Ouranos' strategy in *Pacific Rim* has the Kaiju clones being sent from underground as colonizing agents through a Lovecraftian portal located in an undersea fissure. The invasion of the earth by monsters of escalating size is designed to communicate their creators' mastery of the planet's inhabitants—but instead draws human agents (piloting the jaegars, their god-machines) underground to defeat the Kaiju and their makers.

The potential for altruism is one of the most significant tests that del Toro poses for his creations once they're forced into their respective exiles. To save unsuspecting innocents from the predation of the Judas breed in *Mimic*, Dr. Susan Tyler, Dr. Peter Mann, the shoe shine man, Manny, and the transit system cop, Leonard, have to risk their lives underground; Manny and Leonard lose theirs, while Susan and Peter do what is requisite to end the threat. Dangers are introduced underground in *Hellboy* (the demon Sammael as yet another threat in the subway system; an entire grotto of replicated Sammaels; the blood of a murdered guide in subterranean Antarctica used to resurrect Rasputin), though the ultimate underground threat appears in *Hellboy II: The Golden Army*, with its 4,900 indestructible, self-repairing automatons, built by a goblin blacksmith explicitly to destroy human beings, being mobilized by the quite reasonably enraged Prince Nuada (angry at humans for persecuting anything non-human and for polluting the environment). The unexpected hero of this conflict is Princess Nuala, who performs the ultimate sacrifice in order to stop her royal twin, in effect stabbing him to death by stabbing herself.

Perhaps the most poignant act of altruism in del Toro's films is that of Ofelia in *Pan's Labyrinth*, led by a shape-shifting mantis/fairy underground to meet the Faun who informs her that she's really Princess Moanna, daughter of the King of the Underworld: "You are not born of man. It was the moon that bore you." Her interaction with magical creatures, as she tries to perform a series of tasks assigned to her by the Faun, gives her sufficient hope of being restored to her kingdom that she endures tremendous suffering before being forced to choose between the safety of her infant brother and her claim to the throne. Although idyllic dreams of "blue skies, soft breeze and sunshine" initially led the Princess to escape from her dreary underground realm (despite the fact that there were "no lies or pain" there), she refuses to exchange her brother's life for the chance to return there. Whether the film's closing sequence is just the fantasy of a dying girl or the reward for proving worthy to claim her royal heritage, Ofelia responds heroically when tested underground.

Hesiod's assertion that "the evil deed pleased Ouranos" when he hid away his children in Gaia reveals that the sky god's initial desire to create is subsequently overridden by the desire to maintain dominance over his creations. Dr. Susan Tyler in *Mimic* creates the Judas breed, a hybrid of termite and mantis, to destroy the cockroach carriers of Strickler's Disease, a plague that is striking children. When her mutant insects successfully destroy the carriers, Dr. Tyler is feted as the city's savior. Unfortunately, the creations began evolving with each new generation, producing a threat even greater than the one they were initially designed to eliminate. The Kaiju clones in *Pacific Rim* are created to prepare the way for an alien race to conquer earth—yet the creators' confidence in their tactic of producing ever-larger monsters makes them vulnerable to counter-attack employing those same creatures. In both cases, the monsters that are portrayed onscreen are frightening because of what remains mysterious about them. The Judas breed's seemingly infinite capacity to mimic humanity through evolution raises the question of whether, in time, they might have achieved human-like sentience. The Kaiju are most dangerous for abilities that only superficially seem secondary to their immense size (acid spray; electromagnetic pulse; etc.). Yet these "beautiful" monsters (see del Toro 260), possessing their own dignity as agents of their creators' agendas, are inevitably eradicated as threats to humanity.

Del Toro also problematizes the question of the creator's authority over the created. Although Hellboy grows up under the tutelage of adoptive father Dr. Bruttenholm/Broom, he was conjured by Grigori Rasputin to serve as harbinger of planetary annihilation. This gives Rasputin a sense of proprietary entitlement, falsely seeing himself as creator rather than mere manipulator, his premature gloating about having catalyzed the Apocalypse undercut when a chained Agent Myers tosses Broom's symbolically potent rosary beads to Hellboy, triggering the demon's revolt with the words, "Remember who you are." Rasputin's bid to destroy the world ends with Hellboy breaking off his restored horns, closing a Lovecraftian portal, and stabbing Rasputin with one of the severed horns. Like Ouranos, Rasputin celebrates a bit too proudly and a bit too early.

The creators in del Toro's films who follow Ouranos' strategy for controlling their creations without any regard for the impact of their ambitions and the ambivalence of their desire to create, are inevitably outlived by their creations. Fuchinelli, the alchemist who designs the Cronos device, shuts it away inside an archangel statue and records notes on it in backwards Latin, yet this provides him merely the illusion of control since he's enslaved by the vampiric blood-need the device instills as the price of immortality. His arcane safeguards prove ineffectual when a building collapse mortally wounds him and the Cronos device eventually falls into the hands of Jesús Gris, the most unlikely of inheritors. A similarly thwarted creator is the rigidly authoritarian Captain Vidal in *Pan's Labyrinth*, who shuts away his pregnant wife, Carmen, in an attempt to control her, her daughter, Ofelia, and his unborn son—though ultimately his actions contribute to Carmen's death, he kills Ofelia, and he's informed that his son will never learn his father's true identity. Destruction seems synonymous with creation for him: his one exercise of imagination features him standing before a mirror as he mimes drawing a straight razor across his throat. Truly creative activity, according to Colin Wilson, "cannot flourish in an atmosphere of reductionism and determinism," for the flourishing of invention occurs in proportion to the creator's "degree of freedom."[21] Del Toro's characters like Rasputin, Fuchinelli, and Vidal are ultimately thwarted by their fixations on power and by their own lack of imagination.

Kronos' Solution: It Takes One to (B)eat One

In anticipation of Kronos' future treachery against Ouranos, Hesiod introduces him in the *Theogony* as "the youngest, crafty Kronos, most terrible of children; he hated his lusting father."[22] Gaia "groaned within from the strain" of having the children forced back into her womb, "and planned an evil crafty trick," addressing her fearful children with the plan to "punish the evil outrage of your father."[23] Kronos agrees to do it "since I have no respect for our father unspeakable; since he first planned unseemly deeds."[24] In an ironic allusion to Ouranos' initial aggression, Gaia specifically hides Kronos from his father, puts into his hands "a sickle with jagged teeth," and then from ambush Kronos "quickly severed his own father's genitals."[25] While goddesses like the Meliai (nymphs) and Aphrodite form spontaneously from the bloody phallus, monsters also result: the Erinyes (Furies) "and great Giants, shining in armor, holding long spears in their hands."[26]

Once the children of Ouranos and Gaia are freed from their mother's body, Kronos and his sister, Rhea, produce their own "illustrious children" Hestia, Demeter, Hades, Poseidon, and Zeus.[27] However, Kronos learns from his parents that "it was fate that his own son would overthrow him, although he was powerful," so "he kept no blind man's watch, but alertly swallowed his own children" as each was born, to ensure "that none of Ouranos' proud line but himself would hold the right of king over the immortals" (54). Before bearing her final child, Rhea begs her parents to provide her a plan "by which she might secretly have her son, and make great crafty Kronos pay" for swallowing the children,[28] hence they inform her frankly that Zeus would soon "overthrow him by force and violence and drive him from his honor, and rule the immortals himself."[29] Gaia hides the infant "in a deep cave, down in dark holes of holy earth"[30] while Rhea "wrapped a huge stone in a baby's robe, and fed it to Ouranos' wide-ruling son" who "took it in his hands and put it down his belly, the fool."[31]

Kronos' bold stroke frees his fellow creations from oppression and empowers him as a creator, with new creatures generated as a consequence of removing his progenitor's source of power. In del Toro's films, monsters similarly appear as the products of efforts to displace authorities perceived as tyrannical, though those monsters remain floating signifiers, variously connoting good or evil according to the nature of the authority under attack. Raleigh Becket's voice-over in *Pacific Rim* tells us that the world's nations pooled their resources to address the Kaiju threat: "To fight monsters, we created monsters of our own." Justification of the action is implied in its very description, the variable scale of provocation and morality applied to the directors' individual monster creations. The power to create monsters by bringing to life what was previously dead, for example, appears both positively and negatively in *Hellboy*, where Grisgori Rasputin resurrects the demon Sammael (appropriately aka the Hound of Resurrection), a creature hodge-podge that indicates the viability of Rasputin's intention to provide access for a much greater, Cthulhu-like monster from another dimension. Rasputin's own dying body creates yet another monster through a kind of parthenogenesis. These monsters, however, are all unambiguous extensions of Rasputin's preference for chaos over order, of his colossal hunger for power. In contrast, the corpse that Hellboy reanimates, Ivan Klimatovich, aids him in locating the mausoleum of Rasputin, initiating the events that culminate in the antagonist's defeat.

Some of del Toro's monsters displace tyrants of an intangible or abstract nature. The oppressor attacked by the alchemist in *Cronos* is time, or more precisely, human mortality. His adamantine sickle is an egg-shaped golden device (itself a monstrous hybrid of insect and clockwork mechanism) that produces a vampiric hybrid of human and bloodsucker. By the time his transformation is complete, the now immortal Jesús Gris possesses skin that is puffy, pale, and grub-like—like a bloodless version of the insect inside the Cronos device. The tyranny of time and mortality is replaced by a new tyranny, the need for blood, resetting the cycle of oppression and potential rebellion. *The Devil's Backbone* addresses this by asking the question of what a ghost is: one possibility is "something dead that still seems to be alive." Carlos has no understanding of the political realities behind the Spanish civil war and lives imaginatively in the world of comic books and *The Count of Monte Cristo*. When Dr. Casares tells him about "limbo water," the concoction of very old dark rum and cloves used to preserve deformed fetuses (some with exposed spines, a condition known locally as "the devil's backbone") but poured off and sold by the doctor in town as a potency enhancer, Carlos is simply unsettled by the jars full of monster-infants. Casares recognizes the oppressors here as, "Poverty and disease. That's all it is." But to Carlos, the explanation gives credence to certain other boys' suspicion that Santi was killed for his blood, which they theorize was then sold "to rich people to cure their tuberculosis." Carlos' contact with the ghost of Santi helps him to see that adult greed, personified in the person of Jacinto, is ultimately what killed the boy.[32]

Del Toro also cues viewers periodically to empathize with his monsters' plight by anthropomorphizing their responses; that is, he manipulates reaction by allowing his hybrid creatures to defend their actions with moral and philosophical values that are likely to coincide with many of the viewers' own. This makes it possible for humans to be targeted by monsters as tyrants (and hence *essentially* monstrous) deserving of elimination. The danger of tampering with nature, even for rationally defensible reasons, is exposed in *Mimic* by encouraging sympathy and respect for the Judas breed. Susan Tyler engineered the insects to remove threats, but as her mentor, Dr. Gates, reminds her, "Evolution has a way of keeping things alive." Since human beings want them dead, the Judas breed develop the perfect defense mechanism—mimicry of their most threatening predator. Evolving quickly through short-lived generations, they become a human-insect hybrid ("Lungs. Insects don't have lungs."), though people resist acknowledging the transformation: pulled from the sewer, one of them is described as neither an insect *nor* a human being ("It's a lobster, right?"). The soldier insects among the Judas breed are so successful at their mimicry that they become figures in local urban legends: "Overcoat Slim, Long John." They're merely trying to defend themselves against predation; to encourage even more support for them from the audience, del Toro shows the audience that not all deaths they cause are undeserved—take the example of Ping, the preacher who uses his church as a front for a slave labor ring.

Ambiguously presented to the audience, the elvish Prince Nuada in *Hellboy II: The Golden Army* initiates the unconscionable murder of human beings via calcium-devouring tooth fairies (which look like relatives of the mantis/fairy from *Pan's Labyrinth*) and H.R. Giger-esque face-hugging creatures in order to acquire humanity's portion of the crown that controls the Golden Army. Nuada nevertheless articulates a perfectly legitimate moral defense of his actions when he argues that human beings have been destroying the environment and with it the planet's biodiversity. As reinforcement, a conflicted hybridity occurs at both the micro-level (represented by the infant-like figure[33] at the Troll Market who humorously informs the audience: "I'm not a baby. I'm a tumor.") and the macro-level (when Hellboy is obliged to save the lives of human beings by destroying an elemental that is the last specimen of its kind) of the narrative. Louise Krasniewicz has argued that when considering horror films, "we can and should make distinctions between the moral and the technological, and between the individual and the social," though "we also have to recognize the deep interdependencies and interactions of these arenas."[34] To del Toro, it's not appearance or hybridity that makes a character abominable, it's monolithic thinking that perpetuates self-serving desires without regard for others. "We die," Nuada tells Hellboy, "and the world will be poorer for it."

Having learned from Ouranos' unsuccessful strategy of exiling threats to a remote site, Kronos adopts a policy of keeping everything to himself, under his surveillance, personally controlling all his creations. His motive, however, is the same fear that plagued Ouranos, and prediction of his tactic's inevitable failure comes from the two beings most experienced in the inescapability of fate. Del Toro is well aware that foreknowledge of future disaster doesn't blunt the immediacy of emotions for characters, as when Liz Sherman bargains with the Angel of Death in *Hellboy II: The Golden Army*, despite being told that Hellboy's destiny is to bring about the end of the world. Damaskinos, in *Blade II*, is another father/creator who seeks control by internalizing threats: he creates a Reaper, a monster/vampire hybrid to ensure his control of the vampire nation. Blade likens the Reaper threat to cancer. "Cancer with a purpose," sneers Damaskinos. The original Reaper, however, is Damaskinos' own son, Nomak, who eventually bites and kills his father, then pushes a broken segment of Blade's sword into his own heart. His grieving sister, Nyssa, then passes the final judgment on their mutual progenitor: "Isn't it sad that you die not by the hand of your enemy, but of your own children." Other characters try to internalize their problems (Aurora hides the Cronos device inside the head of her stuffed bear; Dr. Newton Geiszler believes that creating a drift with a Kaiju brain will allow him to understand the plans of its alien controllers), but the result is never control. Supremacy, in theogonic myth, has to come from a complex of empowerment, the same hybridity that is the very definition of monsters.

Zeus' Solution: The Lessons of Titanomachy, Alliance, and the Bigger Gun

In Aeschylus's play *Prometheus Bound*, Prometheus remarks to Hermes regarding the generations of the sky gods, "I have seen / Two dynasties already hurled from those same heights; / And I shall see the third, today's king, fall to earth / More shamefully than his precursors."[35] This prediction, of course, doesn't work out well for Prometheus, but he sees a very familiar future for Zeus: as the previous generations were overthrown by sons, so Zeus eventually will be overthrown. In a stalemate, however, as Zeus' prisoner, Prometheus refuses to divulge the future avenger's identity: consequently, "Force is limited by lack of knowledge; knowledge is limited by force."[36]

Hesiod records that after being "tricked by the clever advice of Gaia, great crafty Kronos threw up his children.... First he vomited the stone he had swallowed last"[37]; Zeus then sets it up at Delphi/Pytho "to be a sign thereafter, a wonder to mortal men."[38] He "released from their deadly chains his uncles [the Kyklopes], Ouranos' sons, whom their father mindlessly bound. They did not forget gratitude for his help, and gave him thunder and the fiery lightning-bolt."[39] Thus Zeus becomes supreme ruler and promises that, "whoever held no honor or right under Kronos would enter upon honor and rights, as is just."[40] When war breaks out between the Titans of Mt. Othrys and Kronos' children of Mt. Olympus, "by Gaia's counsel," Zeus and the other Olympian gods release the Hundred-Handed. The opponents fight for ten years to a draw; but when Zeus gives these latest allies "nectar and ambrosia, which the gods eat themselves,"[41] reminding them of what they owe him for their release, the balance shifts. "They stood against the Titans in grim battle, holding great rocks in their massive hands" till soon "a heavy tremor of feet reached dim Tartaros, and the loud noise of unspeakable rout and violent weapons."[42]

Kottos, Briareos and Gyges "threw three hundred rocks from massive hands at once, and with their missiles overshadowed the Titans; they sent them under the wide-pathed earth, and bound them in cruel bonds, having defeated them by force."[43] In Tartaros, "the Titan gods under the dim gloom are hid away by the plans of cloud-gathered Zeus, in a moldy place,"[44] with the Hundred-Handed serving as their guards. How bad is exile to Tartaros? "Even for the immortal gods this is monstrous,"[45] though it effectively ensures Zeus' sovereignty.

Numerous del Toro characters are tricked into accepting surrogates just like Kronos. The Kaiju masters are tricked by Raleigh and Mako who slip Gipsy Danger through their defenses by employing a dead Kaiju as a Trojan horse; Manuel de la Guardia, the wealthy recluse, accepts a box of locks that he believes to be the Cronos device; to protect themselves from attack by the insect soldiers, Susan, Peter, Leonard, and Manny rub pieces of chopped Judas breed over their bodies; Jacinto is fooled into digging through the explosion's rubble when Carmen cannily hides the gold in her prosthetic leg. Greed and overconfidence create vulnerability, suggesting that if faith isn't tempered by skepticism, unpleasant surprises are likely to result. Like the baby/stone that's set up at Delphi, home of the famous oracle, Carlos treats the bomb that failed to explode as a holy object: "If you're alive," he whispers to it tentatively, "tell me where Santi is."

Zeus capitalizes on having escaped his father's stratagem by forging alliances that quickly make him much more than just a survivor. The lightning that he receives in gratitude, the ultimate weapon, however, is not celebrated in del Toro's films as the end for which alliances are merely a necessary means. Whistler makes ever more devastating weapons for Blade, but Nomak isn't finally defeated until he destroys himself in an unspoken pact to end the Reaper menace; Hellboy employs Big Baby, yet he's still dealt what initially seems to be a mortal wound by Nuada's spear; the jaegars are built in escalating size to address the Kaiju threat, but the counter-response is simply to produce larger Kaiju. Del Toro makes his position on this subject clear in notes for his *The Left Hand of Darkness* project, giving the Count a weapon like Kronos' sickle for enacting revenge: "But there's a moment where the Count goes too far and becomes a monster." He's provided a mechanical hand "that is not good for anything but killing," to illustrate the point that "revenge, when you enact it, ultimately leaves you empty. It makes you feel dirty afterward."[46]

It's not violence that inspires a creator like del Toro (versus a Zack Snyder or Michael Bay), it's the recognition that the hope and empowerment fostered by cooperation is what allows heroes, monstrous or not, to emerge and triumph. Thus Blade works with the Blood Pack, vampires who trained for two years specifically to hunt him; Carlos, Jaime, Owl and the other boys unite to overcome the physical advantage of their adult tormentor, Jacinto; by sacrificing themselves individually, Dr. Ferreiro and other rebels allow the coordinated efforts of Mercedes and Pedro to succeed; the drift, the unique mental rapport between jaegar pilots, allows teams to accomplish what individuals could not. The shortcomings and failures of these characters are aesthetically as important as their successes: "Why enthrone the myth of the perfect, infallible superman," asks del Toro, "if it's always more beautiful to know that the humanity that creates beauty is the same fallible species that can create horror or misery?"[47] In a variant version of Zeus' usurping of Kronos, "the son repeats his father's act, and Zeus plies Kronos with fermented honey, binds him and then castrates him, as he had castrated his father."[48] Perhaps this is why Daniel Bray has argued that in effect the beginning *is* the end in Hesiod's *Theogony*, that the characteristics of the Titanomachy liken it to other prototypical eschatological myths, like the medieval Scandinavian Ragnarök.[49] The fear of being superceded by one's own creation persists in every generation—and is the dominant source of any pejorative monstrosity in Guillermo del Toro's films.

The Maker's/Monster's Aesthetic

Curiously, there are those moments when del Toro seems to be explicitly referencing elements of theogonic myth: e.g., the computer projection of the breach diagram in *Pacific Rim* with its rings at either end looks like a visual illustration of Hesiod's description of Earth and Tartaros ("as far below the earth as sky is above the earth; for it is that far from the earth to dim Tartaros"[50]). The director readily concedes that in some ways he's simply recycling himself in each film—the many repetitions of references, characters, actors, etc. from his previous films confirm this—and reinventing beloved influences, literary and cinematic. His *At the Mountains of Madness* project, adapting Lovecraft's narrative, proposes a version "set during the time of conquest of the New World with a bunch of conquistadors arriving at the Mayan ruins and finding another city beneath,"[51] reminiscent of the political allegory of *The Devil's Backbone*. And the author Arthur Conan Doyle, reinvented as a fiction, succeeds in the proposed *The List of Seven* project "only when he includes Holmes as a character."[52]

Perhaps this is how the director deals with his own anxieties about being superseded by what he's created. Hesiod, after all, didn't invent the notion of a theogony: "Functioning like day residue in a dream, previous myths provided Hesiod with the data that he arranged in a new and satisfying pattern."[53] Guillermo del Toro consistently focuses in his films and his unfinished projects on a creative ambivalence that at its most simple can be expressed as the paradoxical desire for monsters to be stunning and awe-inspiring, but also flawed and vulnerable. Thus the hulking Angel de la Guardia in *Cronos* wants to modify his nose—so he'll look less like the monster that he truly is, and the audience sympathizes with this fleeting glimpse of his ingenuousness. It is in the duality of such moments, reflected in the archetypes of theogonic myth, that del Toro's monsters most resemble their creator.

Notes

1. Abraham Maslow, *The Farther Reaches of Human Nature* (New York: Viking, 1971), 93.
2. Jeffrey Cohen, "Monster Culture (Seven Theses)," *Monster Theory: Reading Culture*, Jeffrey Jerome Cohen, ed. (Minneapolis: University of Minnesota Press, 1996), 7.
3. Ibid., 17.
4. Guillermo del Toro and Marc Scott Zicree, *Guillermo del Toro Cabinet of Curiosities: My Notebooks, Collections, and Other Obsessions* (New York: Harper Design, 2013), 72.
5. Ibid., 58.
6. Richard Caldwell, *The Origin of the Gods: A Psychoanalytic Study of Greek Theogonic Myth* (New York: Oxford University Press, 1989), 33.
7. In some cases he achieves this by suggesting an aesthetic paradigm shift, as when *Cronos*' Manuel de la Guardia pursues an insectophile perspective: "Who says insects aren't God's favorite creatures? Christ walked on water, just like a mosquito. The matter of the resurrection is related to ants, to spiders. They can remain inside a rock for hundreds of years until someone comes along and frees them." Hybridity is itself an aesthetic for del Toro: as Ann Davies has pointed out, by making both English-language and Spanish-language films, the director has also developed "a hybrid cinematic resumé" (135).
8. del Toro and Zicree, *Cabinet of Curiosities*, 51. These early influences continue to inspire del Toro, as demonstrated by the reappearance of the "Gill-Man" in the form of Abe Sapien in the *Hellboy* films; clips from *The Bride of Frankenstein* and *The Creature from the Black Lagoon* also appear in the background of shots in *Hellboy II: The Golden Army*. The protagonist of the unproduced project *Meat Market*, Ernie, is a composite of these early del Toro influences: he'd been dropped as a baby and "had his face broken on the concrete. They had to put him together the best they could, and he became sort of a mixture of the Phantom of the Opera and the Frankenstein monster" (253).
9. del Toro and Zicree, *Cabinet of Curiosities*, 48.
10. Ibid., 254.
11. Piero Camporesi, *The Incorruptible Flesh: Bodily Mutilation and Mortification in Religion and Folklore*, trans. Tania Croft-Murray (New York: Cambridge University Press, 1988), 36.
12. Hesiod, *Hesiod's Theogony*, trans. Richard S. Caldwell (Newburyport, MA: Focus Classical Library, 1987), 35–6.
13. Ibid., 36.
14. Ibid., 36–7. The "theogony," or birth of gods, then, also includes the birth of monsters. *The Library* of Apollodorus, another collection of Greek theogonic myths, lists the offspring of Gaia and Ouranos in reverse order of Hesiod's *Theogony*. The firstborns are the three Hundred-Handed, followed by Arges, Steropes, and Brontes ("of whom each had one eye on his forehead"), but these latter he threw into Tartaros; then they're followed by the Titans and the Titanides. Angered about the cyclops, Gaia "persuaded the Titans to attack their father" and gave Kronos "an adamantine sickle" (5).

And towards addressing the motif of monstrous activity occurring underwater in del Toro's films, Caldwell reminds us that the union of Gaia and Pontos (Seas), "perhaps a reminiscence of the marriage of water and earth as primeval fertility principles, eventually produces most of the major monsters of Greek mythology" (152).

15. Ibid., 37.
16. Ibid., 33.
17. Ibid., 37.
18. Ibid., 64.
19. Ibid., 40.
20. Hence in the unproduced *Meat Market*, del Toro proposes that the protagonist, Ernie, be blamed for his "meat-processing mogul" father's murder (which was committed by his uncle), so he subsequently "goes and hides in the sewers full of chunks of rotting meat" (253). He faces the horror of being surrounded by the putrescent flesh (figuratively representing both his father's power and his dead body), the very act functioning to vindicate his character.
21. Colin Wilson, *New Pathways in Psychology: Maslow & the Post-Freudian Revolution* (New York: Taplinger, 1972), 67.
22. Hesiod, *Hesiod*, 36.
23. Ibid., 37.
24. Ibid.
25. Ibid., 38.
26. Ibid., 39.
27. In a slight variation that reiterates the cyclic nature of the sky gods' oppression of their offspring, *The Library* of Apollodorus reports that the Titans release their cyclops siblings "who had been hurled down" to Tartaros, though once Kronos is granted sovereignty over the other gods, "he again bound and shut them up" in Tartaros (7).
28. Hesiod, *Hesiod*, 55.
29. Ibid., 56.
30. Ibid., 55.
31. Ibid., 56.
32. Santi, the ghost-boy hybrid with dark, fishy eyes and translucent skin from having been waterlogged for years—and hence constructed from a definition of spectral presence that allows for the evolution of the ghost's appearance, rather than a trapped-in-amber image fixed at the time of death—is an excellent example of the synthesizing implicit in what Antonio Lázaro-Reboll has called "transnational horror" (46), drawing visually upon Japanese horror film visuals while recreating in the narrative the social conflicts associated with the Spanish civil war.
33. Babies are a special kind of monster: "they have something which we lack, which we desire," so "adults are looking for their inner child, while children themselves all too often are thought to harbour an inner ogre" (Warner 159). Cf. del Toro's smiling infant grotesque, a human/alien hybrid from one of his notebooks, captioned "Niño con Problemas III: happy, full of life" (71). Yet del Toro also celebrates the brave, miraculous children who avoid becoming monsters despite the provocation of encounters with horrors: Aurora, orphaned and taken in by her grandparents, shows remarkable poise and maturity in the face of her grandfather's metamorphosis; the autistic Chuy, a savant at calculating shoe sizes just by listening to (and replicating with spoons) the footsteps of passersby, successfully communicates his harmlessness to a Judas breed soldier; Ofelia sacrifices everything for her infant brother; the child

who Hellboy meets while shadowing Myers offers mature counsel concerning the demon's feelings for Liz (Hellboy: "You're not old enough to be giving me advice").

34. Louise Krasniewicz, "Cinematic Gifts: The Moral and Social Exchange of Bodies in Horror Films," *Tattoo, Torture, Mutilation and Adornment: The Denaturalization of the Body in Culture and Text*, Frances E. Mascia-Lees and Patricia Sharpe, eds. (Albany: State University of New York Press, 1992), 31.
35. Aeschylus, *Prometheus Bound, The Suppliants, Seven Against Thebes, The Persians*, trans. Philip Vellacott (New York: Penguin, 1978), 48–9.
36. Jan Kott, *The Eating of the Gods: An Interpretation of Greek Tragedy*, trans. Boleslaw Taborski and Edward J. Czerwinski (New York: Vintage, 1974), 11.
37. Hesdiod, *Hesiod*, 56.
38. Ibid.
39. Ibid., 56–7.
40. Ibid., 50.
41. Ibid., 65.
42. Ibid., 66.
43. Ibid., 67.
44. Ibid., 69.
45. Ibid.
46. del Toro and Zicree, *Cabinet of Curiosities*, 258.
47. Ibid., 55.
48. Marina Warner, *No Go the Bogeyman: Scaring, Lulling, and Making Mock* (New York: Farrar, Straus and Giroux, 1998), 57. A telling reiteration of this variation occurs in Sigmund Freud's *Psychopathology of Everyday Life* (1901), where he devotes an entire chapter to correcting errors that he committed in *The Interpretation of Dreams* (1900), one of which identifies Zeus as the castrator of his father, Kronos: "This horror I have erroneously advanced by a generation," he explains, noting that behind "every error is a repression" (142). For del Toro, the ability of fathers to reconcile their differences with their children (like Hercules Hansen with Chuck, or even adoptive fathers, like Dr. Bruttenholm with Hellboy, or Stacker Pentecost with Mako Mori) is what most effectively breaks this pattern of successive generations wishing to avenge themselves on their predecessors.
49. Daniel Bray, "The End of Mythology: Hesiod's *Theogony* and the Indo-European Myth of the Final Battle," *The Journal of Indo-European Studies* Vol. 28, nos. 3–4 (2000): 359.
50. Hesiod, *Hesiod*, 67–8.
51. del Toro and Zicree, *Cabinet of Curiosities*, 260.
52. Ibid., 256.
53. Caldwell, *The Origin of the Gods*, 186.

Bibliography

Aeschylus. *Prometheus Bound, The Suppliants, Seven Against Thebes, The Persians*. Trans. Philip Vellacott. New York: Penguin, 1978.
Apollodorus. *The Library*. Trans. James George Frazer. Cambridge: Harvard University Press, 1921. Volume 1.

Bray, Daniel. "The End of Mythology: Hesiod's *Theogony* and the Indo-European Myth of the Final Battle." *The Journal of Indo-European Studies* Vol. 28, nos. 3–4 (2000): 359–71.

Caldwell, Richard. *The Origin of the Gods: A Psychoanalytic Study of Greek Theogonic Myth*. New York: Oxford University Press, 1989.

Camporesi, Piero. *The Incorruptible Flesh: Bodily Mutilation and Mortification in Religion and Folklore*. Trans. Tania Croft-Murray. New York: Cambridge University Press, 1988.

Cohen, Jeffrey Jerome. "Monster Culture (Seven Theses)." In *Monster Theory: Reading Culture*, Jeffrey Jerome Cohen, ed., 3–25. Minneapolis: University of Minnesota Press, 1996.

Davies, Ann. "The Beautiful and the Monstrous Masculine: The Male Body and Horror in *El espinazo del diablo* (Guillermo del Toro 2001)." *Studies in Hispanic Cinemas* Vol. 3, no. 3 (2006): 135–47.

del Toro, Guillermo, and Marc Scott Zicree. *Guillermo del Toro Cabinet of Curiosities: My Notebooks, Collections, and Other Obsessions*. New York: Harper Design, 2013.

Freud, Sigmund. *The Basic Writings of Sigmund Freud*. Trans. and ed. A.A. Brill. New York: Modern Library, 1966.

Hesiod. *Hesiod's Theogony*. Trans. Richard S. Caldwell. Newburyport, MA: Focus Classical Library, 1987.

Kott, Jan. *The Eating of the Gods: An Interpretation of Greek Tragedy*. Trans. Boleslaw Taborski and Edward J. Czerwinski. New York: Vintage, 1974.

Krasniewicz, Louise. "Cinematic Gifts: The Moral and Social Exchange of Bodies in Horror Films." In *Tattoo, Torture, Mutilation and Adornment: The Denaturalization of the Body in Culture and Text*, Frances E. Mascia-Lees and Patricia Sharpe, eds., 30–47. Albany: State University of New York Press, 1992.

Lázaro-Reboll, Antonio. "The Transnational Reception of *El espinazo del diablo* (Guillermo del Toro 2001)." *Hispanic Research Journal* Vol. 8, no. 1 (2007): 39–51.

Maslow, Abraham H. *The Farther Reaches of Human Nature*. New York: Viking, 1971.

Warner, Marina. *No Go the Bogeyman: Scaring, Lulling, and Making Mock*. New York: Farrar, Straus and Giroux, 1998.

Wilson, Colin. *New Pathways in Psychology: Maslow & the Post-Freudian Revolution*. New York: Taplinger, 1972.

Henry's Kids

Othered Children and Karloff's Frankenstein Monster

JOHN KENNETH MUIR

One of film director Guillermo del Toro's seminal artistic influences, master of suspense Alfred Hitchcock, once observed that audiences enjoy scary movies because they like to be scared when they feel safe. Significantly, however, del Toro's films have not been designed, first and foremost, to generate a sense of fear or terror in audiences. Instead, del Toro's films often serve as emotionally-intimate reflections of his own personal ethos. Specifically, they operate as sensitive explorations of a hated or derided *outsider, or a group of outsiders.*

This is a role that the director has, for much of his personal and professional life, played as well, at least to some significant degree. As a child growing up in Mexico, del Toro was an outsider in his own family because of his love of monsters, fantasy, and insects. Raised as a Catholic, he further separated himself by shunning his Christian faith and becoming an agnostic.

Similarly, as a filmmaker in contemporary Hollywood, del Toro is also counted an outsider by the establishment because of his nationality, but also because of his philosophical views about children, mortality, monsters, and the purpose of horror storytelling itself. These ideas often clash with a corporate hierarchy that seeks economic success above fidelity to art, philosophy, ideals, or even a consistent worldview.

Writing for *Interview* in 2007, journalist Elvis Mitchell elaborated on del Toro's unique approach to visual storytelling, and observed that the artist's films feature a "sensibility" that employs "the tools of horror movie-making to express emotional states other than fear."[1] In broad strokes, those emotional states might include loneliness, alienation, isolation, and even child-like innocence. And to adequately express these human emotions, del Toro has frequently utilized a specific character type in his cinematic endeavors: *a monster.*

As defined by del Toro, a monster is, explicitly, "the ultimate disenfranchised minority,"[2] and the "patron saint of imperfection."[3] Del Toro views monster then, not primarily as destructive, sinister or evil forces out to destroy humanity, but rather as representatives of a different and perhaps unfortunate breed or class. They are imperfect or incomplete beings rendered dangerous by their "unfinished" qualities.

If one gazes a bit more closely, however, at his films, virtually every del Toro silver screen monster shares another important quality. In some fashion, each monster relates to the singular example he first encountered in his much-storied childhood in Mexico: Boris Karloff's (1887–1969) Frankenstein Monster.

Monster vs. Monster and Victor vs. Henry

At this juncture, it is crucial to differentiate between Mary Shelley's literary monster, or so-called "abomination," Adam, and Karloff's memorable movie monster of the early 1930s. The literary Adam can read, for one thing, and possesses a cunning, even strategic intelligence. In the course of the novel, he executes a detailed plot of vengeance against Dr. Frankenstein for failing to create a mate for him, a female, that could end his curse of loneliness.

By contrast, Karloff's monster is a physical powerhouse—the proverbial bull in a China shop—but he is neither a conniving manipulator of men nor an intellect capable of advanced reading. When he speaks, his thoughts are enunciated in awkwardly delivered half-sentences and grunts. Physically, the Monster is like a robust and incredibly strong adult human, but in terms of psychology he is like a newborn attempting without success to learn about the world around him and those with whom he shares it. Everything that he grasps he destroys, not because of malicious intent, but because he has not yet learned how to modulate his strength, or how to be gentle.

Importantly, the literary and movie monsters boast very different fathers as well. The literary Doctor Frankenstein, Victor, is a vain and ambitious man who finally recognizes that his vanity has gone too far, and thus cost him everything of value in his life, including his work, his wife-to-be, Elizabeth, and his very future. The novel's wraparound story or bookend, set in the Arctic, is designed exclusively to excavate this quality in Victor Frankenstein. He encounters Captain Robert Walton at the North Pole, and instructs him to seek happiness in what he *has*, meaning emotional and human connections to family and community, not in those frontiers he wishes to breach, or in the discoveries he hopes to make and announce to the world.

Victor Frankenstein created Adam out of the latter desire. He sought to break new ground in the world of science and the study of mortality, and yet could not view his creation as a child worthy of love and empathy. Overall, this first iteration of Frankenstein—Shelley's iteration—remains a Byronic Hero, an individual of brilliance and power who is tortured by a fatal flaw in his character, but who realizes—much too late, perhaps—how grievously he has erred. The crucial quality of the Byronic hero is that he has lived a troubled life and suffered from his own bad decisions, brought on by arrogance. But he is not delineated as insane or evil. He is, merely, human, and therefore beset by flaws and foibles.

By contrast, Colin Clive's Dr. Frankenstein—named Henry, not Victor—is a very different animal. He seems much more obsessed with negatives, for one thing. He hopes to prove others wrong and establish, by his words, that he is "not crazy." Henry actually states that he knows "how it feels to be God." Where his literary antecedent was a man with a Persian flaw, hubris, Henry is a textbook megalomaniac.

Accordingly, the balance between man and his unholy creation is shifted drastically from literary work to film adaptation. In the movie, the monster is less villainous, and the father figure is much more so. Without being too blunt about it, Boris Karloff and James Whale (1889–1957), not Shelley, created the dynamic that del Toro seems to have keyed so strongly upon as a young man.

Karloff's memorable and widely beloved character was depicted both in Whale's *Frankenstein* (1931) and its sequel, *Bride of Frankenstein* (1936), an artistically superior follow-up that del Toro describes aptly as "moving graveyard poetry,"[4] and it is these images of the Monster—square-domed with electrodes pinned in his neck—that still dominates in American pop culture, despite the Hammer Studios versions of Shelley's tale starring Christopher Lee, David Prowse and others, and despite Kenneth Branagh's big-budget adaptation in 1994 starring Robert De Niro. The 1930s visuals and characterization of the Frankenstein Monster and his father remain the dominant one.

Because del Toro first "met" this particular monster when he was young, and because it is, by nature, the "child" of its ambitious, "mad" creator, del Toro the artist and filmmaker in his own work often equates monsters—that disenfranchised minority—with children, and specifically their innocent nature or qualities.

Children often make strong protagonists (and sometimes villains too) in popular storytelling because, according to David Rudd in *The Routledge Companion to Children's Literature*, their "identities are unfixed, open to otherness, and in the process of becoming."[5] And for a definition of "otherness," one need only to consider Owain Jones' in *True Geography*, quoted in *Lost and Othered Children in Contemporary Cinema*:

> Otherness does not just mean simple separation and knowability. It is a more subtle idea of the knowable and the unknowable, the familiar and the strange, the close and the distance [sic] being co-present in adult-child relations."[6]

Indeed, del Toro films such as *Mimic* (1997), *Pan's Labyrinth* (2006), *Splice* (2011), and even *Pacific Rim* (2013) all feature bad or overtly flawed parents that, like Colin Clive's Dr. Frankenstein, discount, abandon, and seek to destroy their monstrous or quasi-monstrous children. This might be described a "generation gap" of sorts, but it is also, perhaps, a universal standard of the human condition. At some point, children and parents often simply fail to connect with one another, and a distance grows between them. Importantly, children in del Toro's films are often seen experiencing growing pains, learning about humanity, life, and even death, much like Karloff's Monster. Yet their parents knowingly destroy them, even in that formative and questing shape.

Still, this blanket description does not adequately describe entirely the del Toro creative equation, either. Films such as *Blade II* (2002), *Hellboy* (2004), *Hellboy II* (2008), and once more, *Pacific Rim*, showcase instances of positive parental imagery as well.

In the cases of *Blade* and *Hellboy*, the "monster" or other becomes a hero because he is beloved by a caring parent. In fact, he survives his childhood *explicitly* because of his parental care and love. Otherwise the child would have lapsed into monstrousness, and for del Toro, that monstrousness is an assimilation into the conventional adult world.

By exploring innocent monsters and sometimes positive, sometimes negative parents, del Toro uses the horror film not as many other genre filmmakers do, as a venue for generating fear, or for making political or social commentary. Instead, the artist utilizes the form as a personal vessel that attempts to give children, in the spirit of Hitchcock's comment, a "dosage of fear in a safe way," or what he terms "a vaccine against the real horrors out there."[7]

Because of his commitment to this cause, del Toro's films are special, emotionally-resonant works of art, and their "artistic decisions seem guided by a personal integrity and creative integrity,"[8] rather than the vicissitudes of studio politics or economics.

Monster Influences and "Seeing" the Monster: "It's one of the strangest stories ever told"

Guillermo del Toro grew up in Guadalajara, Mexico and was raised as a Catholic. As a young boy, circa 1971, he became obsessed with monster movies and monster magazines such as Forrest Ackerman's *Famous Monsters of Filmland*. According to journalist Daniel Zalewski at *The New Yorker*, young del Toro "filled his bedroom with comic books and figurines, but he was not content to remain a fanboy."[9] Instead, the monster that he saw in *Frankenstein* (1931) resonated with him, and eventually, he sought to dramatize his own stories about similar monsters. But why did the Frankenstein Monster resonate so deeply with young del Toro?

As described above, the monster's status as a misunderstood child emerged at the forefront of Karloff's interpretation. This sense of a monster eternally shut out from the light of reason and love even finds resonance in the movie's vivid imagery, especially in a heart-breaking moment when the Monster reaches out to touch the sun, a kind of brightness and warmth that his life and relationships do not possess.

The Monster's innocence is seen in other haunting ways. In the Whale film's most infamous scene, the monster plucks flower petals on a riverbank with a little girl and then, out of curiosity, tosses her into the water. It's impossible not to understand the creature's naïve thinking at this horrific moment. If petals can float, perhaps girls can too. But the child immediately drowns and the creature is further separated from humanity. He has made a terrible mistake but it is one borne of ignorance and curiosity, not malice.

Whale's sensitive direction, however, makes a point not of the creature's inadvertently or mindlessly violent act, but rather of the villagers' *ensuing pre-meditated* violence. Lacking impulse control, the monster kills out of innocence or perhaps ignorant curiosity. The villagers, however, are a different story.

They are seen in a long tracking shot, carrying the girl's corpse through the streets, stoking rage and violence all the while. "There can be no waiting while the horrible creature is still alive," declares one of the villagers. Another suggests that the Monster should be put down like a savage animal, implying that the monster is inhuman, and therefore, by nature, not entitled to the protections of the law. Yet it is very clear from the scene set at the river that the monster is not monstrous at all, merely lacking in worldly understanding and knowledge. Meanwhile, humans—and adults especially—represent true evil because they could choose not to kill, but instead *knowingly* pursue the cause of vengeance and bloodlust. They allow ignorance and fear to determine their actions.

Del Toro has termed *Frankenstein* "the founding text of modern monster mythology,"[10] but has reserved his greatest praise for Karloff's performance—or embodiment—of innocent monster-hood. He has noted the "enormous humanity" of Karloff's portrayal, its "kinship and empathy" and noted that it is "at once horrifying and vulnerable."[11]

The director has also noted that the portrayal is important because of its focus on so-called outsider-ism. "Karloff embodies the most essential, existential quality of being human—a creature expelled from a womb of darkness and silence by an uncaring creator and thrust upon a world of fire, rain, and hatred."[12] It is not difficult to read this description as being del Toro's universal (Universal?) view of childhood, especially given what is known of his difficult relationship with his own father, who never quite understood his obsessive fascination with horror and fantasy.

Similarly, del Toro described to Terry Gross of NPR's *Fresh Air* how his grandmother feared his interest in monsters, and acted much like the

Piper Laurie character in Brian De Palma's *Carrie* (1976), going so far as to conduct exorcisms on him. She did so "hoping to guard his soul from the monster movie and fantasy stories he loved."[13] Del Toro later called his grandmother an enthusiastic amateur whose efforts simply didn't take, but beneath that humorous comment there surely must have been some emotional pain involved. Not just the pain of being misunderstood as "evil" or a monster, but the pain of seeing the objects, stories, and art he loved equated with devils and demons.

Accordingly, in the short-films of his youth, del Toro sometimes created monsters that, like their cinematic model, were more scared of humans than humans were of them. One such film involved a monster emerging from the slime of a bathroom toilet, only to find humans mystifying and terrifying, and thus retreat to its dark world in terror.[14] Another involved a potato that was a serial killer, at least before being pulped by his family members. Both of these monsters interacted with the human world, and in some sense, were repelled by its confusing contradictions. Both are also stories of monsters that function, structurally and thematically as questing, questioning outsiders who discover in the adult world answers that are not to their liking.

Human Influences: The Child Meets the Monster Again in *The Spirit of the Beehive* (1973)

Not long after he discovered *Famous Monsters* and *Frankenstein*, del Toro encountered another film that reinforced his view of the world, children, and monsters: *The Spirit of the Beehive*. The artist has since termed this film from director Victor Erice "one of the most seminal movies" that "seeped" into his "very soul."[15]

Much like *The Devil's Backbone* (2001) and *Pan's Labyrinth* (2006), *The Spirit of the Beehive* is set at or near the end of the Spanish civil war, in 1940, and much of the action revolves around a six-year-old girl, Ana (Ana Torrent), who sees an ad hoc showing of *Frankenstein* in her village. At home, Ana lives with an emotionally disconnected mother and a largely absent father, who tends studiously to his beehives.

After watching *Frankenstein*, Ana is confused about the reason that the Monster killed the little girl by the river. Her older sister, Isabel (Isabel

Telleria) reports that he didn't, that it was all staged, and that the Monster still lives, as a spirit in the forest. Furthermore, Isabel informs Ana that she can summon the monster at any time by saying, "It's me, Ana."

Later in *The Spirit of the Beehive*, Ana helps to take care of a wounded Republican soldier, until Franco-ist forces intervene to put an end to such ministrations. Finally, she imagines that she meets the Frankenstein Monster by a riverbank, much like the girl with the flower in the Whale film.

In *The Spirit of the Beehive*, a soldier of a (vanquished) ideology is metaphorically compared to a monster, a derided outsider whose humanity cannot be reckoned with, except by an innocent child. But this social critique is likely not what impacted the young del Toro so deeply. Rather, it may have been the idea of a child and monster meeting, and recognizing each other—in a long, hard look at one another—as kindred spirits. Del Toro considers the film a companion piece to *Night of the Hunter* (1955), and has said that both are "sublime fairy tales of despair that depict the adult world as a toxic environment for kids to exist in."[16] Significantly, that description also applies to del Toro's genre pictures. In many of his movie narratives, the monsters are avatars representing the innocence or loneliness of childhood. But the monsters represent not only childhood, but perhaps also del Toro himself, and his own status as outsider.

There's another layer of artistry to consider here as well. *The Spirit of the Beehive, The Devil's Backbone,* and *Pan's Labyrinth* form a Spanish civil war horror-themed trilogy, in a sense. Children in all three efforts are seeking to learn who they are, who they should become, and interact with an adult world that doesn't truly understand them. The existence of the monster in these stories is thus an entry point for the children in their understanding of death, broached as a dream world, a world of spirits, or a fairy world. These other worlds might also represent death. Del Toro's films connect children with the discovery of mortality in a potent fashion, suggesting that the discovery of death is a crucial part of life.

Meet the Bad Parents

Although it was a troubled production that del Toro does not regard highly because of studio interference but also strife in his personal life, his American feature film debut, *Mimic* (1997) is nonetheless a full-fledged

Frankenstein-type film that gazes at irresponsible science and couples that theme with bad parenting. In this case, the Dr. Frankenstein surrogate is Dr. Susan Tyler (Mira Sorvino), who destroys Strickler's Disease—an ailment which threatens the children of Manhattan—by eliminating its carrier: cockroaches. Specifically, Tyler genetically engineers a race of insects called Judas Bugs, and they destroy the threat of Strickler's Disease.

But years later, the Judas Bugs have not expired as they were intended and engineered to do, and instead have formed a sort of thriving hive society underneath the forgotten world of the New York subway system. Susan realizes *"evolution has a way of keeping things alive,"* and even as she struggles to conceive a biological child of her own, must destroy the insect children she has forsaken. The film implies that a parent's mission in the case of Henry Frankenstein and Susan Tyler is actually to kill their unwanted creation.

In the film, the bugs are thus abandoned children, or "the Monster," to continue to the comparison with the Frankenstein template. Although they do commit murder (much like the Monster in Whale's film), they often do so to protect their egg chambers and young. We learn over a period of time that the bugs have not only imitated the human form, but some essential aspect of the human heart too, "mimicking" a human love for their young ...which were not modeled by Susan.

Importantly, *Mimic* also visually quotes Whales' *Frankenstein*, and the famous moment with the little girl on the riverbank, the very moment re-parsed in *The Spirit of the Beehive*. Importantly, however, *Mimic* substitutes an "autistic boy ... for *Frankenstein's* little girl."[17] Here, young Chuy (Alexander Goodwin) recognizes the presence of insects before almost any other character in the story, including the "parent" figure, Susan. He attempts to communicate peaceably with them before being spirited away, an act which reflects his innocence and openness. That the insects don't kill Chuy, perhaps, represents theirs. In *Mimic*, Susan Tyler ultimately participates in the destruction of her insect children, but not before her mentor, played by F. Murray Abraham notes that her "Frankenstein" has "gotten the better" of her, putting a fine point on the connection between the stories.

Pan's Labyrinth similarly features a bad parent, this time in the form of Captain Vidal (Sergi Lopez), a soldier in post-civil war Spain who is not only a committed Fascist, but also a sadistic murderer. He is the husband of Mercedes (Maribel Verdu), who is pregnant with his child. Importantly, Mercedes, not unlike Susan in *Mimic*, is struggling with the process of creating life, and undergoes severe pain as her pregnancy develops. Biological parenthood, from conception (*Mimic*) to delivery (*Pan's Labyrinth*) is a process that can take away a parent's attention and devotion, then, as the Judas Bugs and Mercedes' little girl, would attest.

Mercedes' other child is a young Ofelia (Ivana Baquero) who may either be the daughter of the King of the Underworld, Princess Moanna, or merely a normal human child prone to fantasy and daydreaming. She interacts with fairies and other fanciful monsters in a labyrinth, but is ultimately killed by her stepfather, Vidal, for her decency and humanity. In one version of reality, the one preferred by del Toro, she returns to the Underworld and takes her throne for a long reign. In our world, however, she is dead, but her sacrifice has helped her newborn brother to be born and survive away from the "monster" father that created him. As we have seen before then, the benevolent world is the world of monsters, here the Underworld, and the world of malevolence is in our own: a place of untrustworthy and monstrous adults.

In very similar terms, *Splice* (2010) executive-produced by del Toro, picks up the concerns of the *Frankenstein,* bad-parent dynamic. The film involves genetic engineers, Elsa (Sarah Polley) and Clive (Adrien Brody)—named after Elsa Lanchester and Colin Clive in *Bride of Frankenstein*—who introduce human DNA into chimera experiments. They create a female being called Dren (first Abigail Chu as the child and then Delphine Chaneau as the adult) from Elsa's DNA. Dren is part amphibious, but clearly possessed of curiosity and a soul. Dren also boasts an accelerated lifespan, which means she will live, age, and die while her parents monitor her development.

At first Elsa treats Dren like the biological child that she is, but when Dren reaches moody adolescence something changes. Her mother treats her like a thing or monster instead of as a child, a development which mirrors the real life frisson, perhaps, between parents and their teenagers. At one point, Elsa brutally straps the teenager to a surgical table and cuts off part of her "alien" anatomy, a metaphor perhaps for destroying her autonomy, instead.

Though not Dren's biological father, Clive is not blameless either. When Dren turns her affection towards him, he engages in sexual intercourse with her, a violation of his role in her life as stepfather. This action is a total abdication of that role, and a moral failing of the highest order. Accordingly, *Splice* concerns a key aspect of the Frankenstein story. Specifically, irresponsibility in creating life is trumped only by irresponsibility in rearing that life.

When Dren grows up hating her cruel parents, who now consider her only a mistake, she commits violence and destruction, and her actions (rape, specifically) suggest the real life generational cycle of abuse. As is the case with the Frankenstein Monster, Dren is monstrous only because, finally, she has been treated monstrously and doesn't understand the nature of the world she lives in. She has learned to be a monster during her accelerated process of maturity, because monsters—parents—are her only role models.

Finally, *Pacific Rim* features a most unusual bad parent. In the course of the story, a human scientist is able to "drift" into a shared consciousness with a giant monster called a Kaiju, and he learns that the Kaiju are clones, and indeed, slaves, of alien masters. The Kaiju are thus defined, like Dren, as the "children" of those masters, and in keeping with the Henry Frankenstein model, poorly treated ones. They exist only to fight and conquer, thrown into a world of combat and terror with Earth's population, and the Jaegers. "I grew up with a steady Kaiju diet," del Toro told *U.S.A. Today* about the monsters in *Pacific Rim,* describing them as being "like his children."[18]

In another interview promoting *Pacific Rim,* he likewise reiterated *Godzilla* (1954) director Ishiro Honda's famous description of Kaiju monsters as "not being suited for the world,"[19] a dynamic which makes them not only del Toro's aforementioned children, but also explicitly derided outsiders, rendered imperfect because of their size and strength. In other words, they are very strong corollaries for the Frankenstein Monster, or at least Karloff's iteration of it.

Meet the Good Parents

Above, many instances of bad parents in the film works of del Toro have been noted, but there is another side to the story too. His films also feature, on occasion, good parents. Many critics have thus noted that in del Toro films "benevolent paternalism plays a critical role" as well,[20] though at this juncture benevolent *parental-ism* might be a better, more accurate term since there have also been positive female roles or parental figures that—through their goodness—develop strong and lasting bonds with children.

Cronos (1993), for example, models a positive relationship between a kindly antique dealer, Jesus Gris (Federico Luppi) and his young granddaughter, Aurora (Tamara Sahnath). Aurora's biological parents are mysteriously not involved in the film at all, and that's a key, if unexcavated point of the narrative. Gris pens and sends Aurora letters from her absent parents, but it is suggested strongly that they are actually dead, and that the quiet girl has undergone some sort of terrible trauma from which she has not yet fully recovered or awakened. "Her silence is never explored, Hollywood-style in the film, and one of the interesting questions that the silence triggers is to what extent silence itself activates the fantasy in the film as a form of trauma,"[21] suggests Costas Constantinides in *Screening the Undead*.

Because of this perspective, *Cronos* could be interpreted as a story that occurs from the outsider viewpoint of Aurora herself. She is an orphan who has grappled with the loss of her parents, but also the impending demise of her elderly, gentle grandfather. Of course, the competing explanation is more linear and concrete, that Jesus Gris comes into contact with a gold clockwork device, created in the 1500s by an inventor named Veracruz that can prolong life, but creates the vampire-like appetite for blood at the same time. One might even consider a comparison to Ofelia in *Pan's Labyrinth* here, and the way her story bridges two worlds. Aurora's might be said to do so as well. Just as Don Coscarelli's rubber-reality masterpiece *Phantasm* (1979) serves as a story about a child confronting a real-life monster in the form of mortality, *Cronos* similarly concerns a child's reckoning that death will once again intrude on her life.

What is plain, however, regardless of the interpretation, is that Jesus and Aurora understand each other. Thus when Gris transforms, largely against his will, into a vampire, Aurora demonstrates love and compassion for him, even decorating the coffin he sleeps in with tokens of her affection.

The real monster in *Cronos* is a collector, Dieter de la Guardia, played by Claudio Brooks who covets longevity, but not family bonds. In other words, the things that make life worth living are less important to Dieter than the fact of continued existence itself. Vampirism, then, is the desire to live more, but not to connect meaningfully. Importantly, Gris ultimately makes a different choice and it is the sound of Aurora's voice, finally, that prevents him from seeking her blood. Her voice reminds him of his human connections, and that it is more important to honor those than to seek ever more life, and a corrupted life at that. We see in *Cronos* a father figure, Gris, and a child, Aurora, love and care for one another then, in a positive relationship that keeps evil at bay.

Guillermo del Toro has worked frequently in a horror-tinged superhero milieu, and yet his contributions there all tend to view monsters and parents in a more favorable or positive light than do many of his traditional horror pictures. In *Hellboy* (2004), a film based on Mike Mignola's graphic novel for Dark Horse Comics, a young expert in the occult, Trevor "Broom" Bruttenholm (John Hurt) unexpectedly becomes the father to a demon or monster from another dimension that he names Hellboy.

In both *Hellboy* and its sequel *Hellboy II: The Golden Army* (2008) also directed by del Toro, there are many instances showcasing the loving and healthy relationship that develops between Broom and the child he considers his son. In an early scene of *The Golden Army*, Broom tells his boy a bedtime story, for instance. This is an especially intimate and loving act. It occurs at a time when a child's defenses are down, and slumber is intimate. The act of sharing a story is one that suggests the passage of cherished information and art from parent to child, generation to generation, but also one of gentleness and imagination. Together, new worlds are broached.

Similarly, Hellboy refers to Broom as "Father," and Broom, having raised his son as a human, and in atmosphere of love, considers the adopted boy his child. Shortly before his death, Broom is given a terrifying vision of the apocalypse, one that ostensibly deems Hellboy a monster for the carnage. Yet Broom does not renounce his son on his deathbed, or their family history together. He has faith in Hellboy's choices, a faith that is eventually validated.

The grown Hellboy (Ron Perlman) is depicted in both del Toro films as a dedicated agent for the Bureau of Paranormal Research and Defense. His position there demonstrates, perhaps, that Hellboy is integrated into society and that he functions, more or less, as normal and healthy. Also, he has sawed off the symbols of his demonic birthright—two enormous horns—in an attempt to further integrate with human society and co-workers. Broom's tutelage thus enables him to grow up not as a horrendous, immoral monster or evil creation, but as a man who is capable of loving another outsider, in this case Liz Sherman (Selma Blair), a pyrokinetic with a history of some mental instability.

But over the course of two films, viewers see how Hellboy and Liz heal each other, and form a new family unit. Indeed, they are made for another, as Hellboy is one of the few beings who can stand inside the ring of Liz's fire and not only survive, but actually thrive there.

In *The Golden Army*, Hellboy goes further towards healthy maturity. He learns that he will be a father (to more than one child, no less) and his acceptance of family, and the responsibilities that come with it are another indication, perhaps that a good father, Broom, made all the difference in his life. Broom invested time, energy, and sensitivity in Hellboy, despite his physical differences and status as demonic outsider, and now the cycle of love continues, with Hellboy forming his own close-knit family unit. In this case, the casting also plays a role in fostering our identification with the father of a monster. One of John Hurt's most famous roles is as a gentle monster himself, in David Lynch's *The Elephant Man* (1980).

Although del Toro has made it abundantly clear that *Blade II* (2002) is not quite the "personal movie"[22] that his other movies are, the superhero there actually undergoes a similar type of journey. In the original 1998 film, directed by Stephen Norrington, Blade (Wesley Snipes) is a human-vampire hybrid who is discarded by his mother, Vanessa (Sanaa Latham) after childbirth. Ignoring her responsibilities as a mother, she accepts the vampire life and becomes the lover of the evil Deacon Frost (Stephen Dorff), a vampire warlord. Later, an aimless and hostile Blade is adopted by a human man, Whistler (Kris Kristofferson) who cares for him, teaches him, and trains him to overcome his bloodlust. In the course of the film, Whistler is killed, and Blade mourns the father figure who guided him through youth and adolescence.

However, del Toro's sequel opens with Blade—now the grown child, like Hellboy—returning the love for his father figure. Since the climax of the first film, Blade has been scouring the world for Whistler, who is actually alive, and being tortured by vampires. Showing devotion and determination, he rescues Whistler, and brings him back into the fold, investing in his father the time and energy that was once invested in him.

In both the *Hellboy* and *Blade* films of del Toro, then, we see how a parent's love is carried forward into the next generation and meaningfully embraced by it. We see the son become the father, in a sense, caring for the adopted parent who reared him, or by embracing the prospect of family life itself. Such examples represent is a powerful contrast to the negative "parents" we meet in *Mimic* or *Splice*.

Pacific Rim also splits the difference, or more accurately, compares two kinds of parents. As already established, the Kaiju are the children of bad parents, the uncaring alien clone-masters, but Stacker Pentecost (Idris Elba) is the epitome of a good human father. He too is an "adopted father," a Jaeger pilot who discovers an orphaned girl, Mako Mori (Rinko Kikuchi), in the ruins of a city, and raises the traumatized child as his own. He teaches her with tenderness and kindness, and protects her, so much so that as an adult she begins to rebel against his suffocating brand of protectiveness. But clearly, Stacker is the yin to the aliens' yang, a kind of father who does not abandon his children, or throw them into the dark and confusing world without the tools they need to thrive.

In *Cronos*, *Hellboy*, *Hellboy II*, *Blade II*, and *Pacific Rim*, the parents all take on another very specific nature. They are substitute or adopted parents, not biological ones and that very strongly contrasts them with Elsa, for example, or even Vidal, since he was the biological father of Mercedes' son. Furthermore, if one also considers *Don't Be Afraid of the Dark* (2010), a film produced and written by del Toro (based on a television movie of 1973 directed by John Newland), we witness another example of this trend in parenting.

In *Don't Be Afraid of the Dark*, a young girl named Sally (Bailee Madison) moves into a new home with her father (Guy Pearce), and his girlfriend, Kim (Katie Holmes), unaware that the mansion, Blackwood Manor, is already occupied by malevolent fairies looking to transform a human into one of their number. They settle on Sally because of her youth, but in the end, Kim sacrifices herself, and Sally survives the encounter. Once more, then, a non-biological parent figure steps up to protect and nurture a child, and the biological parents does not.

It is fair to state then, that in the films of del Toro, parent figures can be positive and worthwhile characters who aid the children. But to fulfill that role, apparently, they must be non-biological in nature. Since *Frankenstein* resolutely remains the tale of *non-benevolent* paternalism, many del

Toro films serve as deliberate or pointed contrasts to the legend; ones which re-write "bad fathers" or "bad parents" in more positive, humane terms. Some of these movies are reiterations of the *Frankenstein* myth in the sense that they feature a father or mother of a "monster," but in del Toro's efforts, the parent neither renounces nor destroys the children, as non-biological father Dr. Henry Frankenstein did.

Towards Creating His Own Frankenstein Monster

Del Toro has often stated that it is his deepest dream to create his own cinematic adaptation of *Mary Shelley's Frankenstein*. In 2008, *Variety* reported that the dream might come true, has he had signed a "long-term" commitment with Universal to remake the monster for modern movie audiences.[23] He has called that prospective version of *Frankenstein* the "most personal" film he could possibly make. Del Toro has similarly noted that his long-established and verified personal "connection with the creature is very profound and deep" and that, furthermore, he doesn't believe "there's any other monster" that has affected him "as deeply."[24]

Indeed, these facts are abundantly clear from a survey of his film work, wherein children are frequently portrayed as being of the same outsider status as a "monster," if not a monster themselves, like Hellboy, Dren, Blade, or even the Judas Bugs. Similarly, del Toro—now a parent himself—has demonstrated great trepidation about parental figures in his works, because he remembers the model of Colin Clive's Henry Frankenstein.

When del Toro finally adapts Mary Shelley's classic Promethean story, then, one must wonder: Will his film tell the story of Victor Frankenstein and his cunning, strategic monster? Or will del Toro convey instead the story of Henry Frankenstein and his wayward, lost child? Given the artist's devotion to Karloff's performance and James Whale's 1931 film, we have every reason to suspect the latter, and might expect another tale of an "othered" child—a monster—lost in a cruel, adult world. If that is indeed the case in, and in direct contradiction to Alfred Hitchcock's' theory of horror films—"fear" generated in safety—we can anticipate a story that instead expresses sympathy for a child-like monster, and disdain for the bad, irresponsible parent.

Notes

1. Elvis Mitchell, "Guillermo del Toro," *Interview* 27, no. 2 (March 2007), 98.
2. Mark Kermode, "Guillermo del Toro, Part II," *The Guardian*, November 21, 2006, http://www.theguardian.com/film/2006/nov/21/guardianinterviewsatbfisouthbank1.
3. Guillermo del Toro, "I am Guillermo del Toro, director, writer and producer." *Reddit*, http://www.reddit.com/r/IAmA/comments/2agklw/i_am_guillermo_del_toro_director_writer_producer/.
4. Guillermo del Toro, "Guillermo del Toro." *Newsweek*, July 7, 2008.
5. David Rudd. *The Routledge Companion to Children's Literature* (New York: Routledge, 2010), 166.
6. Andrew Cahill and Debbie C. Olson, eds., *Lost and Othered Children in Contemporary Cinema*, (Lanham: Lexington Books, 2012), 197.
7. Kimberly Chun, "What Is a Ghost? An Interview with Guillermo del Toro," *Cineaste* 7, no. 2 (Spring 2002): 28–31.
8. Scott Baugh, *Latino American Cinema: An Encyclopedia of Movie Stars, Concepts and Trends* (Santa Barbara: ABC-CLIO, 2012), 70.
9. Daniel Zalewski, "Show the Monster," *The New Yorker*, February 2, 2011, 40–53.
10. Ibid.
11. "I am Guillermo del Toro, director, writer and producer," *Reddit*, http://www.reddit.com/r/IAmA/comments/2agklw/i_am_guillermo_del_toro_director_writer_producer/.
12. Jeff Jensen, "Inside the Mind of Guillermo del Toro," *Entertainment Weekly*, July 11, 2008, 44–45.
13. Zalewski, "Show the Monster," *The New Yorker*.
14. Robert K. Elder, *The Best Film You've Never Seen: 35 Directors Champion the Forgotten or Critically Savaged Movies They Love* (Chicago: Chicago Review Press, 2013), 16.
15. Brian Slattery, "Guillermo del Toro and *The Spirit of the Beehive*," Tor.com, http://www.tor.com/blogs/2008/11/deltorobeehive/.
16. The Criterion Collection, "Guillermo del Toro's Top 10," Criterion.com, http://www.criterion.com/explore/125-guillermo-del-toro-s-top-10.
17. Charles Derry, *Dark Dreams 2.0: A Psychological History of the Modern Horror Film from the 1950s to the 21st Century* (Jefferson: McFarland, 2009), 316.
18. Brian Truitt, "It's a duel of del Toro Proportions: Robots vs. Monsters," *USA Today*, February 4, 2013.
19. Daniel Egan, "Robots vs. Monsters," *Film Journal International* 116 (July 2013), 8–10.
20. Yvonne Tasker, *Fifty Contemporary Film Directors*, 2d ed. (New York: Routledge, 2011), 157.
21. Costa Constantinides, "From Mexico to Hollywood: Guillermo del Toro's Treatment of the Undead and the Making of a New Cult Icon," *Screening the Undead: Vampires and Zombies in Film and Television*, Leon Hunt, Sharon Lockyer and Milly Williamson, eds. (London: I.B. Tauris, 2014), 175.
22. Mitchell, "Guillermo del Toro," *Interview*.
23. Katey Rich, *Cinema Blend*, October 4, 2012.
24. Ibid.

Bibliography

Baugh, Scott. *Latino American Cinema: An Encyclopedia of Movie Stars, Concepts and Trends.* Santa Barbara: ABC-CLIO, 2012.

Cahill, Andrew, and Debbie C. Olson, eds. *Lost and Othered Children in Contemporary Cinema.* Lanham: Lexington Books, 2012.

Chun, Kimberly. "What Is a Ghost? An Interview with Guillermo del Toro." *Cineaste* 7, no. 2 (Spring 2002): 28–31.

Costa, Constantinides. "From Mexico to Hollywood: Guillermo del Toro's Treatment of the Undead and the Making of a New Cult Icon." In *Screening the Undead: Vampires and Zombies in Film and Television*, Leon Hunt, Sharon Lockyer and Milly Williamson, eds. London: I.B. Tauris, 2014.

The Criterion Collection. "Guillermo del Toro's Top 10." Criterion.com. http://www.criterion.com/explore/125-guillermo-del-toro-s-top-10.

del Toro, Guillermo. "I am Guillermo del Toro, director, writer and producer." *Reddit.* http://www.reddit.com/r/IAmA/comments/2agklw/i_am_guillermo_del_toro_director_writer_producer/.

_____. "Guillermo del Toro." *Newsweek*, July 7, 2008.

Derry, Charles Derry. *Dark Dreams 2.0: A Psychological History of the Modern Horror Film from the 1950s to the 21st Century.* Jefferson: McFarland, 2009.

Egan, Daniel. "Robots vs. Monsters." *Film Journal International* 116 (July 2013): 8–10.

Elder, Robert K. *The Best Film You've Never Seen: 35 Directors Champion the Forgotten or Critically Savaged Movies They Love.* Chicago: Chicago Review Press, 2013.

Kermode, Mark. "Guillermo del Toro, Part II." *The Guardian*, November 21, 2006. http://www.theguardian.com/film/2006/nov/21/guardianinterviewsatbfisouthbank1.

Mitchell, Elvis. "Guillermo del Toro." *Interview* 37, no. 2 (March 2007).

Rich, Katey. *Cinema Blend.* October 4, 2012.

Rudd, David. *The Routledge Companion to Children's Literature.* London: Routledge, 2010.

Slattery, Brian. "Guillermo del Toro and *The Spirit of the Beehive*." Tor.com. http://www.tor.com/blogs/2008/11/deltorobeehive/.

Tasker, Yvonne. *Fifty Contemporary Film Directors*, 2d ed. New York: Routledge, 2011.

Truitt, Brian Truitt. "It's a duel of del Toro Proportions: Robots vs. Monsters." *USA Today*, February 4, 2013.

Zalewski, Daniel. "Show the Monster." *The New Yorker*, February 2, 2011: 40–53.

Where the Wild Things Are
Monsters and Children
ALEXANDRA WEST

Genre films ask big questions—life-changing questions. What is real? What happens when we die? What happens if we survive? The utilization of fantasy and escapist tropes is what sets genre-films apart from say the Neo-Realists. The ability to project characters into fantastical situations offers filmmakers the opportunity to ask questions surrounding the nature of humanity and of the world we live in. By offering a view of a heightened and fictional world the audience is able to let go of the particulars of everyday life and engage with a story in a more democratic way. Not every audience can let themselves go in the Rome that is visualized through Rossellini's lens but there is a better chance at a more humanistic view of life if the events of a story are taken out of the everyday and exaggerated.

The world of the genre-film is equally dependent on the audience and its creator. The creator must reveal a world that is complete while containing fantastical elements. The audience must arrive to the film open and willing to engage with a new world or a world that is only somewhat familiar to them. These skills, both as storyteller and as audience are present in all of us especially as a child. Which is why utilizing a child as a protagonist is not uncommon but few use this trope with the effectiveness of Guillermo del Toro. A child can be a truly fantastic portal into a world for an audience because we have all been children and can identify with the feelings of dependence, independence, and wonder that are often associated with a child's view of the world. We are willing to suspend our disbelief to engage in a purer and untainted view of things.

For mature viewers we are allowed, for the length of a film, to reengage with a part of ourselves that asked questions without fear. The films of del Toro are filled with a childlike innocence and enthusiasm brought forward in the film by child characters who serve to provide a contrast for the darker world that the adults live in. The role of a child in film has been one that has taken on many different facets. They can easily elicit empathy but they are also resilient and less fractured by the world than their adult counterparts. Popular child characters are littered through cinema in films for adults and young audiences alike. Del Toro, however, uses his child characters to impact his worlds by pulling back the curtain on a bleak reality to explore the possibilities of what is beyond our own worldviews. Del Toro offers his child characters the strength to ask those questions without fear and for a while, his adult audience can ask them too.

Ghosts of a Mexican Childhood

In an interview for an event with *The Guardian* newspaper del Toro spoke of his own childhood:

> I have said sometimes that I have spent 32 years recuperating from my first 10 years. Really. I had a pretty screwed up childhood, living in Mexico. I don't know if it's because I was living in Mexico and I'm a Mexican but I have had a life full of very, very fucked up and strange things. The two events that happen in *Pan's Labyrinth* and *Devil's Backbone* are based on things that happened to me. When I was 12, I heard a ghost that whispered and sighed. I was in my late uncle's room, in the house I inherited. This uncle and I had been very good friends—he introduced me to Lovecraft and horror writers. When we were talking, I said, "When one of us dies first"—of course, that's very easy for a 12-year-old to say—"he has to come back and tell the other that there is something else."[1]

The director's childhood notion that death is not the end of the story but simply a page being turned over is a present theme throughout all of his films. A lover of all things horror from a young age, this is not a shocking revelation but when considering that del Toro was raised Catholic it becomes more interesting. "I really suffered intensely in the first 10 years of my life. I would cry at the concept of burning in hell, or the concept of purgatory and original sin. Mexican Catholicism is very, very brutal and very, very gory. That all affected me."[2] For Catholics, the religion teaches fear. You fear being bad which will ensure your place in the Hell, which they also fear. Del Toro's personal view of life and death comes from transcendence. Letting go or trying to let go of the fear that can freeze a person. Doing only what you are told and never looking beyond that goal. For del Toro, death can be going from one moment to the next, but the next moment could be an entirely new world.

Usually at the center of a conflict the child character is unaware of the stakes and tensions that exist around them in the adult world. Del Toro cleverly uses his child characters to explore the themes and metaphors of the adult struggles. Through the eyes of a child the problems become universal through the use of myths and monsters. The relationship that the child has with the monster is at the heart of the story and that relationship forces the plot forward as the adult caregivers become stuck in time, unable to see beyond their own problems. The monstrous caregiver is a guide and friend to the child protagonist. Sometimes they are good and sometimes evil. By examining the films *Mimic* (1997), *The Devil's Backbone* (2001) and *Pan's Labyrinth* (2006) I will look at the child's experience of humanity through the monster and how del Toro uses the monster as both friend and enemy.

In each of these films, the actual parent to the child characters (Chuy in *Mimic*, Carlos in *The Devil's Backbone* and Ofelia in *Pan's Labyrinth*) is somehow absent. The monstrous characters take up the mantle of a parent or guardian-like figure to introduce them to a new world. The adults who are charged with the child's protection are unable to truly see these worlds, creating a blind spot within the film. The monsters step in as a parent or guardian figure and through their actions they reveal who the true villains of the piece are. By being forced to confront the true monsters, the world of the film is finally able to move forward.

The monsters in these films serve to provoke the plots of these films. They are introduced when the world order has reached a stalemate, but they require a child conduit for them to make an impact on the larger world. In each of these films, the child is able to see the "monster" and therefore is able to see the world much clearer than those who deny their existence.

Epidemic Evolution

Del Toro wrote of *Mimic* in his famous notebooks and spoke of, "An evolutionary leap. Evolution's on their side."[3] In this case "their" does not refer to humans. Del Toro's first foray into the studio system proved to be an arduous one to the say the least, aided by the infamous Weinstein brothers Harvey and Bob, *Mimic* began its life as a short story by Donald A. Wollheim and was initially intended to be part of a series of short films. After the surprising blockbuster success of *Scream* (1996), Dimension Films, a subsidiary of Miramax, decided to green light *Mimic* as a stand-alone feature. To accomplish this, *Mimic* would have to become a sellable commodity, a big, fun and dumb bug hunt. This would be worlds away from the religious parable that del Toro wanted to tell, with God forsaking humankind and favoring the Judas breed insects. While the complexities of del Toro's initial take were whitewashed a great deal of his themes are still presents even if they have devolved slightly.

The fictional Strickler's Disease threatens to kill a generation of children in New York City. Spread by the common cockroach the disease lacks a cure. Dr. Susan Tyler (Mira Sorvino) an entomologist is brought on to help eliminate the cockroach population. Three years later they have succeeded. Susan created the Judas Breed, an insect designed to kill the cockroach population and believing the Judas Breed population to only have female the scientists conclude that the Judas' would only be able to live for one generation. Three years later Susan, her husband Peter, an officer named Leonard and a shoeshine named Manny find themselves trapped in the abandoned New York City subway tunnels with the much evolved Judas Breed attacking them. Susan and Peter caught on to the evolution of the Judas Breed and Leonard brings them down to the subway tunnels to investigate. Manny runs into them as he searches for his son, Chuy. Chuy, labeled "special" and possibly autistic, has spent his days with his father mimicking the sounds of people steps. Chuy speaks minimally throughout the films and very early on identifies someone as "Mr. Funnyshoes." Mr. Funnyshoes is actually a fully-grown Judas Breed who, through its evolution process has grown to mimic the human figure.

The terror in *Mimic* is that the Judas Breed was not only created by humans, but also evolved right under our noses. Chuy spends the early part of the film observing and staying by his father's side. He mirrors back the sounds of steps that he hears through the day using two spoons. Listening out his window at night, he hears the clicking of the Judas Breed coming from the basement of a church across the street. Mimicking those sounds, he follows and becomes ingratiated into the insect colony. Chuy's childlike innocence and ability to listen, rather than simply talking, take him into that world and allows him to survive. The adult characters of Susan, Peter, Leonard, and Manny are constantly at odds arguing and blaming one another. While Susan and Leonard are able to come up with a way to get them out of the tunnels it is not without several heated arguments.

Susan first becomes aware the Judas Breed is still alive when two street kids bring her a "weird bug" in exchange for money. Prior to this exchange, Susan and Peter are quietly going about their lives trying for a family. When the street kids, Ricky and Davis, bring the specimen to Susan they effectively break that curtain of tranquility. Needing money and knowing Susan to be kind, Ricky and Davis are willing to venture into the bowels of the sewer to find a meal ticket, something Susan and Peter wouldn't do without hazmat suits. While Susan and Peter are celebrated for their advancements and for eradicating Strickler's Disease, doubts of their methods are still present as revealed in her exchange with a colleague (played by F. Murray Abraham):

> **Dr. Gates:** Is it answers you want from me, or absolution? ... Three years ago I would called [creating the Judas'] unforgivable. But I have two grandchildren who are alive today probably because of you. It would be a tad hypocritical to pass judgment.
> **Susan:** That's not an answer, Walter.
> **Dr. Gates:** It's not an easy question. As to the Judas,' I think it's likely some survived. Evolution has a way of keeping things alive.
> **Susan:** But they all died in the lab.
> **Dr. Gates:** Yes Susan, but you let them out. Into the world. The world's a much bigger lab.

Susan deduces that there must be a male that is allowing the Judas' to breed and evolve. If they can find the male, they can stop the spread. In the final climatic escape, Manny is killed and Susan takes charge of Chuy. Peter is separated from them and finds himself in the Judas' nest with hundreds of eggs about to hatch, eggs which he manages to blow up and still makes a getaway. Susan and Chuy are attempting to make their way out of the tunnels and to safety when they encounter the male Judas. As the male is about to attack Chuy, Susan draws its attention to her and kills it.

Chuy is emblematic of a pure innocent in the film. Nearly silent and purely trusting, he does not understand he's in danger until the Judas' attack his father. Del Toro's oeuvre is filled with religious imagery and in the scene where Chuy is happily sitting in the nest the Judas's large figures lords over him. The Judas' watching over Chuy owes to a new step in evolution, Chuy's paternal parent will no longer suffice. He needs a new guardian one only he can communicate with and who understands his form of communication. When Manny finds him, Chuy only says "friends" in reference to insects, one of whom promptly descends from above and dispatches with Manny. Chuy's true parent, Manny, is killed by his new family of the Judas.' When Susan finds Chuy she is changed. Covered in grime and shamed by Leonard and Manny for creating something that should have existed and playing God, her previous life is shattered. When she confronts the male Judas to protect Chuy, she knows no fear. She doesn't save a child by working in a medical lab, she saves him by confronting the monster outright.

Mimic exemplifies one of del Toro's favorite themes, the blind spot. The adults are able to deal with the epidemic of Strickler's Disease by creating a new breed of insects. Epidemics have been used in religion and in literature as a metaphor for the Will of God, a force that wipes out something that is wrong with the world in the hopes of starting anew. The children in *Mimic*, as in many of del Toro's other films, are not heeded as truth-sayers because the adults in charge are dealing with their own issues and concerns. Losing a generation of children cannot be abided so the adults find a solution. As the Judas Breed evolves it is the children who see them first and alert the adults. Chuy's descent into the Judas' hive is not shown in the film, it is simply accepted. Chuy, though loved, is not understood by his father as Manny tries to keep Chuy in the world of denial and perceived safety while the insect population grows. Chuy's journey into the lair and eventual rescue by Susan helps illuminate the perversion that Susan has created. Chuy is able to exist among them but in the final scenes when he has lost his spoons and is no longer able to mimic the insect sounds puts him in danger as the male Judas advances on him. Susan must confront the monster she has created. Throughout the film, Susan has been brave, kind and level-headed, but ultimately passive in the action because as Peter puts it in the film, "you understand the creature ... you've got to get back up there. You've got to undo this." When Chuy is face to face with the threat Susan is able to confront what she has created and destroy is to save not only a child, but also humanity.

The final moments of the film show Chuy and Susan with the emergency responders dealing with the explosion that reached the street when it eliminated the nest. Chuy is without a father and Susan believes she is without a husband. Chuy identifies Peter's shoes as they approach and the new family embraces, safe from the threat of the perverted family of the Judas Breed that Susan created. Susan let go of her own innocence thinking that her lab was the same as the outside world, and comes away with the knowledge that the world can deal its own retribution when tampered with.

Abandoned Sighs

After del Toro's frustration with the production of *Mimic* he wanted to make a much more personal film, a film that would come purely from him and not be tampered with by an overzealous studio system. In *The Devil's Backbone*, del Toro creates a world that is frozen in time. In a small boys orphanage, in the midst of the Spanish civil war, Carlos (Fernando Tielve) is abandoned there after his father dies fighting against the Fascists. Carlos tries to make his way in the orphanage helped by the kind owners Dr. Casares (Federico Luppi) and Carmen (Marisa Paredes) who also secretly oppose the Fascists. The groundskeeper Jacinto (Eduardo Noriega) terrorizes the boys in hopes of keeping them in line. Upon his arrival Carlos begins seeing "The One Who Sighs" or Santi, a boy who is believed to have run away from the orphanage who begins to try to communicate with Carlos. While the boys are aware of a ghostly presence the adults laugh it off and speak of it in passing. For them, the notion of something existing on the other side of death is secondary to the brutal and bloody war that is encroaching on their lives.

The Spanish civil war began in 1936 and ended in 1939. The country was heavily divided between those who supported General Francisco Franco and the legally elected Socialist. After the election in 1936 when the Socialist Party won, Franco waged a war to take control of the country and by 1939 he had succeeded. What followed was decades of Fascist rule under Franco's regime and Spain remained a country divided and scared of its leader. Franco remained in power and his supporters remained loyal thanks to a healthy and consistent dose of propaganda. While the civil war was still raging propaganda was heavily relied upon by both sided to shore up support and keep their fighters fighting.

We are not privileged to the world outside the orphanage. When characters drive away or leave we do not follow them, we see only a desert landscape. For the inhabitants of the orphanage, time has stopped. Before Carlos' arrival and on the night of Santi's death, a bomb was dropped on the orphanage by Germans, ardent Fascist supporters, but it did not detonate. It landed upright in the middle of the courtyard where the boys play. While it has been defused and poses no threat, it is a constant reminder of the war that rages. With no information coming in about the war on a regular basis, the orphanage lives in fear of what could come towards them. While *The Devil's Backbone* was initially conceived to take place against the backdrop of the Mexican Revolution, that was dropped in favor of the Spanish Civil war which for del Toro offered more of a mirror to the suffering of the orphans. Just as the children are ignored, so was Spain by the rest of Europe.

The dynamics of the adults are central to the tension within the story. While Carmen and Dr. Casares support the Republican loyalists who oppose the Fascists, they are also storing the Republics gold. Jacinto, formerly an orphan now an angry young man, secretly supports the Fascists. Jacinto sleeps with Carmen, a former mother figure to him, to gain access to her room and take keys from her to see if he can break into the orphanages' safe and take the gold. Carmen's husband died several years ago while fighting and Dr. Casares cares for her deeply but feels that he cannot satisfy her the way the young Jacinto can.

As the adult drama plays out we learn that it was Jacinto who inadvertently killed Santi the night the bomb dropped and left his body in the water tank to cover it up and say that he ran away. Carlos, though initially fearful of Santi, figures out that he was murdered by Jacinto and promises to bring Jacinto to him. While the boys live in fear, initially of Santi then of Jacinto, their well-intentioned caregivers Carmen and Dr. Casares cannot see this. They're fears of the war drawing closer and the lack of food and money to take care of the boys overshadows their fears. While Carmen and Dr. Casares know the rumor of the ghost, they're concerns are seemingly more present. It is Santi who alerts the boys to Jacinto's true nature.

The boys are not only orphaned by their parents, most of whom who have died in the war, but also by Carmen and Casares. The two adults are not only fully aware and fearful of the war on their doorstep but potential romantic relationship also blinds them to the boys. The rumor of the ghost is thought to be frivolous, something that the boys who have time to use their imagination can worry about. The boys see Jacinto for who he is. He is cruel, angry and violent as he of often yells and torments the boys when neither Dr. Casares nor Carmen are present. Santi guides them to the realization of how truly monstrous Jacinto is. When Carmen and Dr. Casares decide that it is too dangerous to stay at the orphanage they begin to pack up with the children but not before Jacinto blows up several parts of the buildings in hopes of finding the gold. Carmen is killed and Dr. Casares is wounded who eventually succumbs to his injuries. The boys are at the mercy of Jacinto who locks them up. Deciding to work together, the boys decide to fight Jacinto. As they plan, the ghost of Dr. Casares opens the door holding the boys. They are able to lure Jacinto, who has tied the gold he has found to his belt, to the lower parts of the orphanage next to the water tank. As they attack, they drive him into the water. After he is submerged, the gold he has spent the whole film trying to find weighs him down as Santi appears and drags Jacinto to a watery grave.

The final shot of the film is the boys leaving the orphanage behind and walking towards something, anything else. As they walk the figure of Dr. Casares appears and repeats the dialogue that opened the film with a slight addendum:

> What is a ghost? A tragedy condemned to repeat itself time and again? An instant of pain, perhaps. Something dead which still seems to be alive. An emotion suspended in time. Like a blurred photograph. Like an insect trapped in amber. A ghost is me.

In the final moments of the film we see that Santi was not simply a metaphor or part of a hubristic imagination, he was a real force within the film. The line between the real and imagined is at constant play in fantasy and horror films and the most shocking moments arise from the perceived imagined world having a direct impact on the real world. The bookend question of the film, "what is a ghost," does not end with Santi and Dr. Casares, *The Devil's Backbone* asks its audience to look around them for the ghosts, the traumatic moments that keep happening. Del Toro, through this film, shows that the past will always inform the present for those who are willing to look back.

Del Toro's films often show us that the monsters are not truly monstrous, humans are. The *Devil's Backbone* celebrates a constant theme in del Toro's films, that innocence and youth are to be acknowledge, the adults have lost the ability to see everything at play and don't gain enough information to save themselves. Interestingly, Dr. Casares becomes a ghost and aids the boys in the climax of the film. By transcending into a new form Dr. Casares is able finally help the boys when they need him the most. As the boys leave the orphanage into an unknown and cruel world it is Casares who stays behind. Casares, as his final voiceover insinuates, was a man who still seemed to be alive but was unable to act during his life. He studied life but did not interact with it. His love for Carmen was never realized, and his ability to help those that depended on him most only came about once he'd passed to the other side. As del Toro spoke of his uncle needing to "come back and tell the other that there is something else," *The Devil's Backbone* posits that the only thing to fear is an unfulfilled life.

While Carmen and Dr. Casares are giving up, the boys do not. The boys fight their own war against an unbelieving world that has forgotten about them. When their home is threatened from within, they rise to the challenge guided by Santi. They drive their own story while the adults only react to the world around them. Dr. Casares evolution into something monstrous creates a morose ending, we know that ghosts are not monsters in this world but it is tragic as he could only impact change in death and will haunt the orphanage while his boys go into an unknown world on their own.

Chalk Outlines

"*Devil's Backbone* is the boy's movie. It's the brother movie. But *Pan's Labyrinth* is the sister movie, the female energy to that one. I wanted to make it because Fascism is definitely a male concern and a boy's game, so I wanted to oppose that with an 11-year-old girl's universe."[4] Alongside *The Devil's Backbone*, *Pan's Labyrinth* may be del Toro's most fully realized personal vision. Again, it combines many of del Toro's favorite themes proving once again that he is not simply a director for hire but artist whose vision of the world around him is so unique and exciting that it is unmistakable.

The events of *Pan's Labyrinth* take place five years after the events of *The Devil's Backbone*. Spain is in the infancy of Franco's rule and World War II is turning for the allies. A young girl named Ofelia (Ivana Baquero) leaves her home in the city to live with her mother and her new husband, the cruel Captain Vidal (Sergi López), in the country as her mother rests in the final months of her pregnancy. Ofelia, wary of the Captain, seeks solace in a world she is brought to by a fairy her first night in the Captain's home. The fairy brings her to the labyrinth where she meets the Faun (Doug Jones) who tells Ofelia that her true identity is Princess Moanna. To take her rightful place as Princess, Ofelia must complete tasks, to prove she is the rightful heir. While Ofelia completes the tasks, the Captain's bloodlust grows increasingly vitriolic as the anti–Franco rebels begin to descend and attack his compound. Vidal's housekeeper, Mercedes, is aiding the rebels and helping care for Ofelia's whose mother's time is taken increasingly by her unborn child. The two stories play out side by side throughout the film. As Ofelia descends further into the fantasy world, the rebels get closer to the compound as the Captain loses his tenuous grip on his power he attained through fear.

Like *The Devil's Backbone*, *Pan's Labyrinth* parallels the stories of a war-torn Spain with the fantastic realm that only a child is able to see. *Pan's Labyrinth* veers from the horror genre to a more purely fantasy film, while the horror of Franco's Spain is in full force the fantasy realm is a place of wonder and horror. The lore of the world of Princess Moanna is heavily based in fairy tales and folklore from all over the world. Del Toro brings back these types of stories to their more sadistic and frightening roots by keeping them violent and aggressive which mirror the violence and decay we are witness to in the Captain's compound and surrounding area. Ofelia's first challenge is retrieving a golden key from the belly of a massive toad which lives under a tree and is draining the tree's life force. Ofelia does this by tricking the toad into eating stones that turn the toad's body inside out in a grotesque regurgitation. Ofelia must use the key to obtain a dagger held captive by the eerie Pale Man who sits silently in front of a large meal. Ofelia easily retrieves the dagger but is too tempted by the ornate food spread before her and eats a grape off the table which awakens the Pale Man who then comes after her. The Pale Man is a terrifying figure whose lair is furnished with not only an elaborate banquet but a pile of children's shoes, presumably those who failed to escape him, which depicts not only the waste of nourishment but a waste of life, which mirror the Captain's own means and ends.

Throughout these tasks, Ofelia is guided by the Faun and the fairies. Ofelia tries to be open and tell her caregivers about them but they fail to listen. Mercedes says, "My mother told me to be wary of Fauns." And later Ofelia's mother tells her:

> You're getting older, and you'll see that life isn't like your fairy tales. The world is a cruel place. And you'll learn that, even if it hurts ... Ofelia! Magic does not exist. Not for you, me or anyone else.

The magic for Ofelia is real, the adults are unable to see it because, for them, the presence of World War II and the fight for their political beliefs has become a life or death situation. As Ofelia completes the tasks the two worlds begin to merge before they are pulled together then forever torn apart. Ofelia's descent beneath the tree in search of the toad that is draining the tree's life mirrors the gestating baby in her mother's womb. The toad represents the relationship between the lifeforce draining out of her mother and the toad becoming more demanding and controlling over her body. Ofelia's journey to the underworld to retrieve the dagger from the Pale Man also mirrors the ornate meal that the Captain is having at practically the same time. As the Fascists eat at the dinner party, the people of Spain go hungry. As the dinner guests tiptoe around the Captain in hopes of pleasing him during the meal, the temptation of support is evident. By supporting the Fascists, the rich are allowed to remain rich. Ofelia gives into her temptation of the food, but in the fantasy world the brutal and violent Pale Man awakes, gruesomely eating two of the fairies. Through both of these trials, Ofelia sees the cause and effect of the tasks unlike the people of Spain. She sees the deterioration of the tree and the moment she takes the Pale Man's bait she is attacked. Ofelia is, in essence, experiencing the same trials as the adults. The worlds begin to overlap when Ofelia feels she is unable to finish the tasks because of her mother's help. The Faun gives her a mandrake root which, when put under her mother's bed in a bowl of fresh milk with a few drops of blood, which help her feel better. The other instance is when the Faun gives Ofelia a piece of chalk to use to draw a door to the other world. The chalk is still in Ofelia's possession when the compound is under attack and the Captain locks Ofelia in a room. Ofelia uses the chalk to escape with her brother.

Ofelia's final task is to bring her baby brother to the center of the labyrinth, once there the Faun tells her to spill her brother's blood, the blood of an innocent, to pass to the other side. Ofelia refuses to hurt her brother, and the Faun leaves as the Captain appears killing Ofelia and taking her brother. Because Ofelia refused to kill her brother she passes the final test and takes her rightful place as Princess Moanna. As the epilogue narration states:

> And it is said that the princess went back to her father's kingdom and that she reigned with justice and a kind heart for many centuries. And that she was loved by all her subjects. And, like most of us, she left behind small traces of her time on earth. Visible to only those who know where to look.

As the Captain leaves the maze with his infant son he is met by Mercedes and the rebels. As Mercedes takes his son from him the Captain says:

Tell my son the time that his father died. Tell him...
Mercedes: No. He won't even know your name.

The rebels achieving a satisfying victory over the Captain, the fear in the film is dominated by his needing to be remembered. The rebels ensure that he will be forgotten, particularly by his son. While the ending to *Pan's Labyrinth* can be read as tragic because of Ofelia's death it is important to remember that she transcends to her true home. The Captain's death is far more tragic because he cared. As del Toro has stated, "the only true immortality is when you don't care if you die. The moment you stop giving credence to gain is when you become invulnerable to pain."[5]

As the parallels between the war drama and the fantasy world show, Ofelia is fighting her own battle to return to her home, while the adults are trying to build a new one. Fairy tales are often about the loss of innocence, the protagonist's life is change and they must move forward of their own accord and by doing so they leave their childhood and begin to forge their way as an adult. Ofelia is living her fairy tale, the people of Spain are living the fairy tale that Franco and his Fascists were selling to them. The notions of permanence and time being held by a high standard by the Captain in the temporal world are part of his downfall, by suppressing all other voices to aid in the birth of a "new, clean Spain" all feed his need to be remembered. Ofelia's permanence is through the story of the fantasy world. Both Ofelia and the Captain tell stories, Ofelia tells them to make sense of the world she is and to change it, while the Captain tells the story of the glory of Fascism which only serves to keep people in line. His story has not worked because his dissenters are drawing closer. Ofelia's stories which serve to protect, allow her to transcend.

While the adults in *Pan's Labyrinth* never truly encounter the monsters of the fantasy world, they are forever surrounded by them. The actions that Ofelia takes in trying to help herself and her mother serve to drive the story forward and change the fates of both worlds. Ofelia's constant challenging of the Captain serves to underscore her idealism and bravery while propelling her towards her true and rightful place in the otherworld. The Faun and the fairies give her ideas and stories credence, after each task the temporal world is changed. Even though she's left the human world by the end of the film, the rebels won by taking the compound and by taking her brother who will never know who his father is. Ofelia's story will live on through the rebels and her brother because stories are what make us human in del Toro's eyes. They serve to contextualize and elevate the world around us, whichever world that may be. In this case, the biggest tragedy is being forgotten.

The Weight of Imagination

"Disbelief isn't light; it's heavy ... whenever I run into someone who expresses a feeling along the lines of, 'I don't read fantasy or go to any of those movies; none of it's real,' I feel a kind of sympathy. They simply can't lift the weight of fantasy. The muscles of the imagination have grown too weak."[6] Echoing these words of Stephen King, the worlds in which these films take place are fantastic, but the adults have lost their ability to see beyond the known world. Their priorities shifted as they grew older and they no longer needed to flex the muscle of imagination. The adults' notion that the worlds the children escape to are light or inconsequential are proof that they have lost the ability to see beyond themselves and what they need. The children, on the other hand, have a far greater ability to intuit beyond the world in front of them. For Chuy, Carlos and Ofelia, they have progressed beyond their adult caregivers and seek a new family who understand the person they are becoming.

Chuy, who is trusting and calm, needs Susan once she is able to face the monster. Susan's jump from passivity to action allows her to care for Chuy more than her own safety, earning her a place in a family. For Carlos and the boys of the orphanage, Dr. Casares also had the best of intentions but was crippled by his own insecurities. Once he lets go of the pain of his life, he is able to help the boys by giving them the ability to leave the orphanage where he is now trapped. In *Pan's Labyrinth*, the realities of the Franco's Spain have consumed the adults and Ofelia is free to discover her true self with those such as the Faun who are invested in her returning to their world. In each case, the children pass from childhood and towards adulthood which signals and forces the adults to move forward in their own ways which cause the events of the film to radically change the world of the film. The adults in the film are unable to be the guides the children need. They are blind to the truths of their collective worlds. As del Toro has said, "I don't really care much for the idea of normal—that's very abstract to me. I think that perfection is practically unattainable but imperfection is right at hand. So that's why I love monsters: because they represent a side of us that we should actually embrace and celebrate."[7]

Del Toro is a true storyteller, not only for his ability to weave a story that is purely his, but also because he understands the power of stories. They are not only designed to be read and enjoyed, they are also meant to be experienced and educate. Del Toro shows his audience that the brave idealists who are kind and fight for what they believe in are the true heroes of the story. The earnestness of the child characters is to be celebrated and not extinguished because the ability to be a hero is all around us, if we know where to look.

Notes

1. The Guardian, "Guardian/NFT interview: Guillermo del Toro," 21 November 2006, http://www.theguardian.com/film/2006/nov/21/guardianinterviewsatbfisouthbank.
2. Richard Crouse, "Guillermo del Toro's 'horrible' childhood at the root of his dark movies," Metro, 15 January 2013, http://metronews.ca/scene/510875/guillermo-del-toros-horrible-childhood-at-the-root-of-his-dark-movies/.
3. Guillermo del Toro and Marc Scott Zicree, *Guillermo del Toro Cabinet of Curiosities: My Notebooks, Collections, and Other Obsessions*. New York: Harper Design, 2013, 91.
4. The Guardian, "Interview Guillermo del Toro."
5. Ibid.

6. Stephen King, *Danse Macabre*, rpt. ed. (New York: Gallery Books), 201, 104.
7. The Guardian, interview with Guillermo del Toro.

Bibliography

Crouse, Richard. "Guillermo del Toro's 'horrible' childhood at the root of his dark movies." Metro. 15 January 2013. http://metronews.ca/scene/510875/guillermo-del-toros-horrible-childhood-at-the-root-of-his-dark-movies/.

del Toro, Guillermo, and Marc Scott Zicree. *Guillermo del Toro Cabinet of Curiosities: My Notebooks, Collections, and Other Obsessions*. New York: Harper Design, 2013.

The Guardian. "Guardian/ NFT interview: Guillermo del Toro." 21 November 2006. http://www.theguardian.com/film/2006/nov/21/guardianinterviewsatbfisouthbank.

King, Stephen. *Danse Macabre*. New York: Gallery Books, 2010.

Bloodsucking Bugs
Horacio Quiroga and the Latin American Transformation of Vampires

Gabriel Eljaiek-Rodríguez

In his 1993 film *Cronos,* Guillermo del Toro introduces a twist to the traditional vampire narrative that threatens to change the iconic—and almost totemic—animal (the bat) representing the monsters that ravage the earth in search of blood. The vampire is in danger of being replaced by an insect, specifically a mechanical one. This strategy, however, is not new, as it was already employed by the Uruguayan writer Horacio Quiroga in 1917 in his short story "El almohadón de pluma" ("The Feather Pillow"). Del Toro defamiliarizes characters and themes of the European and Latin American Gothic tradition, transforming them substantially but not so much as to render them unrecognizable; they remain faithful to the genre, while becoming transgressors of the tradition.

Eighty years before del Toro's film, Quiroga also adapts the themes and characters typical of the vampire narrative, creating a Gothic ambiance in the middle of the Uruguayan jungle, displacing traditional European narratives to a sub-tropical clime. Unlike the crawly bloodsuckers of the Uruguayan pillows—horrific monsters that share with the vampire a taste for blood, but without the anthropomorphic features of the traditional Transylvanians—the vampire device in *Cronos* is "inhabited" by an insect, able to transform humans into creatures recognizable as classic vampires: photophobic immortals who feed on blood and attain it by attacking the neck of their victims. In this sense, I propose to discuss the ways in which Guillermo del Toro transforms and adapts traditional European vampire narratives to a distinctly Latin American literary and sociopolitical context, continuing along the path previously explored by Horacio Quiroga in the first half of the 20th century.

Vampiric Bugs

"The Feather Pillow" ("El almohadón de pluma") is one of Quiroga's most cited and recognized narratives. In this short story the reader contemplates the physical deterioration of a beautiful and healthy woman—Alicia—who, almost immediately after her wedding, begins losing blood in great quantities. She becomes anemic and eventually dies after suffering hallucinations and night terrors replete with monstrous creatures that crawl into her bed. Just as the story seems to be over, the narrator makes the reader return to the bed where the maid and Jordan, Alicia's husband, discover within the cushion, "over the background, between the feathers, moving slowly its hairy legs, ... a monstrous animal, a living, viscous ball. It was so swollen that its mouth was barely visible."[1] This vampiric monster had been feeding on Alicia's blood, sucking her dry during the time she had been in bed. Quiroga concludes the short story in a frighteningly scientific way, literally messing with the head of whatever reader might be unlucky enough to own a feather pillow: "These parasites of birds, tiny in the usual way, can acquire daunting proportions in specific conditions. They seem to be keen by human blood, and it is not uncommon to find them in feather pillows."[2]

"The Feather Pillow" is constructed from the beginning as a Gothic tale, with all the elements that make it recognizable as such: Alicia is the typical heroine of Gothic stories, "blond, angelic and shy" while Jordan incarnates the "impassive" Casanova who loves his wife but cannot prove it, and suffers in silence for that reason. The narrative unfolds in an environment that resembles a castle—despite its location somewhere in the Uruguayan countryside—strengthening the environmental effect, even for the characters: "The house in which they lived influenced their fears. The whiteness of the silent courtyard—friezes, columns and marble statues—produced an autumnal feeling of an enchanted palace"[3]—an environment that Walpole or Radcliffe would certainly appreciate.[4]

Despite the horrific clarity with which it is discovered that the murderer of Alicia has been a parasite/vampire who has drained both her blood and her life, there are elements in the story that suggest that the animal only continued a process that had already been set in motion at the time the protagonists enter the house (the Gothic environment). The first line of the story foreshadows this deterioration process, stating that the "honeymoon was a long shudder," one that continued in the "strange love nest" in which Alicia loses power, weight and becomes sick—all of this even before she starts losing blood. Jordan thus functions as a vampire without fangs, who has kidnapped the girl and unwittingly brought her to an enchanted palace, where she will only find death.

The Uruguayan critic Emir Rodriguez Monegal, states that the bug/vampire is nothing but a mask for the husband: "Quiroga introduced a monstrous insect to say that the one who has emptied this woman is the husband, whom with his monstrous indifference has dried up her sources of life. This seems to be a case of backwards vampirism."[5] Like any good vampire, the parasite only attacks at night, while Alicia is lying on her bed. This fact and the way that her deterioration is described, bring the narrative closer to Gothic vampire stories, and to descriptions of nocturnal vampire attacks such as the one found in "Carmilla" by Joseph Sheridan Le Fanu and *Dracula* by Bram Stoker.

In both cases, loss of vitality, fatigue and consumption are the product of the attack of a bloodsucker (the parasite or the human vampire), which is kept alive through the lives of its victims. Quiroga creates a parasite/vampire who uses the same attack methodology of the European vampires (a barely visible bite at night, committed while the victim is unaware), and stages the attacks in similar environments (a dark and foreboding old house/mansion). However, this particular vampire is unique in its transformation and setting. Quiroga's vampire had been transposed from the European woodlands to the Uruguayan landscape where the story takes place: it is no longer a human nobleman with supernatural powers who is metaphorically called "vampire" (or who really can transform at will into a vampire or other animal), but a real animal, some kind of insect which the narrator calls "bird parasite" and that under certain conditions can attack and feed on human blood.

This shift is so frightening precisely because the author does not appeal to a necessarily supernatural factor (curses, transformations, or mysterious disappearances) but to a fact that could be familiar to anyone, and more so to people that live in a rural environment: the possibility of finding a bug somewhere in the house, and specifically on one's pillow.

Thus, the scientific explanation at the end of the story, powerful in its assertion of the possibility of finding one of these parasites in any feather pillow, constitutes a plausible source of horror for a reader who may consider checking the pillow before bedtime. Despite being a statement, it works the same way as the ambiguous explanations of many Gothic narratives that leave readers with a similar sense of insecurity, accentuated in this case by the ominous familiarity of a feather pillow.

The ending also serves to locate the existence and unbridled development of the parasites/vampires in a particular environment: the narrator affirm that the parasites, "tiny in the usual way, can acquire daunting proportions in specific conditions,"[6] conditions that occur in the context of the short story. The first is the release of energy brought by Jordan's indifference to Alicia coupled with the spooky atmosphere of the house they live in, and the second is the stillness in which Alicia is submerged by the influenza that keeps her in bed until she is sucked dry of blood.

To this should be added the "special disposition" of the Latin American environment to generate monsters, a narrative constructed by Europeans since the dawn of conquest. In this scenery America is the *locus amenus* of the monstrous, habitat of the cannibal, as stated by Carlos Jáuregui: "America [was] imaginary constructed as a Canibalia: a vast geographical and cultural space marked with the image of the American monster eater of human flesh or sometimes, imagined as a fragmented body devoured by colonialism."[7] It is precisely these images and representations that Latin American writers who write in a Gothic way take advantage of.

"The Feather Pillow" along with "The Decapitated Chicken" ("La gallina degollada" [1917]) and "The Specter" ("El espectro" [1924]) are some of Quiroga's masterpieces and fine examples of Latin American Gothic works. His influence can be seen in many Latin American writers and artists (from Julio Cortázar to Alberto Breccia) as well as in film directors like Hugo Covarrubias or Guillermo del Toro, whose movies are a constant exploration of the Gothic, the horror, and the fantastic genres.

Wind Up Bug/Vampires

The resurgence of interest in Mexican horror film was generated, in part, by a series of movies directed by young filmmakers like Guillermo del Toro, Daniel Gruener and Leopoldo Laborde. Despite the quality of Gruener and Laborde's films, del Toro's work is undoubtedly the most widespread in and outside Mexico in recent years, constantly blurring the lines between the horror and fantastic genres. Scholars such as Antonio Lázaro-Reboll (2007) and John Kraniauskas (2003) have characterized del Toro films as transnational and multicultural products that appeal to both the international film industry and spectators from different backgrounds and filmic traditions. As Kraniauskas asserts referring to *Cronos*,

> The Mexican city in the film is not a "national" or "regional" capital in the culturalist sense. It is, rather, bilingual in speech (Spanish and English, the latter being a clear allusion to American economic power), and multilingual in representations of writing. Both the workplace (the de la Guardia factory) and domestic spheres (Jesus's house) have become globalized places permeated by several overlapping forms of writing, visible in billboards and newspapers.[8]

It is with this film—*Cronos* (1993)—that del Toro rose to international recognition, due to its great filmic quality and particularly because of its thematic twist on the traditional vampire story: in the movie we are introduced to a Mexican vampire who is transformed by an alchemical/mechanical device which requires blood to operate. This shift is intentional and despite the change that it implies for the traditional image of the vampire, the character that del Toro creates is still deeply immersed in the Gothic tradition, a choice that is evident in the selection of topics images, as well as the script and notes of the film. Del Toro demonstrates a comprehensive knowledge of the Gothic genre in his description of the characters and preliminary annotations to the screenplay, where he states the transposition (recycling) and use of Gothic elements in his film in the form of a table:

CHIAROSCURO	CHIAROSCURO
NIGHT	NIGHT
RAIN	RAIN that falls harder every time (3 times)
WIND	WIND
HOWLING, OMINOUS SOUND	STEAM ENGINES
CASTLE	FACTORY
PRISION CELLS	FACTORY INTERIOR
FOREST	CITY AT NIGHT
CAVES	ALLEYS
BLOOD	OF COURSE

INNOCENT, PURE HEROINE	AURORA
DEGRADED HERO	JESÚS
LOST LOVE	JESÚS/MERCEDES

And obviously, the ideas of dead time, hunger, thirst, desire repression, etc.[9]

It is clear then that the director is giving us a Gothic vampire film, making a detailed and judicious use of themes, characters and Gothic atmospheres that are recognizable to the viewer. Despite being stated as a list (and be checked by the director in the original manuscript), these elements are sufficiently transformed in the film so as to constitute its own unique form of the genre. Homage and mockery are an important part of the way the movie is constructed, as Carla Gonzalez Vargas asserts: "what del Toro does is not only homage (although it is too), but clever reworking of a cinema that—so to speak—needed a good dose of new blood."[10]

Thus, the film begins in 1535, the year of the founding of the Viceroyalty of New Spain, bringing to the newly founded Viceroyalty the French alchemist Fulcanelli, who according to the narrative of the film worked as a watchmaker for the Viceroy. His knowledge of both alchemy and mechanics helped him to create an artifact that provides its owner with immortality, that it, the Cronos device. The proof of the effectiveness of the mechanism is demonstrated by the encounter, in 1937, of the body of Fulcanelli—with white and translucent skin—in the rubble of a building, as well as his notes and scientific apparatuses in an apartment in the city center. With this preface to his film, del Toro not only situates the legend of the vampire in Mexico, as well as the construction of the transformative device in Veracruz (the Mexican tropics), but also mobilizes the figure of the mad alchemist-scientist, who thanks to his secret scientific knowledge overcomes the constraints of time and attains immortality.[11]

Del Toro masterfully connects the birth-creation of his vampire (and possibly of vampirism) with the birth of the Viceroyalty of New Spain, anchoring the myth to Latin America and making a political commentary on the systematic bleeding of the continent by European conquerors. In this sense, the Spaniards can be seen as vampires that fed on the blood (vital resources) of the civilizations that inhabit Mexico, creating in addition a race of bureaucratic bloodsuckers that continued the bleeding through the centuries. This political undertone permeates the movie and makes clear that Fulcanelli achieved in Mexican lands what no one had ever been able to accomplish, that is, become immortal by using blood as a means of survival.

Thanks to these movements vampires adopt a new nationality and the mechanism by which a human turns into a vampire changes completely. The demonic intervention, by which Vlad the Impaler turns into a vampire in Coppola's version of *Dracula* for example, or the direct transmission of the vampirism through the bite (using fangs as a medium), are replaced in *Cronos* by a mechanical-alchemical device that spreads the condition through a sting.

The exact form in which this device operates is difficult to ascertain given the short and fragmentary shots of the interior of the apparatus as well as the lack of an explanation of it from the characters. However, gleaning some information from its brief appearances, the Cronos device is a mechanical unit connected to/merged with some kind of insect, who "wakes up" and moves in the presence of blood. It is a clear case of the Gothic imaginary meeting with Steampunk aesthetics, since Fulcanelli is presented in the movie as a watchmaker and most of the shots of the interior of the machine show gear wheels and screws in movement, indicative of a technology that is somehow simultaneously primitive and advanced (suggesting that the master alchemist is also a great inventor).[12]

As in Kafka's *Metamorphosis*, the identity of this insect is never revealed—we don't know if it is a worm, a beetle, or a spider, as it seems to incorporate features of all of the above. While its outer shape looks like a golden beetle (one of the Egyptian symbols of immortality, and more specifically of regeneration and resurrection), its inside is more reminiscent of a larva or worm; in addition, the way it stings and draws blood seems to suggest a type of scorpion. The lack of differentiation remains both throughout the film as well as in the advertising associated with it: in some posters and DVD covers the artifact looks like a scorpion, while in others it most resembles a beetle.

What is clear is that del Toro is presenting a vampiric/insectoid creature that hibernates inside a mechanic exoskeleton, waiting for human blood. When activated it enters into a symbiotic relationship with the person that owns the mechanism: it drinks the blood of the human in exchange for an extension of its life, a transmission of its own ability to resist the passage of time. The only explicit description of the artifact in the film comes from the mouth of Didier de la Guardia, a Franco-Mexican businessman who deciphered the manuscripts of Fulcanelli and devotes his life to search for the Cronos device to beat the cancer that is consuming him. As he tells Jesus Gris, accidental finder of Cronos; "the insect is caught in the invention, as a sort of ... living filter," adding that the insects are possibly the "favorite creatures of God" possessing characteristics that could be assimilated to immortality, as self regeneration and the ability to survive environments uninhabitable for other animals ("the issue of the resurrection is not a strange thing for ants or spiders, if caught in the middle of a rock they are able to wait hundreds of millions of years to be released").

The twist that del Toro explores in his movie is so radical that it threatens to change the very figure of the iconic monsters that ravage the earth for blood: the vampire is in danger of being replaced by an insect (a strategy that Quiroga used in "The Feather Pillow" decades prior). Yet just as this total replacement seems poised to occur, as del Toro de-territorializes characters and symbols, all of a sudden he re-territorializes them once again, transformed but recognizable; faithful to the genre, but transgressors of tradition. Unlike the bloodsucking creature that inhabits the Uruguayan pillows (or any other feather pillow, according to Quiroga)—a horrid monster that shares with the vampire a taste for blood but that has no anthropomorphic features and can not transform his victims—the Cronos device is able to transforms humans into creatures recognizable as vampires while all the while drinking their blood.

The vampire created by the mechanical device also shares behavioral and aesthetic characteristics with literary and cinematic vampires. Although Jesus Gris doesn't look like Dracula, there are definite recognizable elements that can be found in the repetition of cinematic clichés recurring in vampire movies: such is the case of the way Jesus positions his arms after his complete transformation into a vampire (after having died and risen), shading himself from the light like Dracula—Bela Lugosi, Christopher Lee, and many others—did before.

Del Toro pays homage to classic vampires and their representations in film and literature, while at the same time profoundly and transgressively transforming them. The director himself acknowledges the influence that literature has on the film by stating that "in Cronos there are more horror literary influences than filmic influences. There are even many references to Gothic novels that few people notice."[13] In this sense, the Jesus Gris who has been bitten (or stung) by the Cronos device can be recognized by any viewer as a vampire, a creature that is receding in age thanks to the effects of the blood and can return from the grave.

However, there are some major changes that complicate this condition. One essential difference is the gradual loss of human skin, a change that occurs after being killed and resurrected, and a phenomenon that again makes this vampire closer in appearance to an insect (many insects lose their exoskeleton, or what at first glance can be misread as skin, in order to grow and continue with their lives). Thus, the Jesus Gris we see the end of the film, dying for a second (and presumably last) time in bed accompanied by his wife Mercedes and his granddaughter Aurora, is more reminiscent of a giant larva—with bright green skin—than of a chiropteran.

The viewer of the film is confronted then with a hybrid vampire that sometimes behaves and looks like any other literary or cinematic vampire but that is slowly acquiring characteristics of an insect (without transforming completely such as in the case of the protagonist of *The Fly* [1958 and 1986], for example) thanks to his encounter and bloody exchange with the mechanical device- part machine, part insect. The cultural heritage of vampirism is mixed and constantly called into question, not only because of the vampire and the device that transforms him, but also from objects and situations that occur throughout the film. As stated before, the Cronos device as well as the vampirism are linked to Mexico's colonial past (the artifact and the viceroyalty are created the same year), a fact that is stated in the prologue of the film and represented by the statue of the colonial angel where the Cronos device was hidden, until it was discovered by Jesús Gris and his granddaughter in the antique shop.

The statue's ability to connect past and present is made clear in the narration when the statue is discovered to be the holder/custodian of the Cronos device, but also through scenes that reveal the connection visually, placing the statue in the same place in the frames that represent past and present, and showing faded the users of the artifact in both times: Fulcanelli and Juan Gris.

The trigger of the discovery, which also functions as an index, is the emergence of multiple cockroaches from inside the statue, revealing the hiding place of the Cronos device. The choice of this animal is not innocent, both because of its omnipresence in horror films such as *Creepshow*

(1982) and *The Nest* (1988), and (especially) for their contemporary relationship with immortality: such as the popular urban myth that purports that cockroaches would be the only living thing to survive a nuclear catastrophe. Del Toro played with and twisted this idea in his 1997 movie *Mimic*, where a special breed of insects, hybrid creatures genetically designed to get rid of a cockroach plague, mutate and take over the subway system in New York. Both *Cronos* and *Mimic* are consistently following the interests and obsessions that del Toro has manifested in his career, as he asserts in an interview on WNYC's *Leonard Lopate Show*: "I have a sort of a fetish for insects, clockwork, monsters, dark places, and unborn things."[14]

In both films insects are presented as images of the possibility of overcoming death (in *Mimic* the insects, called Judas Breed, are expected to die after a short period of time but instead they become human-sized monsters), an event that is fascinating and strange, and even becomes repulsive when the outcome is far from the idealized expectations of resurrection. As Eric White asserts, "del Toro thus references insect life to suggest that disquieting alterity lurks beneath the reassuringly familiar face of conventionally recognizable human identity."[15] Whether through an insect that transforms humans into monsters or through an insect that transforms into—or mimics—a human, the familiar become sinister, unfamiliar, informing the films and creating spaces of horror (whether Gothic horror in *Cronos* or science fiction horror in *Mimic*).

Multiple Mechanical Devices

The colonial angel where the Cronos device was hidden until the moment Juan Gris open it, functions literally as the guardian angel of Fulcanelli's secret. In this sense, and following the game of names that del Toro constructs with all the characters in the film, the custody of the Cronos device seems inherent to the patriarch of the family that holds the name of the angel: De la Guardia. According to this logic, the nephew of Didier is literally a guardian angel, who must protect his uncle until he is able to receive the device and gain immortality. However, this nominal logic that at first glance is transparent (Ángel de la Guardia is the guardian, Jesus Gris is the resurrected, Aurora is the hope), becomes cloudy when the viewer discovers that the characters and their actions do not necessarily reflect the meaning of their names or roles.

This gap has to do with the transpositions that del Toro makes of classic Gothic characters and environments in his Mexican film adaptation. Like the Cronos mechanical device, the movie works as a mechanism that transforms highly recognizable elements of the genre—like the animal that incarnates the iconic monster—into complex hybrids that both pay homage to and mock the conventions of the Gothic. Didier—despite his De la Guardia last name—is an occultist/technocrat who inhabits a castle/factory and would like to purchase immortality to enjoy longer the fruits of his labor, which he has achieved using exploitative ways. Angel cannot be considered angelic neither in appearance nor in his bullying attitude, much less a guardian angel of his uncle, since the only thing he is really hoping for is that Didier will die in order to inherit his money.

Meanwhile Jesus Gris, whom del Toro identifies with the degraded heroes of Gothic stories, is closest in his actions to the protagonist of Mathew Lewis's *The Monk* than to the figure of Christ. In this sense, he is the ambiguously gray (gris) copy of the savior of the Christians, a character who is neither very good nor very bad, but nevertheless is recognizable as a biblical figure. He gets the vampiric message through an angel, resurrects on the third day, gives his life for others, and needs blood to survive. Even though his love for his granddaughter and his wife does not stop him from acting selfishly for most of the film, he sacrifices himself to save Aurora, coming closer to the image of Jesus as savior. As Marta Sorensen asserts, "[m]ost filmmakers dealing in vampire fiction have a tendency to ignore a certain fact. Guillermo del Toro, on the other hand, has embraced it as a major aspect of his debut film Cronos. The fact is this: Vampires have a lot in common with Jesus Christ."[16] This ignored relationship is stressed in *Cronos*, showing a reverse Christic image.

Aurora shares with Gothic heroines a halo of purity and fragility, augmented by the fact that she is nearly mute (this condition is never explained in the film and the only time she speaks in the movie is to prevent her grandfather from attacking her). However, with the development of the film this fragility seems porous: the girl, who always accompanies her grandfather and does not have a good relationship with her grandmother, seems to understand and accept like a mature adult everything that happens to Jesus. Unlike many female protagonists of Gothic stories who reject the encounter with the monstrous, this little girl appears to embrace it and even have a certain affinity for it. Aurora is present every time Jesus has a craving for blood (besides being dressed in red throughout the film) and is the only character that welcomes him after he returns from the grave, by arranging a coffin no other vampire would dream of: a toy chest where the vampire sleeps accompanied by a teddy bear and a doll.

Aurora's familiarity with the horrible (de-familiar familiarity in every sense) makes her a more complex character than a simply heroine who gets scared, screams and must be constantly rescued from the clutches of the monster. Despite her age and the moments in the film when she is scared or worried about her grandfather, she is generally shown as a serious girl, who perversely enjoys a little danger (evidenced in her slow, deliberate smile in response to her father's warning of the dangers they would face) and is able to defend herself by hitting De la Guardia with his own cane.

The setup of the story also adds to the hybridity of the Gothic story. The film is set in a dark and rainy Mexican city (that can be Veracruz or Mexico City), where old and new—or "industrial" if we follow the Steampunk thread—clashes in the form of Gris and De la Guardia, respectively. Gris is an aged antiquarian, who spends his life surrounded by both fragments of Mexico's past (colonial and nineteenth-century objects) as well as his own (memories of his childhood, old photos, tangos and boleros). De la Guardia, on the other hand, is a businessman who lives surrounded by technology in an aseptic environment (his apartment is completely isolated inside his factory), who refuses to accept his own deterioration despite the disease that is slowly destroying his body.

In this space, cursed devices, vampires, and occultists move between antiquities, families, and day laborers. The chaotic and crowded streets of the city, where it is potentially difficult to distinguish between a vampire and a homeless man, also serve as the perfect background for a new breed of vampire: a bloodsucker insectoid that keeps losing his skin after being bitten by a mechanical device. In a sense, then, the metropolis is also presented as a bloodsucking creature that attempts to eat, or at least suck the life of those that resist its expansion.

Part of the problem in recognizing precisely where the action takes place (while knowing that the action takes place in a major Mexican city) has to do with the lack of what filmmakers and directors have constructed as geopolitical signposts: markers such as tourist spots, street signs, governmental buildings. With no more than a few "vochos" (the colloquial name of the white and green Volkswagen Beatles, typical taxis of Mexico's capital) to serve as a clue and little dialogue between the characters regarding their origins, it is not easy to pinpoint exactly where the story develops.

However, this does not imply that it is not a uniquely Mexican story—the filmic space is marked from the very beginning with such important elements as the colonial angels, showing at once the plasticity and mobility of the mechanism that del Toro constructs. The filmmaker introduces elements that situate the narration in Mexico that nevertheless fit in with the genre perfectly: such is the case of the scenes in the morgue, where the mortician works on Jesus Gris's body to the rhythm of *rancheras* on the radio. Both the man's language as well as the song playing in the background serves to locate the scene in a populist Mexico, a different version of the country that we have seen and heard throughout the film.

Del Toro uses the song lyrics and the nonchalant attitude of the mortician to address the way that Mexican culture and society typically broach the subject of death, an approach that is at once both respectful and playful; religious and pagan. The song is clearly enunciating the romance of "little dead man" with the "pelancha" (the bald one, the skull): "at that time was the deceased/ cold and well tidied up, the pelancha found him / that dead man was on the metal sheet, and the pelancha came to reclaim him love" (my translation). This staging echoes the point made by Octavio Paz in the article "All Saints Day of the Dead" ("Todos santos día de muertos," included in *The Labyrinth of Solitude*):

> To the inhabitants of New York, Paris or London death is a word that is never uttered because it burns the lips. The Mexican, on the other hand, frequents it, mocks it, entertains it; it is one of his favorite playthings. It is true that in his attitude there is perhaps the same fear that others also have, but at least he does not hide this fear nor does he hide death; he contemplates her face to face with impatience, with contempt, with irony.[17]

The mocking spirit in relation to death resurfaces in other parts of the film, significantly in the moment when Angel goes to the funeral home to ensure that Jesus is dead and, when trying to see the body—which is now supposedly in the incinerator—is questioned by the morgue's employee as to the type of cooking he prefers: "medium or well done?" Although the staging is cartoonish these short scenes locate the narration in a Mexico that welcomes death in a sarcastic way, that is, a perfect place to host vampires, mad scientists and other Gothic horrors and their creators.

Cronos reveals itself as a movie that is not only connected with classics of Gothic literature and film (*Dracula*, "Carmilla," *The Monk*, and its respective filmic version), but also with less canonical approximations to the Gothic and to vampire myths—ones that use mockery and black humor to address topics of death, resurrection, and immortality. Among these figure such literary works as *The Heroine* (1813) by Eaton Stannard Barrett and *Northanger Abbey* (1818) by Jane Austen, and movies like *Abbott and Costello Meet Frankenstein* (1948) by Charles Barton (all in the Anglo-Saxon and American tradition), as well as the many Mexican films where Tin Tan or El Santo face off monsters, vampires, and other ghouls.[18]

Bugged Vampires

One of the most significant changes that Latin American writers and filmmakers have brought to the Gothic is the transformation of seminal figures of the genre, who mutate and enrich their narratives and representations as they pass through the American continent, and in some cases decide to permanently settle. The vampire figure is not indifferent to this transmutation, as I have shown: it has changed quite significantly under both Horacio Quiroga's pen and Guillermo del Toro's camera. What is significant in both cases, and what del Toro recuperates from Quiroga's story, is the fact that their narratives are hybridizing a character that has a long and structured trajectory inside the genre as well as within the popular imagination. The vampire as a monster has been understood in its connection with the vampire bat and the act of sucking blood, a dyad that is broken when the vampire bat is replaced either by a parasite or a compound bug that is at the same time larvae, scarab, and scorpion.

Del Toro's film is not presenting monstrous insects that try to eat humans or conquer the earth—what happens in movies like *Them* (1954) by Gordon Douglas, *Phase IV* (1974) by Saul Bass, or even *Mimic*—or even humanoid insects—like *The Fly* (1958 and 1986). He is instead interested in taking elements of vampire folklore and film and mixing them with elements of creature movies. The result is a Gothic hybrid that transcends the traditional image of the vampire while maintaining the ability to criticize the context from which it emerges, all the while maintaining its essential character as a bloodsucker (in a literal and a metaphorical form).

The director locates his mechanical vampire in Mexico because, besides being a place where representations of death could be easily "welcome," it is a country inhabited by lots of literal bloodsuckers, wealthy industrialists and businessmen (many of them foreigners) who will do anything to get what they want, and "feed" off the lives of their workers. As in many other stories and movies (*Dracula*, *The Vampire*, and soon) the ruling bourgeoisie is portrayed as vampires—or at least as aspiring vampires: Didier de la Guardia dedicates his life to find the object that will return his health and will make him immortal. What he fails to anticipate, however, is that a normal man like Jesus Gris (a gray man) would find and use the mechanism first, prompting a clash between men, social classes, and distinct forms of inhabiting the world.

The movie is highly innovative and still disruptive even after the dozens of vampire films that have emerged since its release in the last decade of the 20th century, and its relevance is assured, in part, by highlighting the vampirism of those that still control politics and the economy in Mexico to this day. Both the film and the short story go beyond the simple repetition or translation of the myth (or myths), displacing and adapting the mainly European monster to Latin American environments, giving birth to new horrors that make the reader or viewer think twice about old clocks and feather pillows.

Notes

1. Horacio Quiroga, "El almohadón de pluma," *Cuentos escogidos* (Buenos Aires: Alfaguara, 2008), 42. Author's translation throughout.
2. Ibid., 43.
3. Ibid., 40.
4. Quiroga was a reader and admirer of the work of Edgar Allan Poe, like he demonstrates in the first point of his *Decalogue of the Perfect Story Teller*: "Believe in a master—Poe, Maupassant, Kipling, Chejov—like in God himself."
5. Emir Rodríguez Monegal, *El desterrado. Vida y obra de Horacio Quiroga* (Buenos Aires: Losada, 1968), 116.

6. Quiroga, "El almohadón de pluma," 43.
7. Carolos Jáuregui, *Canibalia. Canibalismo, calibanismo, antropofagia cultural y consumo en América Latina* (Madrid: Iberoamericana-Vervuert, 2008), 18.
8. John Kraniauskas, "Cronos y la economía política del vampirismo: apuntes sobre una constelación histórica," *Heterotropías: narrativas de identidad y alteridad latinoamericana* (Pittsburgh: University of Pittsburgh Press, 2003), 121.
9. Guillermo del Toro, "Director Notes," *Cronos* (Criterion, 2010), DVD.
10. Carla González Vargas, *Rutas del cine mexicano 1990–2006* (México, D.F.: Landucci/IMCINE, 2006), 58.
11. Fulcanelli was the name used by a French alchemist about whom little is known. In the "Preface to the Second Edition" of *The Mystery of the Cathedrals* Eugène Canseliet affirms that "[w]e must say, certainly, that this man of another age, with his strange appearance, his old-fashioned manners and his unusual occupations, involuntarily attracted the attention of the idle, the curious and the foolish. Much greater, however, was the attention he was to attract a little later by the complete disappearance of his common presence." Eugène Canseliet, "Preface to the Second Edition," *Le Mystère des Cathédrales* (Las Vegas: Brotherhood of Life, 1990), 8.
12. The Merriam-Webster dictionary defines Steampunk as a form of "science fiction dealing with 19th-century societies dominated by historical or imagined steam-powered technology."
13. José Antonio Valdés Peña, *Óperas primas del cine mexicano 1988–2000* (México, D.F. Cineteca Nacional, 2004), 59.
14. Guillermo del Toro, "Pan's Labyrinth," *The Leonard Lopate Show*, BBC World Service, December 29, 2006, http://www.wnyc.org/story/53045-pans-labyrinth/.
15. Eric White, "Insects and Automata in Hoffmann, Balzac, Carter and del Toro," *Journal of the Fantastic in the Arts* 19, no. 3 (2008): 375.
16. Marta Sorensen, "Jesus Christ is a vampire," *The Ooh Tray*, 2010, http://www.theoohtray.com/2010/12/10/modern-classic-film-review-cronos/.
17. Octavio Paz, *El laberinto de la soledad* (Madrid: Cátedra, 1993), 193.
18. Germán Valdés *Tin Tan* (1915–1973) was a Mexican actor, comedian, and singer. In most of his movies he incarnated (and immortalized) the character of the *pachuco* giving visibility to Mexican Americans and being one of the first artists using *Spanglish* in his films. Rodolfo Guzmán Huerta (1917–1984), better known as *El Santo* was a professional Mexican wrestler and actor, considered to be one of the best wrestlers of the country and a Latin American cultural icon. As Greene asserts: "Santo's illustrious career spanned four decades in which he wrestled in over 5,000 matches, won numerous wrestling championship titles, and undoubtedly became Mexico's most famous luchador" (50). El Santo starred in 52 movies in a period of 30 years.

Bibliography

Canseliet, Eugène. "Preface to the Second Edition." *Le Mystère des Cathédrales.* Las Vegas: Brotherhood of Life, 1990.
Cronos. Dir. Guillermo del Toro. Federico Luppi, Ron Perlman, Claudio Brook, Margarita Isabel, Tamara Shanath. 1993.

del Toro, Guillermo. "Pan's Labyrinth." *The Leonard Lopate Show.* BBC World Service. December 29, 2006. http://www.wnyc.org/story/53045-pans-labyrinth/.
_____. "Director Notes." *Cronos.* Criterion, 2010. DVD.
González Vargas, Carla. *Rutas del cine mexicano 1990–2006.* México, D.F.: Landucci/IMCINE, 2006.
Greene, Doyle. *Mexploitation Cinema. A Critical History of Mexican Vampire, Wrestler, Ape-Man and Similar Films, 1957–1977.* Jefferson: McFarland, 2005.
Jáuregui, Carlos. *Canibalia. Canibalismo, calibanismo, antropofagia cultural y consumo en América Latina.* Madrid: Iberoamericana-Vervuert, 2008.
Kraniauskas, John. "Cronos y la economía política del vampirismo: apuntes sobre una constelación histórica." *Heterotropías: narrativas de identidad y alteridad latinoamericana.* Ed. Carlos A. Jáuregui and Juan Pablo Dabove. Pittsburgh: University of Pittsburgh Press, 2003. 115–34.
Mimic. Dir. Guillermo del Toro. Mira Sorvino, Jeremy Northam, Josh Brolin, Charles S. Dutton, Giancarlo Giannini, F. Murray Abraham. 1997.
Paz, Octavio. *El laberinto de la soledad.* Madrid: Cátedra, 1993.
Quiroga, Horacio. "El almohadón de pluma." *Cuentos escogidos.* Buenos Aires: Alfaguara, 2008.
Rodríguez Monegal, Emir. *El desterrado. Vida y obra de Horacio Quiroga.* Buenos Aires: Losada, 1968.
Sorensen, Marta. "Jesus Christ is a vampire." *The Ooh Tray.* 2010. http://www.theoohtray.com/2010/12/10/modern-classic-film-review-cronos/.
Valdés Peña, José Antonio. *Óperas primas del cine mexicano 1988–2000.* México, D.F.: Cineteca Nacional, 2004.
White, Eric. "Insects and Automata in Hoffmann, Balzac, Carter and del Toro." *Journal of the Fantastic in the Arts* 19, no. 3 (2008): 363–78.

The Birth of Fantasy
A Nietzschean Reading
of Pan's Labyrinth

Jack Collins

> *We must now avail ourselves of all the principles of art considered so far, in order to find our way through the labyrinth, as we must call it, of the origin of Greek tragedy.*[1]
> —Friedrich Nietzsche

While Friedrich Nietzsche's 1872 *The Birth of Tragedy from the Spirit of Music* is a problematic work (both as a history of Greek theater and in relation to Nietzsche's later philosophy), it nonetheless represents one of the first truly modern attempts to generate a psychology and sociology of tragic drama, to understand why humans have chosen to create art that portrays the suffering of others. Nietzsche argues that Greek tragedy sought to combat nihilism through a balance between the individual "Apollonian" drive for beauty and order, and the chaotic "Dionysian" forces of collective frenzy. Guillermo del Toro's film *Pan's Labyrinth* (*El laberinto del Fauno*, 2006) contends with much the same nihilistic impulse as Nietzsche's work, and, I will argue, does so through the interplay of many of the tensions Nietzsche identified in classical tragedy. Beginning with a brief synopsis of Nietzsche's argument, I will move on to a close reading of the film in light of the themes of *Birth of Tragedy*, and then examine del Toro's own words regarding the role of fantasy. Based on this, I will argue that *Pan's Labyrinth* manipulates both the conventions of traditional fantasy and those of classical drama in order to deconstruct the historically escapist function of fantasy and regenerate it as a post-modern analog to Nietzsche's "goat song," but one where the abyss is not embodied in the inhuman, chaotic, Dionysian Faun, but in the cold, too-human order of Fascism. Del Toro thus expands the symbolic vocabulary of tragedy and reappropriates fantasy to force the audience to confront what it once only allowed them to escape, yet does so in a manner that conveys hope and redemption.

The Birth of Tragedy in Brief

The Birth of Tragedy is both the first major work of Nietzsche's career as a philosopher, and the final one of his brief tenure as a classical philologist. It provoked controversy in its time with its content, its methods, and its style, all of which broke from the traditions of Enlightenment scholarship against which Nietzsche would rail throughout his philosophical career. This controversy arose in no small part because the book's agenda is more polemical and political than historical, using the decadence of later Greek art as a type of the decadence Nietzsche saw in his German contemporaries, and setting up the (pre–Socratic, pre–Euripidean) Greek culture as an ideal toward which the revitalization of the Germans should strive. At the root of Nietzsche's argument are two "spirits": the Apollonian and the Dionysian. The Apollonian (named for the god of light) represents the ordered, civilized, individuated structure of human experience, while the Dionysian (named for the god of wine) represents the chaotic, untamed, undifferentiated aspects of life. To Nietzsche, both these spirits played a vital role in true tragedy, working in concert to force the audience to confront the chaotic meaningless of life, and show them that this pessimism can be overcome through art.

In terms of art, the Apollonian corresponds most closely to the visual arts, to art as a representation of the world, or of idealized visions thereof. The Dionysian corresponds to music, which Nietzsche (after Schopenhauer) sees as unique in that it does not attempt to copy what already exists. It is pure creation, "an immediate copy of the will."[2] Neither of these forms of expression, however, can generate the true redemptive power of art alone; that requires tension between the two forces. Nietzsche believed this synthesis was most fully realized in the Greek tragedy of the fifth century BCE, typified by the works of Sophocles and Aeschylus.

The purpose of tragedy, according to Nietzsche, was to counteract the pessimism that results from the understanding of the futility of existence. The first remedy for this pessimism that was devised by the Greeks was the Apollonian vision of the Olympian gods. This glorious illusion of a higher world served, for a time, to shield the sensitive Greek spirit from the Dionysian chaos that surrounded them in real life. The "naïve" art of Greece's archaic period, including the works of Homer, reflect this Apollonian striving for deceptive beauty. According to Nietzsche, it was not until to arrival of the cult of Dionysus from the east that the stage was set (so to speak) for the development of an art form that synthesized the Apollonian drive for beauty and order with the awesome and terrible chaos of Dionysian ecstasy. The tragic chorus, he contends, had its origins in the frenzied dithyramb of the cult of Dionysus, in which the chorus originally took on the roles of satyrs. Only later did individual actors step forward from the undifferentiated mass, and begin to impose an Apollonian order on the chaos.

Attic tragedy, as typified by Aeschylus and Sophocles, combined the powers of Apollonian myth with the Dionysian music to produce a redemptive synthesis. Instead of subsuming the individual entirely in the manner of Bacchic rites, tragedy used the beauty and structure to expose the audience to the Dionysian without the complete loss of identity. Through the tragic hero, the audience participated in a collective experience of idealized virtue in the very face of death and meaninglessness. It is only in the face of chaos that order can be fully appreciated, and only restrained by order and veiled with beauty that the chaotic passions can be faced without despair.

This "metaphysical comfort" that Nietzsche finds in Greek tragedy results, he says, from the realization that the Apollonian beauty of artistic creation, of individual existence, is necessarily grounded in the chaotic and incomprehensible. In order to live, one must die, and in order for there to be new life, the old must pass away into the flux. The beauty of tragic art "shows us how necessary is the entire world of suffering, that by means of it the individual may be impelled to realize the redeeming vision."[3] Because the incomprehensible void at the root of life is undifferentiated life itself, in facing that void, the tragic hero acknowledges that life continues regardless of the hero's individual fate. And this realization itself redeems all of the suffering necessary to achieve it. Individual life in all its woes is justified—through a sort of metaphysical bootstrap—by art's ability to bring about this very revelation.[4]

The balance between the two spirits was short-lived, according to

Nietzsche, and the end of true Attic tragedy resulted from a new shift towards the Apollonian. In contrast to the naïve wonder of epic, however, this shift was one toward rationalism. Typified by the plays of Euripides and the philosophy of Socrates, this new approach found beauty only in what is comprehensible, and thus fled from any Dionysian mysteries. There arose a new standard in which beauty was subordinated to reason, "whose supreme law reads roughly as follows, 'To be beautiful everything must be intelligible.'"[5] In drama, it marked a movement away from the universal, archetypal characterizations of myth, and towards a naturalistic depiction of individual *qua* individuals. This, says Nietzsche, robbed tragedy of its redemptive universal power. Without the collective Dionysian experience, the audience no longer shared in the hope of enduring life engendered by their participation in the primal unity. Euripides also introduced the device of *deus ex machina*, in which the tragic hero's sufferings were alleviated at the end of the play by divine intervention. To Nietzsche, this defeated the very purpose of tragedy, where redemption does not come from above, but from facing the primordial chaos.

The purpose of *Birth of Tragedy*, at its core, is to make a call for a revival of the mythic and tragic in German art. Valorizing Wagner as the embodiment of such a movement (a sentiment he would later regret), Nietzsche looked to overcome the historicizing, rationalizing tendency in society which he would later blame for the death of God. By reintroducing the passionate music of Dionysus into art, by embracing mythic archetypes over naturalistic representations of the everyday, Nietzsche believed that Germany could be saved from the decadence overtaking the modern world. Beyond its immediate agenda, however, *Birth of Tragedy* provides us with a model—albeit a flawed one—with which to begin to understand tragedy as a genre. Going beyond the idea of mere imitation of real suffering, or the classical notion of cathartic release, Nietzsche sought to disclose a vital social function behind tragic drama by explaining it in terms of the dialectic between two divergent human impulses.

Fantasy and Tragedy in *Pan's Labyrinth*

Guillermo del Toro's *Pan's Labyrinth* can, in many ways, be read as a tragedy in Nietzsche's sense. It tells the story of Ofelia, an 11-year-old girl growing up in the wake of the Spanish civil war, who goes with her pregnant mother to live with her stepfather, the brutal Fascist Captain Vidal. Against the backdrop of Vidal's vicious campaign against a band of rebels, Ofelia encounters a series of fantastic creatures. An ancient Faun sets her on three tasks in order to prove herself the lost princess of the underworld. After her mother dies in childbirth, Ofelia sneaks away and brings her baby brother to the Faun's labyrinth. But her refusal of the Faun's demand to sacrifice a drop of the baby's blood bars her re-entry into the other world. The pursuing Vidal catches her and she is shot. As her life slips away, she sees a vision of her underworld kingdom, but the film ends with the audience unsure if this vision—or any of the supernatural elements—were ever truly real. Despite the film's adherence to the conventions of fantasy and fairy tales, this tragic (if ambiguous) ending, and the harrowing real-world violence portrayed alongside the fantastic elements, sets *Pan's Labyrinth* apart from the mainstream of fantasy fiction.

A charge often leveled against fantasy as a genre is that it represents a mere escape from the real world.[6] The other worlds of fantasy are often perceived as irrelevant to real human experience, serving no function beyond entertainment and distraction from more vital matters. J.R.R. Tolkien himself, in his essay "On Fairy Stories," defended the escapist, happy-ending character of fantasy, arguing that it provides a necessary consolation for the audience by showing that even the most negative circumstances can "turn," something he called "eucatastrophe."[7] This sort of consolation, however, is diametrically opposed to the metaphysical comfort of Nietzsche's tragedy, and seems likewise opposed to del Toro's approach to fantasy. Indeed, del Toro himself (prior to his abortive stint directing *The Hobbit*) expressed his disdain for "heroic fantasy … little guys and dragons, hairy feet, hobbits. I've never been into that at all. I don't like sword and sorcery, I hate all that stuff."[8]

We may look at modern fantasy as closely akin to the naïve Apollonian impulse of Homeric epic. Tolkien often spoke of his work, particularly the *Silmarillion*, as an attempt to create a national mythology for the English.[9] In this respect, traditional fantasy does represent a break from the overly rationalistic approach to art disparaged by Nietzsche. But Tolkien and most purveyors of fantasy evince far more interest in the function of myth as a veil against the horrors of the world, rather than as a means of confronting them in the style of Nietzsche. Traditional fantasy heroes defeat the forces of chaos and evil; theirs are stories of "an exuberant, triumphant life,"[10] not of "the terror and horror of existence."[11] Like the heroes of Ofelia's story of the flower, the heroes of myth value survival as the greatest victory. It is these very conventions of triumph and survival that are inverted to tragic effect in *Pan's Labyrinth*.

So ingrained has this Apollonian expectation of fantasy become that numerous reviews of *Pan's Labyrinth* summarize the plot in terms of a little girl turning to an imaginary world to *escape* the horrors of war. But regardless of how real the film's other world is understood to be, it provides horrors of its own that match anything the real world has to offer, and thus provide little escape. *Pan's Labyrinth*, we must remember, begins with the story of a princess who escapes *from* the world of fantasy. Del Toro has said that the fantastic world is not an alternative to the mundane one, but intrinsically linked to it: "I find that the girl in the movie is not so much trying to escape reality, which is the way that it would normally go. She's actually articulating the world through her fantasy. So the things in her fantasy would reflect things in the real world. It's not really her way of coping with the real world, more like interpreting."[12] The notion of escape is rejected in favor of a model where fantasy and reality stand in tension without either taking precedence.

What is especially distinct in *Pan's Labyrinth*, then, is how and when it chooses to deploy fantasy. When the film begins, it follows many of the conventions of the genre. It introduces the fantastic elements when the protagonist is alone, leaving doubt in the minds of the audience. These encounters often follow immediately upon acts of violence and cruelty in the real world, turning the narrative away from reality in escapist fashion when reality becomes too terrible to bear. Del Toro admits, "The intent was for the violence to make you more susceptible to fantasy, and the fantasy to make you more vulnerable to the brutality in the movie,"[13] and his juxtaposition of real-world reality and fantastic beauty was a deliberate device for manipulating the audience's response.

As *Pan's Labyrinth* progresses, however, and the lines between the two worlds blur, the escapist element becomes more and more attenuated. The pure fantasy scenes depart when the Faun rejects Ofelia for her disobedience, and the final supernatural element, the mandrake, literally goes up in flames. What follows is perhaps the most harrowing sequence of the film—including the deaths of the doctor and Ofelia's mother, and the interrogation and escape of Mercedes—during which no fantastic escape is offered. When the Faun returns, the audience is given a brief hope that Ofelia had not been abandoned to the horrors of reality. So when Ofelia is cornered by Vidal at gunpoint in the labyrinth, the audience not only expects, but longs for the escape of fantasy. But that longing is denied. The Faun simply vanishes. Ofelia is shot, falls, and lies dying, and the audience is given no relief, no Apollonian veil to shield them from the Dionysian void. The final glimmer of hope, when Ofelia sees herself in the otherworldly throne room, is snatched away as well. Rather than closing with this happy ending, del Toro cuts back to Ofelia's final breath.

In this way, del Toro has appropriated the motifs of fantasy to a function quite opposite of escapism. Where traditional fantasy tends toward an Apollonian ideal, a vision of a beautiful other to hide the ugliness of our existence, del Toro uses fantasy not simply to hold up a mirror to reality, as he has stated,[14] but to magnify and focus the horrors in the audience's mind. Without the fantasy, *Pan's Labyrinth* would have been a disturbing—perhaps unbearable—story of powerlessness before evil, but it would not confront the audience so starkly if it did not provide us a vision of escape denied. It is the audience's very expectation of escapism that gives this denial its power and redemptive quality. As Nietzsche's asserts, "to make the drama as vivid as possible—it would certainly be necessary to add a very important qualification: at the most essential point this Apollonian illusion is broken and annihilated.... Tragedy closes with a sound which could never come from the realm of Apollonian art."[15] The power of tragedy comes not from the experience of beauty alone, but in the revelation of the ugliness upon which beauty is founded.

It is also notable that Ofelia refuses the Faun's demand of an innocent sacrifice, for even a drop of blood. The motif of child sacrifice is one with deep roots, both in Greek drama (Iphigenia, Polyxena), and in the Bible (Isaac in Genesis 22:1–18, Jephthah's daughter in Judges 11:30–39). In her refusal, Ofelia embodies the Nietzschean tragic hero, violating the cosmic order in the name of right. She is, in del Toro's words, "a girl that needs to disobey anything but her own conscience."[16] She rejects the promise of a Euripidean, *deus ex machina* ending because it is wrong, and instead she faces the void defiantly. Like Prometheus and Oedipus, Ofelia accepts her fate in order to lay the foundation for a greater good: the rescue of her brother, the death of Vidal, and the (temporary) victory of the rebels.

And like these tragic heroes, her very being represents a violation of the order of the universe. Just as, Nietzsche argued, Oedipus' "excessive wisdom" and Prometheus' "titanic love of man" are the very qualities that position them to transgress the Apollonian order,[17] just so Ofelia, the defiant changeling child of another world, is positioned to stand at the threshold between the real and fantastic.

Ofelia's refusal to sacrifice her brother, despite her promise to obey the Faun without question, also betrays a very Nietzschean critique of religion. Ofelia is an anti–Abraham, rejecting Judeo-Christian notions of unquestioning faith, eternal reward, and especially substitutionary atonement. She rejects the offer of eternal life in exchange for the innocent blood of another. (Contrast this to the sacrifice of Aslan in *The Chronicles of Narnia*, the film of which del Toro turned down because he "wasn't interested in the lion resurrecting."[18]) Whether or not Ofelia's vision of her return to the other realm is "real" is beside the point. Even if, as the Faun implies, restoration is her reward for refusing to spill her brother's blood, she nevertheless made the choice believing it meant her death. Hers was not an act of faith but an act of conscience. Contrary to T. S. Miller, who argues that rejecting the fairy tale ending "forces the viewer to come close to rejecting narrative itself," because there can be no victory if Ofelia does not survive,[19] reading the film's conclusion on Nietzschean terms makes the victory all the greater, because she triumphs over both fear of the primal chaos, and over the Apollonian illusion.

Individuation and Immortality

To Nietzsche, "the hero is the suffering Dionysus of the Mysteries, the god experiencing in himself the agonies of individuation."[20] This struggle with individual identity can also be seen in *Pan's Labyrinth*, which, according to del Toro's commentary, "was not about a girl dying, but a girl giving birth to herself the way she wanted to be."[21] This, he explains, was the meaning of the reverse shot of Ofelia's blood flowing back into her that opens the film. Elsewhere, he repeats this sentiment: "*Pan's Labyrinth* is a movie about a girl who gives birth to herself into the world she believes in. At that moment, it doesn't matter if her body lives or dies."²² This conception of immortality was also shaped by del Toro's own experiences with death:

> [I]n my personal life dying is as unimportant as changing my shoes and my socks or brushing my teeth. It's just another thing I have to do. It's part of the laundry list. So at that moment you become somewhat immortal, which means you're immune to death. That is in *Pan's Labyrinth* actually. If people watch it carefully, the precise wording of the Faun's words to the girl is: "You have to pass three tests before the full moon shines in the sky. We have to make sure that your spirit is intact and not become mortal." That's the real purpose of the tests.... She fucks up here and there but—when the real test come, when she is cornered with no other options but to either kill or give her own life— she chooses to put her own life at risk rather than the kid's. That's a real test. That's what makes her immortal.²³

Ofelia's immortality comes not from being transported into another world but from her willingness to paradoxically face the loss of her individual identity in order to be the person she was. This paradox is also evident in the story Ofelia tells her unborn brother, in which great men are so in love with life that they dare not risk death to seek immortality. Like the heroes of archaic myth, the men of Ofelia's story see only the joy of living, and dare not defy that order and look beyond that veil at the truly eternal. They do not recognize that true immortality proceeds from robbing death of its power by embracing it as an inevitability. To be sure, del Toro's conception of immortality may have more in common with Catholic martyrdom than it does with Nietzsche's primordial oneness,²⁴ but it again speaks to the degree to which del Toro and Nietzsche found similar solutions to the seeming pessimism of tragic art.

Nietzsche argued that the Dionysian despair of pure music (he uses the third act of Wagner's *Tristan und Isolde* as an example) would overwhelm the listener were it not tempered with some sort of Apollonian vision.²⁵ In the same way, del Toro uses the visual beauty of *Pan's Labyrinth* (for which it won three Academy Awards) as a sort of a balm against the horrors encountered in both worlds. While the fantasy elements do not ultimately provide an escape, their sheer beauty makes the horrors of the film more endurable. Del Toro has said, "If [audiences] are enraged by the bleak hopelessness, or they are enthralled by the beauty and the poetry and the hope in the film, it's equal to me."²⁶ So where Nietzsche believed only the fusion of music and epic in the form of tragedy could provide the healing "metaphysical comfort" necessary to overcome pessimism (for *Birth of Tragedy* is, ultimately, an argument about opera), del Toro offers a recipe of his own, in which the Dionysian element comes not from music, but from horror and violence—both human and supernatural—and the Apollonian from his exquisite vision of the fantastic.

For del Toro, as for Nietzsche, the experience of tragedy is intended to be a source of comfort and consolation, not horror and anguish. This comfort does not come from the escapist eucatastrophe of traditional fantasy, in which the protagonist triumphs over the forces of chaos and lives happily ever after. Tragedy instead confronts the audience with the suffering of individual existence, but does so through a framework of moving beauty, and brings the audience to recognize that there is more to life than individual survival. By manipulating audience expectations of fantastic escapism, and shielding the viewer with a glimpse of the beautiful, del Toro is able to force the real, deadly horrors of the world into a sharper focus than they could be otherwise. Where the audience would normally look away, they are compelled by Apollonian hope and beauty to stare into the darkest night.

Apollo and Dionysus in the Labyrinth

Given these affinities between Nietzsche's conception of tragedy and the use of fantasy in *Pan's Labyrinth*, it is tempting to map Nietzsche's two spirits onto the films two narrative threads. As we shall see, however, the Apollonian and Dionysian permeate both the real and fantastic storylines. This is to be expected, as neither of the two forces is meant to be dominant, and it is only when they work in concert that they achieve the tragic effect. But beyond that, by concealing chaos under apparent order, and hope beneath the guise of the wild and untamed, del Toro plays with audience expectations in a fashion that intensifies the tension between the two worlds.

The most obviously (if deceptively) Dionysian symbol is the Faun himself. The earliest Greek choruses (at least according the Nietzsche) were understood to represent wild, goat-like satyrs, whose song introduced the Dionysian to Greek drama. (The very word *tragedy* may derive from the Greek for "goat song.") It was the satyr Silenus, according to myth, who dared to reveal to King Midas the Dionysian truth that the best thing for a human is never to have been born. The Faun identifies himself with "the mountain, the woods, and the earth"—the very primal forces of nature that Nietzsche associated with Dionysus—and the fantastic scenes are composed in curved, natural lines, in stark contrast to the rigid, mechanical visuals of the real world. Nevertheless, the world that the Faun opens up is not the world of Bacchic drunkenness, but that of dreams, the domain of Apollo. It is the golden vision (quite literally, given del Toro's distinctive color palette for that world) that makes the chaos and meaningless suffering tolerable.

If the Faun is not simply a Dionysian figure, then, what are we to make of him? Del Toro described the Faun as "by definition a creature that is both a giver of life and a dangerous, savage creature, so it's sort of an ambivalent character."[27] He is like Silenus, an embodiment of both wisdom and chaos. His labyrinth functions as his gateway between worlds, with its green color palette that stands between the cool colors of the real world and the warm of the fantastic. The Faun thus represents a liminal state, the intersection of the Apollonian and Dionysian. Just as the Attic chorus was for Nietzsche the synthesis of the mythic drama and the musical frenzy, the Faun is the synthesis of the fantasy and the real. And like the chorus, he narrates the events and judges their outcome.

The mountain-dwelling rebels form a sort of chorus as well, assembling at the film's conclusion to witness and pass judgment on Vidal. They too are associated with nature, living outside the bounds of civilization, and the coloring of their scenes comes closest to that used for the otherworld. Yet they symbolize an Apollonian hope of their own, representing the same escape for Mercedes that the otherworld offers to for Ofelia. But their victory is an illusion, the audience knows, that will be torn away by the course of history just as Ofelia's hope was torn from her by Vidal's bullet.

The person of Vidal presents a similar puzzle to the Faun, as Fascism at least perceives itself in Apollonian terms, as a source of order, structure, and beauty. (It is no coincidence that the swastika began as a symbol of the sun.) The symbols of clockwork surround him, but it is a broken watch, an order out of order. In one of the paradoxes of Fascist mythology, he is the heroic individual, the pseudo-superman, fighting to subsume the individual to the state. And yet it is his world, the world of war and torture, that fulfills the Dionysian function in the film. Del Toro identifies him with the Big Bad Wolf, the archetypical chaos-monster whose defeat marks the victory in conventional fairy tales, but this monster is disguised not in grandmother's clothes, but in the fastidious order of Fascism.

It is perhaps in terms of function, then, that we can best understand how the dialectic of Apollonian and Dionysian plays out in *Pan's Labyrinth*. For while the fantastic elements of the film contain many of the thematic features of the Dionysian, within the narrative, they function as an Apollonian ideal. The tragic power of the film, the reconciliation of Apollo and Dionysus, comes when the veil of Apollo is lifted, when any hope of escape is denied. Del Toro's use of the Apollonian and Dionysian can be seen as a cunning inversion: he disguises the beauty of Apollo in moss, soil, and insects, in the curves of the natural world, while at the same time clothes chaos and violence in the elegant, clockwork trappings of Fascism. Here again he manipulates audience expectations, leaving them unprepared for the real ugliness hidden behind the handsome façade of Vidal, or the beauty that the shaggy Faun would unveil.

Del Toro's Redemptive Tragedy

There is no reason to believe del Toro has any great familiarity with Nietzsche. While an aphorism from *Beyond Good and Evil* was used in the marketing of *Pacific Rim*, del Toro has not spoken of Nietzsche as an influence on his work. Given the (mostly unfair) association between Nietzsche's thought and Fascism, the two would seem strange bedfellows. And, indeed, the divergences between *Pan's Labyrinth* and *Birth of Tragedy* include some of the matters most central to Nietzsche's case. (Notably, music plays little role in the film beyond the lullaby *leitmotif*.) I am not arguing, however, for any direct dependence upon Nietzsche on del Toro's part. Rather, I contend that del Toro is participating in the same struggle against nihilism and pessimism in the face of chaos that Nietzsche projected onto the Attic tragedians, and that he has found another set of tools for reconciling the forces of order and chaos in human existence.

Del Toro's insight into the tragic can be traced, not to Nietzsche's influence, but to his own life experiences. We need look no further than his self-described "fucked up childhood" in order to understand how he came to reinvent the classical struggle between Apollo and Dionysus.[28] Del Toro has confessed a certain autobiographical element in *Pan's Labyrinth*, telling of a recurring dream of his childhood in which he would see a Faun emerge from behind his grandmother's dresser.[29] Like Ofelia, del Toro turned to the fantastic as a means of contending with the pain of his existence—in his case, the psychological and physical abuse of his zealously Catholic grandmother.[30] He began to create monsters, not as an escape, but as a way of imposing an order on the chaos he witnessed. One particular episode highlights his encounters with the unmitigated meaninglessness of human existence:

> [I]t was a visit to a morgue that really engraved itself on the young del Toro's memory. Near a window, in bright sunlight, he saw a "pile" of aborted foetuses. He rubs his beard; the jovial smile has gone. "What was horrible was the casualness of it. And something snapped—I just knew that, OK, there is no benevolent being overlooking everything."[31]

This incident, among other horrors he was exposed to as a child in violence-plagued Guadalajara, led del Toro to abandon the oppressive Catholicism of his youth and become a "raging atheist."[32] Instead, like Nietzsche's Greeks, he turned to art as a means of contending with a world without order.

The kidnapping of del Toro's father in 1997 provides perhaps the best example from del Toro's life of the redemptive hope that can be found in the confrontation of suffering. He relates how the revelation of his father's—and by extension his own—mortality was in fact liberating: "I highly recommend you save your father's life once. It transforms you, that's all I know. You learn that your father is a man. A vulnerable man."[33] Elsewhere he speaks of the pain of the experience as "a good teacher" and "that pain should not be sought, but, by the same token, it should never be avoided."[34] Like the death of Ofelia, coming to terms with the potential death of his father robbed death of its power by looking at it face-to-face. So while his path was very different, del Toro arrived at much the same conclusion that Nietzsche did.

Del Toro perhaps comes closest to Nietzsche in his desire to articulate his vision in mythic terms. He rejects the Euripidean innovation of naturalistic characterization, arguing that "characters can be types and still have an emotional reality."[35] Instead, he turns to the "very simple and very brutal" conventions of the fairy tale in order to connect directly to the audience at a more primal level.[36] Just as Nietzsche's lyric poet is able to transcend subjectivity and speak from the "I" of primordial unity,[37] del Toro uses these simplified archetypes to give universal import to a story with an otherwise very specific *Sitz im Leben*. It ceases to merely be a story about one little girl in Franco's Spain and allows the audience to participate in a universal struggle with fate, obedience, and identity.

In contrast to the mythopoesis of Tolkien, however, del Toro's new mythology draws from the Dionysian, chthonic aspects of myth and folklore, and recognizes their role in the divergent social functions of the fairy story:

> Even when I was a kid, funny enough, I used to be able to find those fairy tales that felt preachy and pro-establishment, and I hated them. I hated the ones that were about, "Don't go out at night." There are fairy tales that are created to instill fear in children, and there are fairy tales that are created to instill hope and magic in children. I like those. I like the anarchic ones. I like the crazy ones. And, I think that all of them have a huge quotient of darkness because the one thing that alchemy understands, and fairy tale lore understands, is that you need the vile matter for magic to flourish. You need lead to turn it into gold. You need the two things for the process.[38]

Here del Toro acknowledges that the stories that are the source of hope are the darkest and most chaotic. He reconciles this paradox by embracing a dialectic much like Nietzsche's. Just as the Apollonian and Dionysian need each other, tempering one another against their extremes, so too, according to del Toro, is it necessary to delve into darkness, into "vile matter" in order to recognize the light of hope.

Paradoxically, in generating his new mythology, del Toro acknowledges that he must depend upon the very generic conventions that he wishes to subvert. In order for the archetypal characters to have the universal impact he desires, there must be an established symbolic foundation from which to draw. The tragic effect of Ofelia's death depends on the reversal of the audience's shared hope for a traditional, eucatastrophic ending. Del Toro has noted that, even as an atheist or "semi-agnostic,"[39] he is still a Catholic, and the symbols he works with depend—even if only by rejection—upon Mexican Catholicism, and more broadly, upon the European fairy tale tradition.[40]

Del Toro also agrees with Nietzsche's criticism of Socratic rationalism in art. "Reason over emotion is bullshit, absolute bullshit," he remarks in one interview, also noting, "If you're not operating on an instinctive level, you're not an artist."[41] This artistic irrationalism is typical of Nietzsche, for whom "the existence of the world is justified only as an aesthetic phenomenon."[42] To both del Toro and Nietzsche, the pursuit of art is the pursuit of meaning that transcends reason. Del Toro places art on the level of religion as a source of understanding: "When you have the intuition that there is something which is there, but out of the reach of your physical world, art and religion are the only means to get to it."[43] So del Toro, unable to accept the Apollonian veil offered by traditional religion in the face of the Dionysian horrors he had experienced, still recognizes that there is a potential for redemption by embracing the chaos through the beauty of art.

The Birth of Tragedy and *Pan's Labyrinth* are works that seek to harness this redemptive power of the tragic. Both reject the false comfort of happy endings, and instead find a paradoxically healing power in the defiant suffering of the hero. While Nietzsche's problematic categories of the Apollonian and Dionysian cannot be applied uncritically to del Toro's film, *Pan's Labyrinth* nonetheless reflects a dialectical relationship between order and disorder, between hope and despair, and acknowledges that both of these elements are essential for what Nietzsche called the "metaphysical comfort" of art. But in contrast to Nietzsche's idealized conceptions of mythic tragedy and Wagnerian opera, del Toro finds his own path to redemption by both exploiting and inverting the generic conventions of fantasy and fairy tales. He lures the viewers in through a fantastic vision of hope and eerie beauty, only to pull back the beautiful mask and force them to look upon the ugliness of human existence. But this confrontation engenders hope rather than nihilism, because of the shared experience of the hero's defiance and the recognition that life endures beyond physical death.

Pan's Labyrinth is not simply a fantasy; it is a fantasy *about* fantasy. It explores why we fashion fantastic, sometimes terrifying worlds alongside the real one, and does so by drawing on the characteristic motifs of the very traditions it deconstructs. Del Toro goes beyond Nietzsche in not simply exploring tragic art, but in creating tragic art in the process of that exploration. Ofelia thus takes on the role, not just of tragic hero, but also of the tragedian. If the fantasy world is to be understood as her method of interpreting with the horrors of the real world, then the other world can be seen as Ofelia's own attempt to temper Dionysian reality with Apollonian vision. The fantasy scenes therefore do not *remove*—or even minimize—the horror of her experience, but they clothe it in a veil of compelling beauty. Rather than escaping the horror that surrounds her, she transforms it into a form that can be tolerated (by the audience and herself) without pessimism or nihilism. But like the tragedian, she tears away the veil of beauty in the end. She rejects the beautiful lie and looks into the abyss behind it. In the same way, del Toro, the master monster-maker, in his very telling of these stories, positions himself as tragic hero as well, confronting the Dionysian terrors of his own childhood through his Apollonian vision of beauty.

Notes

1. *Birth of Tragedy*, 7.1.
2. BT, 16.2, trans. Kaufmann throughout.
3. BT, 4.3.
4. BT, 7.9.
5. BT, 12.9.
6. T. S. Miller, "The Two Kings and the Two Labyrinths: Escaping Escapism in Henson's *Labyrinth* and del Toro's *Laberinto*," *Extrapolation* 52, no. 1 (2011): 26–28.
7. J. R. R. Tolkien, "On Fairy-Stories," in *The Monsters and the Critics and Other Essays*, Christopher Tolkien, ed. (London: George Allen and Unwin, 1983), 153–154.
8. Salon Staff, "Conversations: Guillermo del Toro," *Salon*, October 13, 2006, http://www.salon.com/2006/10/13/conversations_toro/.
9. Humphrey Carpenter, ed., *The Letters of J.R.R. Tolkien* (Boston: Mariner Books, 2000), #131.
10. BT, 3.2.
11. BT, 3.5.
12. Steve Prokopy, "Capone chats with Guillermo del Toro about PAN'S LABYRINTH, HELLBOY 2, 3993, SILVER and more!!!" *Ain't It Cool News*, 2007, http://www.aintitcool.com/node/31084.
13. Guillermo del Toro, dir., *Pan's Labyrinth*, Blu-ray (Burbank: New Line Home Entertainment, 2007).
14. Sam Adams, "Fantasy films? There's truth in there too," *Los Angeles Times*, December 10, 2007, http://www.latimes.com/entertainment/la-et-fantasy10dec10-story.html.
15. BT, 21.11.
16. Javier Soto, dir., *The Power of Myth* (Bonus Feature), Blu-ray (Burbank: New Line Home Entertainment, 2007).
17. BT, 4.4.
18. Mark Kermode, "'Pain should not be sought—but it should never be avoided,'" *The Guardian*, November 4, 2006, http://www.theguardian.com/film/2006/nov/05/features.review1.

19. Miller, "Two Kings," 39.
20. BT, 10.2.
21. del Toro, *Pan's Labyrinth*.
22. Kermode, "Pain."
23. Michael Guillen, "The Evening Class: PAN'S LABYRINTH (2006)—The Evening Class Interview With Guillermo del Toro," *The Evening Class*, December 14, 2006, http://theeveningclass.blogspot.com/2006/12/pans-labyriththe-evening-class.html.
24. Ibid.
25. BT, 21.4.
26. Rebecca Murray, "Guillermo del Toro Interview—Pan's Labyrinth, Fairy Tales," *About.com Hollywood Movies*, 2006, http://movies.about.com/od/panslabyrinth/a/pansgt122206.htm.
27. del Toro, *Pan's Labyrinth*.
28. Murray, "Interview."
29. Prokopy, "Capone."
30. "BIOGRAPHY: Guillermo del Toro," *Lifetime*, 2014, http://www.lifetimetv.co.uk/biography/biography-guillermo-del-toro.
31. Sanjiv Bhattacharya, "Guillermo del Toro: 'I want to make Slaughterhouse Five with Charlie Kaufman,'" *The Telegraph*, July 10, 2013, http://www.telegraph.co.uk/culture/film/film-news/10162218/Guillermo-del-Toro-I-want-to-make-Slaughterhouse-Five-with-Charlie-Kaufman-.html.
32. Daniel Zalewski, "Show The Monster," *The New Yorker*, February 7, 2011, http://www.newyorker.com/reporting/2011/02/07/110207fa_fact_zalewski. This self-description should be held in tension with del Toro's other identification as an agnostic, and his use of the fantastic in a spiritual sense.
33. Bhattacharya, "Slaughterhouse Five."
34. Kermode, "Pain."
35. Soto, *Power of Myth*.
36. Ibid.
37. BT, 5.
38. Murray, "Interview."
39. Guillermo del Toro, "Big Think Interview with Guillermo del Toro" transcript, http://bigthink.com/videos/big-think-interview-with-guillermo-del-toro.
40. Guillen, "The Evening Class"; Cynthia Fuchs, "A Symbol of Transition: Interview with Guillermo del Toro," *PopMatters*, January 11, 2007, http://www.popmatters.com/feature/a-symbol-of-transition-interview-with-guillermo-del-toro/.
41. Erik Henriksen, "A Few Notes on Guillermo del Toro's Q&A," *Portland Mercury Blogtown*, September 30, 2010, http://www.portlandmercury.com/BlogtownPDX/archives/2010/09/30/a-few-notes-on-guillermo-del-toros-qanda.
42. BT, 5.1.
43. del Toro, *Pan's Labyrinth*.

Bibliography

Adams, Sam. "Fantasy films? There's truth in there too." *Los Angeles Times*. December 10, 2007. http://www.latimes.com/entertainment/la-et-fantasy10dec10-story.html.

Bhattacharya, Sanjiv. "Guillermo del Toro: 'I want to make Slaughterhouse Five with Charlie Kaufman.'" *The Telegraph*. July 10, 2013. http://www.telegraph.co.uk/culture/film/film-news/10162218/Guillermo-del-Toro-I-want-to-make-Slaughterhouse-Five-with-Charlie-Kaufman-.html.

"BIOGRAPHY: Guillermo del Toro." *Lifetime*, 2014. http://www.lifetimetv.co.uk/biography/biography-guillermo-del-toro.

Carpenter, Humphrey, ed. *The Letters of J.R.R. Tolkien*. Boston: Mariner Books, 2000.

Crouse, Richard. "Guillermo del Toro's 'horrible' childhood at the root of his dark movies." *Metro*. January 15, 2013. http://metronews.ca/scene/510875/guillermo-del-toros-horrible-childhood-at-the-root-of-his-dark-movies/.

del Toro, Guillermo, Dir. *Pan's Labyrinth*. Blu-ray. Burbank: New Line Home Entertainment, 2007.

Fuchs, Cynthia. "A Symbol of Transition: Interview with Guillermo del Toro." *PopMatters*. January 11, 2007. http://www.popmatters.com/feature/a-symbol-of-transition-interview-with-guillermo-del-toro/.

Guillen, Michael. "The Evening Class: PAN'S LABYRINTH (2006)—The Evening Class Interview with Guillermo del Toro." *The Evening Class*. December 14, 2006. http://theeveningclass.blogspot.com/2006/12/pans-labyrinththe-evening-class.html.

Henriksen, Erik. "A Few Notes on Guillermo del Toro's Q&A." *Portland Mercury Blogtown*. September 30, 2010. http://www.portlandmercury.com/BlogtownPDX/archives/2010/09/30/a-few-notes-on-guillermo-del-toros-qanda.

Huston, Johnny Ray. "Guillermo del Toro on eggs, ghost sightings, lucid dreaming, Catholicism, the 'supranatural,' uterine imagery and more." *Pixel Vision: SFBG Arts and Culture Blog*. December 29, 2006. http://www.sfbg.com/pixel_vision/2006/12/29/guillermo-del-toro-eggs-ghost-sightings-lucid-dreaming-catholicism-supranatu.

Kermode, Mark. "'Pain should not be sought—but it should never be avoided.'" *The Guardian*. November 4, 2006. http://www.theguardian.com/film/2006/nov/05/features.review1.

Lawrence, Will. "'I try to pour a lot of me into every film.'" *The Telegraph*. November 24, 2006. http://www.telegraph.co.uk/culture/film/3656718/I-try-to-pour-a-lot-of-me-into-every-film.html.

Miller, T. S. "The Two Kings and the Two Labyrinths: Escaping Escapism in Henson's *Labyrinth* and del Toro's *Laberinto*." *Extrapolation* 52, no. 1 (2011): 26–50.

Murray, Rebecca. "Guillermo del Toro Interview—Pan's Labyrinth, Fairy Tales." *About.com Hollywood Movies*, 2006. http://movies.about.com/od/panslabyrinth/a/pansgtl22206.htm.

Nietzsche, Friedrich. *The Birth of Tragedy and The Case of Wagner*. Translated by Walter Kaufmann. New York: Random House, 1967.

Orme, Jennifer. "Narrative Desire and Disobedience in 'Pan's Labyrinth.'" *Marvels & Tales: Journal of Fairy-Tale Studies* 24, no. 2 (2010): 219–234.

Prokopy, Steve. "Capone chats with Guillermo del Toro about PAN'S LABYRINTH, HELLBOY 2, 3993, SILVER and more!!!" *Ain't It Cool News*, 2007. http://www.aintitcool.com/node/31084.

Salon Staff. "Conversations: Guillermo del Toro." *Salon*. October 13, 2006. http://www.salon.com/2006/10/13/conversations_toro/.

Soto, Javier. *The Power of Myth*. Blu-ray. Burbank: New Line Home Entertainment, 2007.
Tolkien, J. R. R. "On Fairy-Stories." In *The Monsters and the Critics and Other Essays*, edited by Christopher Tolkien. London: George Allen and Unwin, 1983, 109–161.
Zalewski, Daniel. "Show The Monster." *The New Yorker*. February 7, 2011. http://www.newyorker.com/reporting/2011/02/07/110207fa_fact_zalewski.

Menstruation as Heroine's Journey in *Pan's Labyrinth*[1]

RICHARD LINDSAY

Since the 1949 publication of Joseph Campbell's *The Hero with a Thousand Faces*, scholars in fields of psychology, anthropology, and cultural studies have sharply critiqued the "hero's journey" and its concept of the unfolding of human psychological development along a stable mythological story arc. Additionally, since Campbell's death, biographers have struggled over his right-wing political views and possible anti–Semitism, positions that seem inconsistent with his expansive interest in global cultures.[2] The most important critiques leveled against the content of the mythology itself focus on the male-centeredness of the hero's journey, its immersion in discredited psychoanalytical theories of gender, and the imposition of a meta-narrative on the distinct and detailed mythologies of the world. Postmodern suspicion of overarching narrative structures would seemingly have driven the final nail in the coffin of Campbell's Monomyth. As one student in a recent film seminar I attended stated, with a doctrinal certainty typical of the ostensibly non-dogmatic field of cultural studies, "But we just know that Campbell is not *true*."

"True" or not, there is perhaps no modernist convention in film studies that has been more durable in defiance of postmodern academic wisdom than the hero's journey. In part because of the popularizing of Campbell's scholarship through the 1988 PBS television series, *Joseph Campbell and the Power of Myth*, and its purported influence on *Star Wars* creator George Lucas, the mythology continues to be essential to constructing and interpreting North American and Western European film narratives. Particularly in film, the mythology plays itself out again and again in darkened movie theaters, especially in blockbuster franchises like

Spider-Man, The Lord of the Rings, Pirates of the Caribbean, and Harry Potter. This essay and analysis does not present the hero's journey as the key to all mythologies, but as an observable phenomenon in story, myth, and popular culture, one that must be understood by serious students of Western cinema. To say the hero's journey is not at the heart of every mythology is not to say it doesn't exist; just as to acknowledge Campbell's reactionary politics is not to eliminate a lifetime of influential scholarship. Most important to this essay will be analyzing possible meanings behind the subtle but significant departures taken from the structure of the hero's journey in *Pan's Labyrinth* (2006) as written, directed, and visually conceived by Guillermo del Toro.

"A fallopian palette of colours"

The most notable shift from the typical narrative of a hero's journey in *Pan's Labyrinth* is that the film is written from the perspective of a girl. Hero's journeys are often tales of initiation, the death of the child and birth of the adult. But this form of initiation, whether in rituals of ancient cultures or modern adventure stories, is frequently practiced in the socialization of male children, where the threshold between childhood and adulthood is not as easily divided. In the lives of most females, however, there is a distinct and naturally regulated moment when a girl becomes a woman, at the beginning of menstruation.

On viewing *Pan's Labyrinth*, one is struck by the repeated symbolism of the Faun's head, echoing the goat-like visage of Pan, with its triangular face and curling horns. The Faun's head appears in the form of a fig tree into which the heroine crawls, on the headboard of the bed where her mother sleeps, and in numerous architectural elements in the film. The Faun's head mimics the appearance of a uterus, fallopian tubes, and ovaries. In addition to the uterine symbolism, the film also repeatedly presents instances of bloodletting, through the troubled pregnancy of the protagonist Ofelia's mother, and culminating in the bleeding and dying adolescent Ofelia at the end of the film. The recurrence of the uterine/bloodletting symbolism leads to speculation that the story may be representing some other drama, something that may be taking place almost unconsciously in the life of the young protagonist. *Pan's Labyrinth* is a hero's journey told as a young girl's fairy tale, with the historical drama playing out around her paralleling her own drama of reaching sexual and spiritual maturity.

In a *Guardian*/National Film Theater interview in London in November 2006, del Toro confirms much of this analysis of the film:

> **Mark Kermode:** Obviously watching *Pan's Labyrinth*, there are Jungian archetypes in it, and there's definitely uterine imagery. I'm assuming that's not just me being crass.
> **Del Toro:** No. I very deliberately designed the idea of the fantasy world to be extremely uterine. We used a fallopian palette of colours: we used crimsons and golds, and everything in the fantasy world is very rounded while everything in the real world is cold and straight. You can see it in the not-so-subtle entrance to the tree. When we did the poster for the movie for Cannes, somebody said they wanted to call the movie A Womb with a View.[3]

Understanding del Toro's film also calls for examination of his creative process. He has a strong sense of film as a visual medium, and carefully crafts the visual details and symbols in his movies. This is becomes apparent in the recent publication of del Toro's notebooks.[4] Here we see the stirring images and characters of *Pan's Labyrinth* sketched in detailed drawings in the midst of pages of scrawled notes in Spanish, English, and the occasional Latin (revealing del Toro's Catholic heritage). There can be no doubt, therefore, that the visual symbolism of his films is a carefully chosen, not accidental, element.

Pan's Labyrinth and "Folk Perception"

Reading *Pan's Labyrinth* requires a similar kind of folk reading as Norman Iles attempts in his book, *Who Really Killed Cock Robin?* Taking an approach almost opposite from Joseph Campbell's wide-ranging and intensive academic survey of world mythology, Iles attempts to reconstruct the true meaning of European nursery rhymes using only the varying versions of the texts as supplied by the *Oxford Dictionary of Nursery Rhymes*.[5] His hunch is that most nursery rhymes actually deal with very adult themes having to do with life, death, and sex. As he says of the nursery rhyme "Jack and Jill," "Let us not forget that this pair did *not* go up the hill to fetch a pail of water."[6] According to Iles, most of these tales have been bowdlerized, rendering them nonsense rhymes that have no real meaning for children *or* adults.[7] His project requires that readers try to restore the rhymes' internal logic, and therefore, their wisdom. As he states:

> The knowledge we want is folk-knowledge. All the slang, jokes, rugby songs, writing on bathroom walls ... pub signs, patterns; the art in folk museums, the carvings in old churches. All these are from the same folk culture and relate to the same songs and carols. Books on them may, or may not, be enlightening. What you ought to know you may have to find out for yourself.[8]

Because *Pan's Labyrinth* is a fairy tale, there is a sense in which no analysis based solely on the surface story of the film will do. My folk perception is that in addition to the historical drama playing out on the screen, the movie is about the uterine and menstrual drama experienced by adolescent girls. The reading is a "viewer's hunch," something implicitly understood, not something that is overtly stated in the film. In working on the level of mythos, *Pan's Labyrinth* conjures up a pre-modern humanity that works by its own organically unfolding logic. In initiation myths, there is always a surface story that is adventurous and fantastical combined with a subtext—the real purpose of the story—that deals with the more mundane, but nonetheless vital dramas of everyday life.

The dramas of everyday life are essential to the structure of the hero's journey, because, as Campbell states, the hero emerges out of the quotidian:

> The mythological hero, setting forth from his common-day hut or castle, is lured, carried away, or voluntarily proceeds, to the threshold of adventure. There he encounters a shadow presence that guards the passage.... Beyond the threshold, then, the hero journeys through a world of unfamiliar yet strangely intimate forces, some of which severely threaten him (tests) some of which give magical aid (helpers).[9]

In *Pan's Labyrinth* the heroine Ofelia is an 11-year-old girl who still immerses herself in storybooks and fairy tales. As a dreamer on the border between childhood and adulthood, she is particularly susceptible to instruction from mythical beings. Alienated and lonely, she is the daughter of a widow who has remarried a Fascist captain after Ofelia's father was killed in the Spanish civil war. Her mother is pregnant with the captain's child, and she has taken Ofelia to join her stepfather at a rural outpost where he has been sent to suppress the last vestiges of the Republic carrying out an insurgency in the forests and hills.

A "Sister Movie" to del Toro's *Devil's Backbone*

In choosing a female heroine, del Toro takes an important departure from the traditional hero's journey mythology. Throughout history, men have created stories of heroes, knights, and warriors who commit and survive acts of bloodletting as a means of attempting to create worlds in the same way women create worlds through the natural processes of their bodies.[10] According to Judith Ann Johnson, menstruation has traditionally represented a "taboo" in the truest sense of the term, in that it is both sacred and impure. As Johnson writes, "As much as a woman is capable of giving life, she is on the border of life and nonlife, and she should, therefore [according to patriarchal religions] be kept away from the sacred."[11] The tradition of blood sacrifice used in religion, including the Christian cycle of crucifixion and resurrection, comes in part from the attempt of men to create a "pure" that is, non-female, form of bloodletting that has the same power over life and death as the bloodletting of menstruation and birthing.[12] And even beyond the need for a masculine form of spiritual re-creation, the male line must be cleansed from the "evil" of intercourse with and birth through a woman.[13] The hero's journey thus represents the blood sacrifice of the male warrior, a descent into death, and a resurrection into semi-divinity without the spiritually "tainted" blood of a woman.[14] In appropriating the hero's journey as a metaphor for female menstruation, therefore, del Toro transgresses the patriarchal cycle of womanless regeneration. In this way, although the film follows closely to and in some ways reaffirms the hero's journey as outlined by Campbell, it may also be read as a feminist critique of this mythology.

Ofelia is, in Campbell's words, "lured to the edge of adventure," when she follows a fairy disguised as an insect to the edge of her stepfather's compound. The fairy leads her into an ancient and overgrown labyrinth, and down a set of stairs into a deep well in the ground. Campbell calls this place where the hero meets adventure "the threshold."[15] At the bottom of the well, she meets her "shadow figure," Pan. (He actually introduces himself as "The Faun.") The Faun is a satyr, the goat-man, a Greek god of revelry and fertility that was associated with the rustic countryside. The most famous satyr was Pan, son of Hermes.[16] According to Paul Grootkerk, the Roman name for Pan was "Faunus," "derived from the Latin *fari* meaning 'the speaker,' since the god could reveal the future through dreams."[17] (This is an ability Ofelia is to find in her friend Pan.) Being creatures of fertility, satyrs were often portrayed in Greek art and literature with massive erections.[18] It is not surprising then that in a tradition as suspicious of sexuality as Christianity, such graphic representations of pagan sexuality would become associated with the demonic. In fact, the common horned, hoofed creature associated with the Christian Satan is a derivative of the Faun.[19] During the Renaissance, the more pastoral form of the Faun came back to the fore, as poets and artists celebrated Pan as a figure of music, storytelling, and love.[20]

Although the perception of this magical creature in mythology varies, there is a charged sexual symbolism of a young girl on the verge of adolescence encountering a creature with Pan's fertile history. In a discussion with Ofelia after the girl discloses meeting the Faun ("He smelled like earth," she says, with a slight smile) the adult woman character Mercedes says, "My mother told me never to trust Fauns." Good advice. And yet the Faun is the mythological figure with whom Ofelia must spar in order to achieve spiritual and physical maturity. Read this way, the implied menstrual meaning of the film sprouts from the earth like the mossy form of Pan, who represents fertility and chaos, self-fulfillment and self-denial. He is not to be trusted, and to be trusted implicitly.

The Faun tells Ofelia she is a princess of an underground kingdom, born of the moon. Ofelia resists this story of origin at first, saying she was born of her mother and a tailor. This reflects another part of the hero myth Campbell mentions, the "refusal of the Call."[21] But the Faun has no time for this and dismisses her objection. She is given a book, which she is told will show her future. The Faun tells her she must complete three tasks by the full moon to see if she is worthy of ruling the underground kingdom. As he reveals later, her completion of the task is also essential to the survival of this underground kingdom and its mythological inhabitants.

Ofelia's battle to save the underground kingdom is a parallel battle to the fight against Fascism taking place around her. The fact that she is female is essential to her mythological resistance of the Fascist system.

Comparing *Pan's Labyrinth* to his earlier film, *Devil's Backbone*, del Toro states in The National Film Institute interview:

> I had to make a movie that structurally echoed *Devil's Backbone*, and that you could watch back to back. *Devil's Backbone* is the boy's movie. It's the brother movie. But *Pan's Labyrinth* is the sister movie, the female energy to that other one. I wanted to make it because Fascism is definitely a male concern and a boy's game, so I wanted to oppose that with an 11-year-old girl's universe.[22]

Margrit Shlidrick discusses feminine associations with monster figures like the Faun as part of the "othering" that takes place in the western binary between male and female.

> In light of the longstanding association of the feminine with disorder, in terms both of the rational mind and the leaky body … the conflation of women and monsters should come as no surprise. For all our cultural and technological sophistication, we have inherited, in western countries, an ideological burden that explicitly associates women with danger, particularly in the spheres of sexuality and maternity.[23]

Rather than resisting or redefining the male/female binary as might take place in contemporary forms of feminism and queer studies, del Toro has proposed the monstrous possibilities of "feminine" "dis-order" and associations with nature as qualities to be embraced and preserved. In del Toro's conception, the idea of Fascist Spain is a representation of the worst of the masculine principle—cold, mechanical, and unfeeling—that must be resisted. Ofelia's world of the Faun, and symbols like the moon and the labyrinth represent a wilder, less controlled, and ultimately more humane and feminine principle.

The embodiment of cold, Fascist masculinity is Ofelia's stepfather, himself a kind of monster—a ruthless military man of unspeakable cruelty who tortures and shoots victims at whim. In his daily life, he is stickler for detail, regulating the world with a pocket watch, carefully shaving and grooming himself, and upbraiding his servants for slightly burning the coffee. The precise, mechanistic symbolism of his character is maintained in the placement of his headquarters in an old mill, with the giant wooden gears of the mill's wheel looming behind him in his office, framing him as he sits at his desk.

Ofelia's stepfather is what Campbell calls the "tyrant-monster," the "hoarder of the general benefit" that is the true adversary of the hero/heroine.[24]

Menstruation as Heroine's Journey (Lindsay)

The inflated ego of the tyrant is a curse to himself and his world.... Self-terrorized, fear-haunted, alert at every hand to meet and battle back the anticipated aggressions of his environment, which are primarily reflections of the uncontrollable impulses to acquisition within himself, the giant of self-achieved independence is the world's messenger of disaster, even though, in his mind, he may entertain himself with humane intentions. Wherever he sets his hand there is ... a cry for the redeeming hero, the carrier of the shining blade, whose blow, whose touch, whose existence, will liberate the land.[25]

The Moon vs. the Mechanical

Set against mechanical, and in del Toro's view, masculine, symbols of the tyrant, is the important feminine symbol of the moon. As a marker of months, tides, and seasons, and associated with the menstrual process of women, the natural, feminine time keeping device of the moon as it is used as a symbol in the film stands in direct contrast to the mechanical male time-keeping device of Ofelia's stepfather's watch. (The words

"A womb with a view." Just one example of the repeated uterine symbolism in *Pan's Labyrinth*.

"moon," "month," and "menstruation" share the common Latin root *mensis*.)[26] In addition to harkening back to Ofelia's mythical lunar mother, the moon acts as a tension-building device in the film.

As an example, the day after Ofelia is given her initial task from the Faun, she prepares to take a bath. The light in the room is natural, emanating from three non-symmetrical, moon-like windows above the bathtub. Here Ofelia sits and runs her hands over the previously empty book that Pan gave her, causing white pages to dissolve into an intricately-illustrated instruction of her first task. Once her first task is completed, she returns to the bathroom, and the scene is cropped to show only two moons looming behind her, suggesting the second task is at hand. This two-moon symbolism is paralleled in a scene where Mercedes, who is actually a spy for the Republicans, walks to the edge of the woods to signal the guerrilla fighters using a tin lamp with two asymmetrical holes cut in it. Even Ofelia's stepfather has the lunar imagery imposed on his body, as he wears a pair of round sunglasses that reflect light in a parallel of the two-moon symbolism. As Ofelia moves on to her final task, which must be completed by the full moon deadline imposed by Pan, the viewer waits for the final, singular moon that signals the completion of Ofelia's trial. The single moon appears, ironically, as Ofelia lays dying on the edge of the labyrinth at the end of the film. As her blood drips into the deep well at the center of the labyrinth, the full moon reflects in the blood that has collected at the bottom. When the camera pulls back to show Mercedes weeping over the dying Ofelia, the moon shines in its tragic fullness in the upper left hand of the night sky.

Although Ofelia is very close to her mother, she is closer in character to Mercedes. Ofelia and Mercedes represent adult and child versions of the same struggle: Mercedes is carrying out the adult struggle of resisting Fascism and Ofelia is carrying out the child's struggle of preserving the world of the Faun and the underground kingdom. There are clear parallels in the actions of the two characters. For example, in order to enter a vault for her second task, Ofelia must create a magic door using a piece of chalk. Likewise, Mercedes is shown in the kitchen of the house clearing away dirt from a floor stone to reveal a secret vault in which she hides supplies and messages for the resistance fighters. As mentioned before, Mercedes signals the guerrilla fighters with the two moons of her lantern as Ofelia is preparing to undertake her second task under the two moons in the bathroom. Ofelia must also use a golden key in the second task that she retrieves in the first task, just as Mercedes gives a copy of a key to her guerrilla brother, which opens a storehouse of supplies on the grounds of the mill. The juxtaposition of these symbols suggests that Mercedes and Ofelia are fighting the same fight, one of liberation from the tyranny of masculine symbols imposing themselves on feminine symbols of a more natural, spiritual, and humane existence. The two characters may even be seen as alter egos.

The First Test: The Golden Key

Having met her shadow figure and crossed the threshold of adventure, Ofelia begins her "tests," these "unfamiliar yet strangely intimate forces" that she must face and overcome along her journey.[27] Her first trial involves finding a golden key, which she must extract from the belly of a frog by getting him to eat three stones. Led by the magically appearing instructions in the book the Faun has given her, Ofelia finds the frog inside an old, dead fig tree that echoes the uterine imagery of Pan's head,

Three-moon imagery at the start of Ofelia's journey.

the "womb with a view" that del Toro mentioned. Ofelia crawls through the base of the tree and through the mud and muck below it, and finds herself covered with squirming bugs. When she meets the frog, he sits fat and impassive, shooting his slimy tongue out and devouring bugs off her body. She gets the frog to eat the stones by getting him to shoot his tongue out at a bug disguised among the stones in her hand. The frog begins to vomit, and eventually a giant yellow ball of slime emerges from his mouth as his body deflates and collapses into the ground. In the ball of slime, Ofelia finds the key.

Continuing the parallels between Ofelia's struggle and the fight against Fascism, the frog scene is juxtaposed with the servants in Ofelia's stepfather's household complaining about the cruel perfectionism of the captain as they prepare a feast for him, his family, and supporters. The frog represents Ofelia's stepfather, feasting in luxury while the country scrapes by on ration coupons. The task is also representative of Ofelia's childlike desire to re-enter the womb of her mother. Ofelia emerges from the womb of the tree, undergoing a tentative rebirth, covered with the mud and muck of the earth like the afterbirth of a baby. As del Toro states, "This girl's idea of heaven, ultimately, is to go back into her mother's belly."[28]

But ultimately, returning to the womb is not a possibility for a girl on the verge of adulthood. This resistance to her physical destiny, a second manifestation of the "refusal of the call," leads to disaster. After undergoing her symbolic rebirth through the tree, Ofelia's determination to carry out the tasks is tested. As she consults the Faun's book to try to find out her second task she again finds the book blank. Instead of illustrated instructions of the next task, two red swirls appear on either page of the book. A flow of red begins to trickle down the pages into the center of the book and down the center of the book. The shape formed by the flow of red is the familiar Pan's head/uterus image. Ofelia is horrified when the red liquid shape begins to spill and flow out of its uterine parameters and cover the blank pages in bloody pigment. Frightened, Ofelia rushes from the bathroom into the bedroom to find her mother bleeding from the womb and gasping for breath. The bleeding uterus that appears on the book turns out to be an omen of ill will, acting as foreshadowing of Ofelia's mother's troubled pregnancy and death. But more important, considering the Faun said the book would tell Ofelia *her* future, it represents Ofelia's coming menstruation and adulthood. At one point, faced with the reality of her emerging fertility, Ofelia even denies her body's potential for reproduction. Mercedes explains to Ofelia after she witnesses her mother's bleeding and sickness, "Having a baby is complicated." Ofelia responds, "Then I'll never have one." As in life, however, Ofelia will have no choice but to take on the burden of maturity and loss of innocence, a process that is central to the next task.

Campbell uses a mythological description particularly suitable to Ofelia's situation:

> Refusal of the summons converts the adventure into its negative. Walled in by boredom, hard, work, or "culture," the subject loses the power of significant affirmative action and becomes a victim to be saved. Like King Minos ... whatever house he builds, it will be a house of death: a labyrinth of cyclopean walls to hide him from his Minotaur.... One is harassed both day and night, by the divine being that is the image of the living self within the locked labyrinth of one's own disoriented psyche.[29]

The Mandrake and the Second, Failed Test of Purity

Ofelia is delayed in her second task by her concern for her mother, and in order to move her along, the Faun appears again to motivate her. He gives Ofelia a mandrake root, which he refers to as "a plant that dreamt of being human." Ofelia is instructed to put the mandrake in a bowl of milk and place it under her mother's bed, feeding it with two drops of blood. This will help her mother to get well, and will allow Ofelia to get on with the tasks. When she places the mandrake in the bowl and drips some blood from her finger over it, it squirms and cries like a grotesque infant. In a way, Ofelia has become a mother through the expenditure of her own blood, presaging her mother's letting of blood, and self-sacrifice, in the birthing of Ofelia's brother.

The mandrake represents the legend of the "Mandragora." As recounted by Carol Rose, "Like the appearance of the roots, the spirit of the mandrake is described as resembling a youthful, naked male or female human.... The plant was used from earliest times for its alleged fertility and curative powers."[30] The root is a symbol of the dual association of birth and death, as a mandrake's scream is supposed to produce death in the hearer.[31]

Another folklore reference suggests darkly that the mandrake is "said to germinate from the spilled semen of hanged felons."[32] With the legend of the mandrake, there is a strong association with Original Sin—with the powers of creation usurped from the Divine, and the tragic consequences of this false appropriation.

Once Ofelia figures out the second task, the viewer can sense it has a strong association of sexuality in the context of the Christian doctrine of Original Sin. The instructions in the magical book include a drawing of a skeletal "Pale Man" Ofelia will meet in the chamber she enters during the task, and the illustration shows a girl opening the small door with a key that is placed provocatively between his arched legs. Invoking the biblical forbidden fruit, Pan's instructions to her include an admonishment that she will see tantalizing food in the chamber, and that her life depends on not eating it.

After entering and being led through the chamber by three fairies given to her as helpers by Pan, Ofelia finds the Pale Man to be grotesque and bulbous, with flaps of skin flowing over his emaciated body, a hideous adult manifestation of the infant mandrake root. He is seated at a table laden with sumptuous, but strangely bloody-looking food and drink. Painted on the ceiling of the room are ancient frescoes of the Pale Man impaling and eating small children. The Pale Man is surrounded by hundreds of old leather children's shoes, piled in a corner of the room, with an arched furnace-like fireplace flaming in the background. Here del Toro borrows imagery from the Holocaust to magnify the feeling of the impending death of innocents (and innocence).

Ofelia uses her golden key from the first task to retrieve a shining dagger from one of three small doors placed in the wall behind the Pale Man. As she is leaving, however, she finds herself tempted by the food sitting on the table. In a moment of sensual bliss, she lifts a large, sugar-encrusted grape to her lips, swatting the fairies away as they try to stop her. As she eats the fruit, the pale man comes to life, places his eyes in his hands and glares at her with his palms. He begins chasing after Ofelia, devouring two of the fairies that have swarmed him to save her life. Ofelia escapes, but only one fairy makes it out alive.

Upon hearing of her misadventure, Pan is livid. He shouts, "You failed! You can never return…. Your spirit shall forever remain among the humans. You shall age like them, you shall die like them, and all memory of you shall fade in time." And, revealing his and all the mythical creatures' interest this struggle, he says, "And we'll vanish along with it." There are echoes of the Fall and expulsion from Eden in her failure and in Pan's reaction. In eating the forbidden fruit, laden with sexual symbolism, Ofelia becomes mortal and subject to being lost to memory. The Pale Man, as an adult version of the mandrake baby, could be seen as the inevitable offspring of all humanity, which in its living automatically brings about dying. As with the disturbing imagery painted in the chamber, death is the monster that eats all human babies eventually, either as children or as adults. If the first task represented Ofelia's avoidance of adulthood by a symbolic re-entry of the womb, the second task represents the inevitability of sexual maturity, lost innocence, and, eventually, death.

As suggested from del Toro's interview, the failure of Ofelia's second task is a necessary part of Ofelia's development as a character: "Frankly, I think that everything we try to deny about our bodies and our lives—about being fallible and mortal, that we're going to rot, and that our armpits smell, that we are imperfect, that we sin and screw up—all these are the things that actually make us human."[33]

Ofelia's fallibility, her sin, has consequences. When Ofelia goes to feed the mandrake again, her stepfather discovers what she has been doing and pulls the now stillborn mandrake baby out from under the bed, sniffing the curdled milk in the bowl and wincing from its sourness (like the human stench del Toro mentions). Her mother follows with her disapproval and throws the mandrake into the fire, where it begins to move again, squirming and screaming hideously. Her mother immediately lurches into labor, and after hours of suffering, the real human baby is born. It is a boy, and Ofelia's mother dies in childbirth. Ofelia is left in the house of her hostile stepfather, alone and bereft, her innocence gone.

The Third Test and the Possibility of Resurrection

This leads to the final stage of the hero's journey, the apotheosis, or breaking open and dissolution of the ego, which is integrated into Ofelia's third and final task.[34] Shortly after Ofelia's mother's death it becomes apparent to Mercedes that the captain has figured out she is a spy for the Republicans, and she realizes she must escape into the woods with the guerrillas. Taking Ofelia with her, the two try to leave the compound, but are captured and taken captive. Ofelia is banished back to her bedroom while Mercedes is taken away, presumably to be tortured into giving information about the guerrillas. Ofelia is about to despair, when suddenly Pan appears in her bedroom. He has decided to give her another chance. In order to survive, Pan and Ofelia must both accept her humanity and fallibility. Her innocence is gone, but the purity of her spirit remains, as will be demonstrated in the last test. Pan tells Ofelia to go get her infant brother and come to the center of the labyrinth.

Ofelia does as instructed, but her stepfather follows her into the labyrinth as she runs with her brother. She gets to the center and finds Pan standing menacingly with the dagger she pulled from the chamber of the Pale Man. Pan instructs her to give him the infant, so that the final task can be completed by spilling "just a drop" of the blood of an innocent, "A pinprick, that's all." (Having committed mortal sin in the chamber of the Pale Man, Ofelia is no longer innocent.) Here Ofelia follows the advice of Mercedes, not trusting the Faun to take "just a drop" of her brother's blood. She refuses to hand him the child. Pan bristles and shouts at her, "You would give up your sacred rights for this brat you barely know? … You would give up your throne for him? He who has caused you such misery, such humiliation?" She answers yes. At this point her stepfather catches up with her and takes the baby. Having retrieved his son, he shoots the now expendable Ofelia.

Ofelia's reaction to being shot by her stepfather is not horror or pain, but more a look of shock and sickness. We do not see the wound; the camera frames her from the chest up. We see her look down, "below," and hold up her hand, which is covered in blood, in a shade of red in considerable contrast to the blue filtered background. At this point, the climax of the film, the music swoons as she watches the blood drip from her hand. The wound she receives is both literal and symbolic. It represents the bloodletting of the bullet wound, but also the inevitable death of all little girls in adolescence, in the bloodletting of menstruation.

Joseph Campbell outlines this stage of the hero's journey: "When he arrives at the nadir of the mythological round, he undergoes a supreme ordeal and gains his reward. The triumph may be represented as the hero's … divinization (apotheosis) … intrinsically, it is an expansion of consciousness (illumination, transfiguration, freedom)."[35]

And indeed, Ofelia does gain a reward. As she bleeds and dies in the real world, in the fantastical world she is brought to the underground kingdom, ruled by her real father and mother and attended by Pan. Ofelia is dressed in a red satin jacket, and takes note of her red sneakers, symbols of both her sacrifice and her menstruating adulthood. The court applauds her loudly, and Pan and her parents welcome her, saying that she has passed the final test, spilling her own blood rather than that of an innocent. Although in the real world she dies, here she is reborn to reign as the princess of the underworld. Demonstrating the unmistakable subtext of Ofelia's fertility in the film, in the last scene, the final image on the screen is the uterus-shaped fig tree, the "womb with a view," which had been barren and void, sprouting a white flower on one of its fallopian tube branches.

As Campbell writes, evoking the book of Jonah, "The idea that the passage of the magical threshold is a transit into the sphere of rebirth is symbolized by the worldwide womb image of the belly of the whale. The hero, instead of conquering or conciliating the power of the threshold, is swallowed into the unknown, and would have appeared to have died."[36] But in Campbell's model, the mythical death is supposed to be followed by a resurrection a "flight" from the "threshold forces," and a return "from the kingdom of dread."[37]

Here, del Toro resists the mythological model, and does not give Ofelia a literal resurrection. In del Toro's world, Ofelia's death must be real. Del Toro explains his aversion to resurrection scenes in the National Film Institute interview. He recounts that he was the first director to be contacted to direct *The Lion, the Witch, and the Wardrobe*. Fitting with del Toro's pattern of almost masochistic denial of lucrative film projects (he also turned down the first two *Harry Potter* films) he said he would only direct the *Narnia* movie if Aslan the lion wasn't resurrected. (Obviously, this wasn't acceptable to the film's Christian backers.) As del Toro says,

> What is the worth of that sacrifice if he knows he's coming back? I really enjoy the uncertainty of a guy or a creature going to die for something without knowing if there's anyone to bail him out. What's beautiful about the death of Jesus is him saying to his father, "Why have you forsaken me?" That incredibly mysterious and moving passage is so precious because he doesn't know. If he knew, screw that.[38]

The only possible reading of *Pan's Labyrinth* where a resurrection of sorts happens is in the life of Ofelia's parallel character Mercedes. With her help, the rebels succeed in destroying the outpost and killing the captain, taking the baby brother and presumably saving him from being raised by a sadistic father. The hero's journey started by the child may be seen to carry on in the figure of Mercedes as an adult woman. In this way, the image of Mercedes kneeling and weeping over the dead Ofelia at the end of the film could be seen as the necessary grief of all adults, weeping for the loss of innocence, as the child disappears to reign as monarch of the "underground" realm of the psyche, to be re-summoned in myths and fairy tales. In many ways, Mercedes is weeping for herself.

Echoing this adult need to contact the fantastic world of the child that reigns within, Campbell writes:

> The first step [to spiritual and psychological wholeness] consists in the radical transfer of emphasis from the external to the internal world, macro- to microcosm, a retreat from the desperations of the waste land to the peace of the everlasting realm that is within.... All the ogres and secret helpers of our nursery are there, all the magic of childhood.... In a word: the first work of the hero is to retreat from the world scene of secondary effects to the causal zones of the psyche where the difficulties really reside.[39]

"Transformed by monsters"

Informed by this understanding of the power of mythology as an exploration of internal conflicts, a suspicion about barely disguised uterine imagery, and del Toro's own words, the symbolism of this strange and fantastic film opens like the blooming flower of the final scene. Del Toro brings this resonance with Campbell's model full circle in a quote posted as part of a review on the British Film Institute website. Quoting a Clive Barker story, he mentions the line "Deep in her, in a place touched only by monsters." He explains, "In my case, I really think that the most creative, most fragile part of the child that lives within me is a child that was literally transformed by monsters. Be they on the screen, or in myth, or in my own imagination."[40]

Notes

1. This essay was originally published in the *Journal of Religion and Film* 16, no. 1 (April 2012), Article 1, http://digitalcommonsunomaha.edu/jrf/vol16/iss1/1.

2. Robert Ellwood addresses these concerns in a careful and balanced assessment of Campbell's political views in *The Politics of Myth: A Study of C.G. Jung, Mircea Eliade, and Joseph Campbell* (Albany: State University of New York Press, 1999).

3. Guillermo del Toro, Mark Kermode, Guardian/National Film Theater Interview, November 21, 2006, http://film.guardian.co.uk/interview/interviewpages/0,,1955212,00.html.

4. Guillermo del Toro and Marc Zicree, *Guillermo del Toro Cabinet of Curiosities: My Notebooks, Collections, and Other Obsessions* (New York: Harper Design, 2013).

5. Norman Iles, *Who Really Killed Cock Robin?* (London: Robert Hale, 1986), 13.

6. Ibid., 51.

7. Ibid., 16–18.

8. Ibid., 14.

9. Joseph Campbell, *The Hero with a Thousand Faces*, commemorative ed. (Princeton: Princeton University Press, 2004), 227.

10. Judith Ann Johnson, "Shedding Blood: The Sanctifying Rite of Heroes," in *Wholly Woman, Holy Blood: A Feminist Critique of Purity and Impurity*, eds. Kristin De Troyer, Judith A. Herbert, Judith Ann Johnson, Anne-Marie Korte (Harrisburg, PA: Trinity Press, 2003), 190.

11. Ibid., 206.

12. Ibid., 190–191.

13. Ibid., 205.

14. Ibid., 203.

15. Campbell, 54.

16. "Faun," Paul Grootkerk, *Mythical and Fabulous Creatures: A Sourcebook and Research Guide*, ed. Malcolm South (Westport, CT: Greenwood Press, 1987), 207–208.

17. Ibid., 208–209.

18. Ibid., 208, 210.

19. Ibid., 211, 212.

20. Ibid., 212–213, 216.

21. Campbell, 54

22. del Toro, Kermode.

23. Margrit Shildrick, *Embodying the Monster: Encounters with the Vulnerable Self* (London: SAGE, 2002), 30.

24. Campbell, 14.

25. Ibid.

26. *Merriam-Webster Online Dictionary*, s.v. "moon," http://www.merriam-webster.com/dictionary/moon.

27. Campbell, 227.

28. del Toro, Kermode.

29. Campbell, 54–55.

30. Carol Rose, *Spirits, Fairies, Gnomes, and Goblins: An Encyclopedia of the Little People* (Santa Barbara: ABC-CLIO, 1996), 210.

31. Ibid.

32. Alison Jones, *Larousse Dictionary of World Folklore* (New York: Larousse, 1995), 217.

33. del Toro, Kermode.

34. Campbell, 138.

35. Ibid., 227.
36. Ibid., 83.
37. Ibid., 228.
38. del Toro, Kermode.
39. Campbell, 16.
40. Mark Kermode, "Girl Interrupted," *Sight and Sound*, December 2006, http://www.bfi.org.uk/sightandsound/feature/49337.

Bibliography

Campbell, Joseph. *The Hero With a Thousand Faces*. Commemorative ed. Princeton: Princeton University Press, 2004.
del Toro, Guillermo, and Mark Kermode. *Guardian/National Film Theater Interview*. November 21, 2006, http://film.guardian.co.uk/interview/interviewpages/0,,1955212,00.html.
Ellwood, Robert. *The Politics of Myth: A Study of C.G. Jung, Mircea Eliade, and Joseph Campbell*. Albany: State University of New York Press, 1999.
Grootkerk, Paul. "Faun," *Mythical and Fabulous Creatures: A Sourcebook and Research Guide*. Malcolm South, ed., 207–208. Westport, CT: Greenwood Press, 1987.
Iles, Norman. *Who Really Killed Cock Robin?* London: Robert Hale, 1986.
Johnson, Judith Ann. "Shedding Blood: The Sanctifying Rite of Heroes." In *Wholly Woman, Holy Blood: A Feminist Critique of Purity and Impurity*. Kristin De Troyer, Judith A. Herbert, Judith Ann Johnson, Anne-Marie Korte, eds., 189–222. Harrisburg, PA: Trinity Press, 2003.
Jones, Alison. *Larousse Dictionary of World Folklore*. New York: Larousse, 1995.
Kermode, Mark. "Girl Interrupted." *Sight and Sound*, December 2006. http://www.bfi.org.uk/sightandsound/feature/49337.
Merriam-Webster Online Dictionary. s.v. "moon." http://www.merriam-webster.com/dictionary/moon.
"Pan's People." *The Guardian*, November 17, 2006. http://film.guardian.co.uk/flash/page/0,,1949730,00.html.
Rose, Carol. *Spirits, Fairies, Gnomes, and Goblins: An Encyclopedia of the Little People*. Santa Barbara: ABC-CLIO, 1996.
Shildrick, Margrit. *Embodying the Monster: Encounters with the Vulnerable Self*. London: SAGE, 2002.

About the Contributors

Jessica **Balanzategui** is pursuing a doctorate at the University of Melbourne, Australia, where she also teaches film and cultural studies. She has published work on the uncanny child, madness, and asylums in the horror film in refereed journals such as *Etropic* and *Refractory: A Journal of Entertainment Media*, and she reviews for *Media International Australia*. She co-edited the special issue of *Refractory* titled "Transmedia Horror."

Karin **Brown** is undertaking a master of philosophy degree at the University of Birmingham, writing on fantasy and politics in contemporary Spanish and Mexican cinema. She is the librarian of the university's Shakespeare Institute. For the University of Warwick she wrote 22 performance histories for the Royal Shakespeare Company *Complete Works* project. These were published by Palgrave Macmillan, 2008–2011.

Jack **Collins** holds a Ph.D. in religious studies from the University of Virginia. While his specialty is ancient apocalyptic literature, he has written on topics as varied as demonology in science fiction and castration in early Christianity. He is working on his first book, *Worthless Mysteries: The Secret Teachings of the Fallen Angels*. His blog, also called Worthless Mysteries (www.worthless mysteries.com), features commentary on biblical studies, academia, and religion in popular culture.

Ann **Davies** is the chair of Spanish and Latin American studies at the University of Stirling, Scotland. She is the author of *Spanish Spaces: Landscape, Space and Place in Contemporary Spanish Culture* (2012), editor of *Spain on Screen: Developments in Contemporary Spanish Cinema* (2012) and *Penélope Cruz* (2014), and co-editor (with Deborah Shaw and Dolores Tierney) of *The Transnational Fantasies of Guillermo del Toro* (2014).

Gabriel **Eljaiek-Rodríguez** is a visiting assistant professor at Lawrence University. He received a Ph.D. in Hispanic American literature from Emory University. His areas of specialization include Latin American Gothic cinema and literature fantastic literature, and museum and cultural studies. He has published in journals such as *Hispanic Research Journal*, *Imagofágia*, *Intinerarios*, *Mandorla* and *La Habana elegante*, as well in the edited volume *Horrorfílmico* (2012).

About the Contributors

S. T. **Joshi** is the author of *The Weird Tale* (1990), *The Modern Weird Tale* (2001), *Unutterable Horror: A History of Supernatural Fiction* (2012), and the award-winning *I Am Providence*, on H.P. Lovecraft (2010). He has prepared annotated editions of works by H. P. Lovecraft, Arthur Machen, Lord Dunsany, Ambrose Bierce and Clark Ashton Smith. A two-time winner of the World Fantasy Award, he has also won the Bram Stoker and British Fantasy awards, among others.

Richard **Lindsay** has a master of divinity degree from Yale University and a Ph.D. in art and religion from the Graduate Theological Union in Berkeley, California. He is a scholar and teacher, focusing on religion and film, media and cultural studies, and sexuality and gender. His book, *Hollywood Biblical Epics: Camp Spectacle and Queer Style from the Silent Era to the Modern Day*, will be published in 2015. He is co-editor of the blog PopTheology.com.

John W. **Morehead** is a scholar working in the area of religion and popular culture. He has contributed to the *Journal of the Fantastic in the Arts*, *Extrapolation*, *Cultural Encounters*, and *The Australian and New Zealand Theological Review*. He has also co-edited and contributed to various books, including *Halos and Avatars* (2010), *Handbook of Hyper-Real Religions* (2012), *The Undead and Theology* (2012), and *Joss Whedon and Religion* (2013). He also writes for TheoFantastique.com and Cinefantastique Online.

John Kenneth **Muir** has written more than 25 film and television reference books, including *Terror Television* (1999), *Horror Films of the 1970s* (2002), *The Encyclopedia of Superheroes on Film and Television* (2004), *Horror Films of the 1990s* (2011) and *Horror Films FAQ* (2013). In 2009, his blog Reflections on Film and Television (http://reflectionsonfilmandtelevision.blogspot.com) was named one of the 100 best film study sites on the Internet. The creator of the 2008 and 2009 "best web production" nominee *The House Between*, he is a director of the indie horror anthology *Volumes of Blood* (2015).

Sidney L. **Sondergard**, a professor of English and Asian studies at St. Lawrence University, is the author of *Sharpening Her Pen: Strategies of Rhetorical Violence by Early Modern English Women Writers* and co-author (with Thomas L. Berger and William C. Bradfor) of *An Index of Characters in Early Modern English Drama*. He is co-translator (with Madison V. Sowell) of Giordano Bruno's *The Cabala of Pegasus* and author of an English translation of Pu Songling's *Strange Tales from Liaozhai*. His essays have appeared in *Studies in Philology*, *Critique*, and *The American Journal of Semiotics*.

Alexandra **West** is a freelance entertainment journalist who lives in Toronto. Her work has appeared in the *Toronto Star*, *Rue Morgue*, and *Post City Magazine*, and she is a regular contributor to *Famous Monsters of Filmland* and a columnist for *Diabolique*. She has given lectures at Toronto's Black Museum series on found-footage horror and the films of New French Extremity. She co-founded, with fellow writer Andrea Subissati, the Faculty of Horror podcast, exploring the analytical side of horror and the darkest recesses of academia.

About the Contributors

Kevin J. Wetmore, Jr., has written or edited more than a dozen books and is the author of a dozen short stories. He has written articles about Godzilla, vampires in Shakespeare, exorcism films, Hell Houses, Greek tragedy and the Scream films, children in Hitchcock films, and American adaptation of Japanese horror, among other topics. His books include *Back from the Dead: Remakes of the Romero Zombie Films as Markers of Their Times*, *Post–9/11 Horror in American Cinema*, and *The Theology of Battlestar Galactica*. He is an actor, director, and stage combat choreographer in Los Angeles.

Index

Abbott and Costello Meet Frankenstein 159
Abe Sapien 2, 17
Ackerman, Forrest 116
agnosticism and atheism 11, 13, 24, 175, 176
The Alchemist 26
alchemy 13, 27, 100, 102, 150, 151, 152, 176
Angel of Death 24–25, 37, 44, 104
apocalypse 44, 52
Apollonian and Dionysian forces 163–178
archetype 8, 9, 94, 96, 107, 166, 174, 176
art 2, 3, 8, 30, 33, 48, 60, 72, 90, 93, 94, 95, 96, 97, 112, 115, 116, 118, 119, 127, 149, 163, 164, 165, 166, 167, 169, 171, 175, 176, 177, 185, 187
At the Mountains of Madness 13, 19–20, 22, 35, 107

The Birth of Tragedy 163–164, 166, 172, 174, 177
Blade 115, 126
Blade II 7, 18, 30, 43, 53, 54, 104, 115, 125, 126
The Blessing of Pan 29, 30
Branaugh, Kenneth 115
Bride of Frankenstein 114, 121

Cabinet of Curiosities: My Notebooks, Collections, and Other Obsessions 8, 78, 95
Campbell, Joseph 182, 184, 186, 193, 196, 197
Carrie 24
Chaney, Lon 95
The Charwoman's Shadow 29
children 8, 9, 14, 31, 33, 35, 46, 48, 51, 52, 58, 63, 66, 71, 76–90, 94, 112–127, 131–144, 170, 174, 183, 185, 190, 198
clockwork mechanism 27, 28, 65, 68, 69, 70, 85, 102, 123, 151, 152, 155, 160, 173, 174, 188

Cool Air 25, 26, 28, 38
cosmic horror 23, 25, 36, 38
The Creature from the Black Lagoon 17, 95
Creepshow 154
Crimson Peak 7
Cronos (1993) 1, 7, 13, 24, 25–28, 31, 36, 38, 42, 43, 44, 52–55, 80, 97, 100, 102, 123–124, 126, 146, 150, 155, 156, 159

death 14, 24, 25, 26, 27, 43, 45, 46, 51, 52, 55, 59, 61, 62, 63, 66, 68, 70, 71, 72, 81, 83, 86, 87, 88, 97, 98, 100, 103, 115, 119, 123, 124, 131, 132, 136, 137, 139, 141, 148, 155, 158, 159, 160, 165, 166, 171, 175, 177, 183, 184, 192, 193, 195, 196, 197, 198
De Niro, Robert 115
desacralization 36–38
The Devil's Backbone 7, 9, 14, 30, 31, 35, 42, 43, 44, 44–48, 51, 52, 58–64, 65, 66, 71, 72, 77, 79, 80, 84, 85, 86, 88, 102, 107, 118, 119, 131, 132, 136–139, 140, 186, 188
Don Rodriguez: Chronicles of Shadow Valley 29
Don't Be Afraid of the Dark 7, 9, 77, 79, 89, 126
Dracula 54, 148, 152, 153, 159, 160
The Dreamquest of Unknown Kadath 24
Dunsany, Lord (Edward John Moreton Drax Plunkett) 8, 12, 22–38

The Elephant Man (1980) 125
Erice, Victor 118

fairies 33, 37, 79, 95, 98, 103, 119, 121, 126, 140, 141, 143, 186, 194
fairy tales 32, 34, 35, 44, 49, 51, 68, 69, 79, 85, 87, 119, 140, 141, 142, 167, 174, 176, 177, 184, 185, 198
Famous Monsters of Filmland 116, 118
fantasy 8, 10, 22, 23, 24, 25, 28, 29, 30, 31, 32, 35, 41, 43, 49, 50, 52, 67, 68, 69, 76,

Index

79, 80, 85, 96, 99, 112, 117, 118, 121, 123, 130, 138, 140, 141, 142, 143, 163, 164, 167, 168, 169, 171, 172, 173, 177, 178, 184, 198
fascism 14, 15, 16, 29, 32, 45, 46, 49, 59, 60, 61, 63, 64, 65, 66, 68, 69, 70, 72, 83, 85, 87, 120, 136, 137, 139, 141, 142, 143, 164, 167, 173, 174, 185, 187, 188
Faun 3, 16, 24, 29, 34, 43, 50, 51, 68, 79, 85–86, 96, 98, 140–142, 143, 144, 167, 168, 169, 170, 171, 172–173, 174, 175, 183, 186, 187, 188, 190, 191, 192, 196
feminine 10, 64, 70, 182–198
The Fly 154, 159
Franco, General Francisco 14, 15, 42, 45, 46, 49, 51, 52, 59, 60, 64, 83, 84, 87, 136, 140, 142, 144, 152, 176
Frankenstein 2, 9, 95, 112–127
Freud, Sigmund 65

ghosts 9, 14, 45–48, 58–72, 80–83, 88–89, 102, 131, 136, 137–138
gods 11, 13, 16, 17, 18, 23, 24, 25, 36, 37, 38, 93, 94, 96, 104, 105, 165
Godzilla (1954) 122
grotesquerie 94, 95

Hamlet 58, 65, 68, 69
Hammer Studios 115
Harry Potter 183, 197
The Haunting 67
Hellboy 2, 4, 7, 16, 31, 41, 42, 43, 52, 98, 101, 115, 124, 126
Hellboy II: The Golden Army 2–3, 7, 18, 22, 23, 24, 25, 30, 31, 35–38, 42, 44, 69, 98, 103, 104, 124–125, 126
The Hero with a Thousand Faces 182
hero's journey 182, 183, 184, 185, 195
Hispanic cinema 9, 44
Hitchcock, Alfred 63, 65, 112, 116, 127
The Hobbit 167
Hogan, Chuck 7, 55
horror 9, 12, 18, 22, 23, 24, 25, 26, 28, 34, 35, 36, 38, 41, 45, 47, 48, 52, 55, 63, 71, 76, 77, 78, 79, 89, 90, 93, 103, 106, 112, 116, 117, 119, 124, 127, 131, 138, 140, 149, 150, 153, 154, 155, 159, 160, 167, 168, 169, 171, 172, 175, 177, 178, 196
hybridity 17, 44, 94, 95, 99, 102, 103, 104, 125, 154, 155, 156, 157, 159, 160

insects 9, 13, 27–28, 44, 98, 99, 102, 103, 104, 105, 112, 120, 146, 148, 153, 154, 155, 157, 159, 174

Jacob's Ladder 67–68, 152
Jesus Christ 156
Jones, Doug 1–5, 140
Joseph Campbell and the Power of Myth 182
Jungian psychology 8, 184

Kaiju 31, 44, 98, 99, 101, 104, 105, 106, 122, 126
Karloff, Boris 2, 9, 113, 114, 115, 116, 117, 122, 127
King, Stephen 143
The King of Elfland's Daughter 23, 30, 31–38

Latin American Gothic 9, 146, 149, 159
Lee, Christopher 115, 153
The Left Hand of Darkness 106
liminality 80, 83, 84, 94, 173
The Lion, the Witch, and the Wardrobe 170, 197
local horror 23, 25, 36, 38
The Lord of the Rings 183
Lovecraft, H.P. 8, 12, 13, 14, 16, 17–18, 19, 22–38, 98, 99–100, 107, 131
Lucas, George 182
Lugosi, Bela 54, 153

Machen, Arthur 12, 22
magic 2, 15, 16, 29, 32, 33, 34, 35, 36, 37, 38, 49, 50, 51, 52, 63, 98, 141, 176, 185, 187, 190, 191, 194, 197, 198
Mama 7, 9, 77, 79, 89
A Matter of Life and Death 67–68
Mephisto's Bridge 96
Mexico 1, 7, 9, 12, 13, 22, 24, 26, 27, 46, 52–53, 60, 80, 112, 113, 116, 131, 154, 158, 159, 160
Mimic 1, 7, 9, 31, 41, 42, 80, 98, 99, 103, 115, 119–120, 121, 126, 132–136, 150, 151, 155, 159
Monomyth 182
monsters and monstrosity 8, 9, 43, 44, 45, 48, 51, 52, 54, 55, 77, 83, 86, 89, 93–107, 112–127, 130–144, 146, 147, 148, 157, 178, 188, 195, 198
myth 8, 9, 10, 36, 87, 93–107, 117, 127, 132, 151, 160, 165, 166, 167, 168, 171, 173, 175, 176, 177, 182, 183, 184, 185, 186, 187, 188, 190, 193, 195, 196, 198

The Nest (1988) 155
Nietzsche, Friedrich 10, 163–178

Index

Night of the Hunter (1955) 119
9/11 64
notebooks 8, 78, 95, 132, 184

orphanage 14, 48, 60, 61, 62, 63, 65, 66, 80, 82, 84, 88, 136, 137, 138, 139, 144
The Orphanage 7, 9, 46, 47, 63, 71, 77, 79, 88

Pacific Rim 7, 31, 41, 42, 43, 45, 55, 98, 99, 101, 107, 115, 122, 126, 174
Pacific Rim II 7
paganism 7, 15, 30, 158, 187
Pale Man 3, 24, 33, 35, 43, 50, 51, 52, 140, 141, 194-196
Pan 183, 186, 187, 190, 191, 194, 195, 196, 197
Pan's Labyrinth 3-4, 7, 9, 10, 15, 23, 24, 25, 29, 30-34, 35, 38, 41, 43, 44, 45, 48-52, 63, 61, 64-72, 77, 79, 84-88, 95, 98, 100, 103, 115, 118, 119, 120-121, 123, 131, 132, 144, 163, 166, 167, 168, 169, 170, 171, 172, 174, 175, 177, 183, 184, 185, 188, 197
parenthood 9, 14, 29, 31, 32, 33, 36, 37, 51, 80, 101, 115, 116, 119, 120, 121, 122, 123, 124, 126, 127, 132, 135, 137, 197
Phantasm (1979) 123
Phantom of the Opera 95
Phase IV 159
Pinocchio 7
Pirates of the Caribbean 183
Poe, Edgar Allan 12, 22, 23
Prowse, David 115

Quiroga, Horacio 146-160

religion 7, 8, 10, 12, 13, 14, 15, 20, 24, 131, 135, 170, 177, 186; *see also* spirituality
Roman Catholicism 4, 7-8, 12, 14, 15, 17, 24, 28, 45, 86, 112, 116, 131, 171, 175, 176, 184

Scream (1996) 133
Shelley, Mary 2, 22, 113, 127
Silmarillion 167
space 9, 13, 18, 23, 27, 65, 67, 72, 79, 83, 88, 94, 149, 155, 157, 158
Spain 9, 15, 24, 27, 29, 32, 45, 46, 47, 49, 58, 59, 60, 61, 63, 64, 65, 72, 80, 87, 88, 120, 136, 137, 140, 141, 142, 144, 151, 176, 188
Spanish and Mexican cultural elements 8, 22, 24, 46, 71
Spanish civil war 8, 14, 15, 42, 45, 46, 47, 48, 49, 51, 58-75, 77, 80, 82, 83, 84, 87, 102, 118, 119, 120, 136-137, 167
Spider-Man 183
The Spirit of the Beehive (1973) 118-119, 120
spirituality 8, 11, 13; *see also* religion
Splice 7, 115, 121-122, 126
Star Wars 182
The Strain 7, 53, 55
supernatural 9, 12, 13, 15, 24, 28, 36, 37, 38, 58, 62, 63, 66, 76, 77, 79, 82, 88, 89, 148, 167, 168, 172

Them! (1954) 159
Theogony 93-107
time 64-72, 79, 83, 137
Tolkien, J.R.R. 19, 36, 167, 176
trauma 8, 9, 58, 59, 61, 64, 65, 67, 68, 72, 76-90, 123, 126, 138

The Uses of Enchantment 68

vampire 9, 14, 25, 28, 43, 44, 53, 54, 55, 102, 104, 106, 123, 125, 146-160
Vertigo 65

Whale, James 2, 9, 114, 116, 117, 119, 120, 127

www.ingramcontent.com/pod-product-compliance
Ingram Content Group UK Ltd.
Pitfield, Milton Keynes, MK11 3LW, UK
UKHW042003140426
5217IPUK00015B/955